FAKE, FRAUD, OR GENUINE?

FAKE, FRAUD, OR GENUINE?

IDENTIFYING AUTHENTIC AMERICAN ANTIQUE FURNITURE

BY

MYRNA KAYE

A NEW YORK GRAPHIC SOCIETY BOOK
LITTLE, BROWN AND COMPANY · BOSTON

FIRST EDITION

LIBRARY OF CONGRESS CATALOGING-IN-PUBLICATION DATA

Kaye, Myrna.
   Fake, Fraud, or Genuine?

   Bibliography: p.
   Includes index.
    1. Furniture — United States — Expertising.
   2. Furniture — United States — Collectors and collecting. I. Title.
   NK2240.K39 1987   749.213   87-2809
   ISBN 0-8212-1666-X

New York Graphic Society books are published by
Little, Brown and Company (Inc.).

*Published simultaneously in Canada by
Little, Brown & Company (Canada) Limited.*

PRINTED IN THE UNITED STATES OF AMERICA

DESIGN BY JEANNE ABBOUD
EDITORIAL ASSISTANCE BY PATRICIA ADAMS
COPYEDITING BY DOROTHY STRAIGHT
PRODUCTION COORDINATION BY CHRISTINA M. HOLZ
COMPOSITION BY DEKR CORPORATION
PRINTING BY MERCANTILE
BINDING BY NICHOLSTONE BOOK BINDERY, INC.

Author's Note

"I'm looking for fakes and frauds. What do you have to show me?" Although asking museum curators and directors, antiques collectors, and dealers to show me their problem pieces would not seem a surefire unlocker of doors to cherished collections, it worked.

"I'm looking for genuine antiques to illustrate as well," I added, not to mollify the antiques lover before me but because fakes and frauds are easiest to discern when they come up against the genuine. Fine as well as fraudulent antiques fill these pages.

No curator replied that his collection had hardly a question mark. No collector coyly claimed never to have been taken. As the reader will soon discover, so many people shared so many objects that I was able to pick and choose and pack the book with fabulous examples.

I present mystery after mystery of detection to challenge the eye and wit of the reader. Sleuths must be aware of problems if they are to avoid them, and with each intrigue the reader discovers more about how antiques were constructed, how to conduct inspections, and how furniture detectives can spot the work of fakers and defrauders.

This is a detective's manual. Because in a manual you see the object in a photograph instead of meeting it face to face, I have taken extra precautions. Many of the objects are illustrated in an overall view and also in one, several, or many details; cross references are numerous. For most of the objects, the captions include dimensions. For fine antiques, the dimensions are clues to what to expect; in the cases of fraud, they are often telling tip-offs. Height (H), width (W), and depth (D) signify maximum measurements unless otherwise specified. Seat heights are given because that statistic often points the way to cut-off feet. "Left" and "right" indicate the sides as seen by a viewer looking at the facade.

The antique furniture covered in this book was made in the seventeenth, eighteenth, and nineteenth centuries. Figures 22–26 illustrate some of the terms used by furniture investigators. Elsewhere trade terms are defined in parentheses or illustrated with diagrams. The chapter on technology is a treasury of simple techniques, new ways of looking and seeing, and valuable bits of specialized knowledge.

In these pages I have drawn not only on my own experiences examining over a hundred museum collections in the last decade but also on investigations conducted by others. Reference notes appear at the end of the book and include full citations for those sources not cited in the bibliography. In the bibliography, I commend some general and specific readings.

I am especially indebted to the following — most of them longstanding members of the fakes-and-fraud squad — who shared their problem pieces, their knowledge about suspects, and mug shots of goodies and baddies alike. They gave a good deal of time and a wealth of expertise to enable readers to join the squad:

Robert F. Trent of the Connecticut Historical Society, an outstanding sleuth and a patient sharer, and Christopher P. Bickford, director of CHS; Philip Zea of Historic Deerfield, with whom it is a joy to delve and discover; Brock Jobe of the Society for the Preservation of New England Antiquities, whose eye is as unfailing as his generosity, and Caroline Hughes, Morgan Phillips, and Richard Nylander, also of SPNEA; Patricia E. Kane of the Yale Art Gallery, an extraordinary scholar in charge of an extraordinary collection; Nancy E. Richards, Donald L. Fennimore, and Deborah Federhen of the wondrous Winterthur Museum; Morrison H. Heckscher and Frances G. Safford of The Metropolitan Museum of Art, Edward S. Cooke, Jr., and Jonathan L. Fairbanks of the Museum of Fine Arts, Boston, and Patricia Keller-Conner of the Heritage Center of Lancaster County, all of whom proved to be valuable resources; Robert Blair St. George of Boston University, who gave me the freedom of his splendid negative file; and Walter E. Simmons II, an informed scholar, formerly of the Henry Ford Museum. I also thank the Essex Institute, the Wadsworth Atheneum, and the administrators and trustees of all the above institutions.

Some of the savviest sleuths are not at museums. Sam Pennington graciously lent many of the photographs and some of the words that have enlivened his *Maine Antique Digest*. The magazine *Antiques* allowed photographs and quotes. Albert Sack of Israel Sack, Inc., of New York; John Leonetti of John Walton, Inc., of Jewett City, Connecticut; Christie's of New York; and Phillips of New York all contributed photographs.

I learned much from two able cabinetmakers, Allan Breed, who works independently in York, Maine, and Robert Mussey, who runs the restoration shop for the Society for the Preservation of New England Antiquities, and enjoyed the assistance of an eminent scholar of wood technology, R. Bruce Hoadley of the University of Massachusetts at Amherst.

Jonathan S. Nerenberg's pen has made the craftsman's joints clear, some characteristics of wood understandable, and the glossary of parts concise. Several photographers have captured revealing — sometimes damning — details: Joe Ofria, David Bohl, and Robert J. Bitondi did original photography; Richard Cheek shared his extant photographs.

Sabra Morton, Shirley Moskow, Janet Tassel, and Roberta Leviton made the storytelling smooth. Pat and Dick Warner put much of the manual to the test. Sharon Kaye Smith indexed the objects under study; Anne Rogers checked the bibliography. My editor, Betty Childs, encouraged me; my agent, Susan Urstadt, always had faith in the subject. My husband, Murray, had faith in me; it sustained me until the last fraud was finished off.

Table of Contents

A Gothick Tale

At an auction preview some years ago, my friend Eve and I spotted a double-backed settee whose design was what Chippendale called "Gothick." Eve was excited at the possibility of acquiring such a rare and beautiful seat, and we began to look it over. Everything was looking good until we checked the back seat rail; it was made of three pieces. Why, we wondered, would a chairmaker piece a rail together when good structure and ease of construction called for one long piece of wood? The settee made no sense until we turned into skeptics.

What if it was faked? We reasoned that, for a faker, sound practice and economy of labor might mean making a rare and expensive form from a couple of old chairs. In a fake, a three-part back rail would make sense — two chair rails and a joiner between. We noted that most of the settee — the several elements of the back, the arms, the legs, and the side seat rails — could have been armchair parts. We looked at the front seat rail; it did not look the same as the side rails.

Eve was still interested in the fraudulent made-up settee, but as attractive furniture, not as an antique. She showed the auctioneer what we'd discovered, and he promised to note our findings when the settee was on the block. With the other bidders knowing the truth, Eve reasoned, "it will go at far less than its estimate as an authentic antique settee."

Abiding strictly by his word, the auctioneer announced, "There's been some work on the back rail and some new wood in the front rail of this beautiful Chippendale settee." The bidding flew past the price of a made-up piece, slowed at the estimate, and then topped it.

As we left, I said to the successful bidder, "That's a pretty settee. Did you hear what the auctioneer said about it?"

"Sure," he responded. "At its age, I expect some work to have been done here and a little new wood to be used there. When it's antique, it can't be perfect."

I wrote this book for that man.

FAKE, FRAUD, OR GENUINE?

The Villains

THE path we will take to the genuine is the bypass, passing by way of all the frauds. Using a list of the rascals, we will consider each fraudulent possibility, discard one after the other, and, by elimination, ascertain the genuine antique. (If all of this seems simple, let me throw in the monkey wrench: the biggest aid in discerning the fraud is knowing the look, feel, and smell of the genuine antique, including the repaired antique and the honest reproduction. But despair not, style and technology provide clues to the genuine.) First, the fakes and frauds.

We use the two terms: "fake" refers to a completely made phony; "fraud" designates an antique that has been altered, misattributed, or otherwise disguised or misrepresented as what it is not.

The enemy has several disguises. Full MOs (modi operandi), many with mug shots, follow the simple listing of the nongenuine.

MOST UNWANTED LIST

Entirely Made Fake
Old Parts/New Object
Made-up Set
Remade Object
Old Piece Enhanced
Married Piece with Two Old Spouses
Married Piece of the May–December Sort
Englishman with an American Address
Reproduction Honestly Made but Now Misrepresented

(The Most Unwanteds are not to be confused with the perfectly acceptable although not perfect.)

WANTED (IF NOT MOST WANTED) LIST

Reproduction Recognized as What It Is
Honest Repairs on a Genuine Object

By having these lists with you at all times (you may find yourself antiquing when you least expect to), you can look out for each villain, following any order but covering the entire slate. Now, to know each rascal better.

ENTIRELY MADE FAKE

This object was made from scratch to fool you. It is the object many buyers fear most but is in fact the one they need fear least.

Publicity about fakes — paintings reputedly by old masters, sculptures by the ancients — leads to the feeling that the complete fake is the primary villain. While this may be the case for paintings, sculpture, ceramics, and glass, it is not so for furniture. The astronomical prices paid for paintings make faking well worth the effort; the relative ease of producing copycat ceramics and glass does the same. In the field of furniture, however, neither price nor ease of production fosters the complete fake.

In 1978, a story made the rounds that put the fear of the fake into many. As featured in *Yankee* magazine, in the "Antiques to Look for" department, retitled "Antiques to Look Out for," Wayne Worcester told of Armand LaMontagne, a Rhode Island wood sculptor who set out to fool museum people by faking a three-hundred-year-old turned chair. Eventually, the "Ford Museum paid over $9000 . . . [LaMontagne] spent $2 and two months' time to make it."[1]

LaMontagne had built himself a house in seventeenth-century style and filled it with reproduction furniture he made when he was not working on busts of former Presidents and other wood sculptures. He "confessed" because his idea from the first was to embarrass "the experts." Once, on a visit to a museum, LaMontagne had been asked to leave when his derogatory comments about evident repairs and alterations to antique furniture on display were overheard. LaMontagne sought revenge.

He chose to fake a rare form, a seventeenth-century great chair

with turnings in the back, beneath the seat, and under the arm, and he modeled his, with variations, after an extant example at Pilgrim Hall in Plymouth, Massachusetts (fig. 131). LaMontagne felled a tree and lathe-turned the elements while the wood was still green so they would shrink somewhat out of round. He used a modern drill and a modern bit, which saved him time and enabled him to later prove the chair was a fake. He assembled it and then attacked it, denting it, bruising it, and gouging out bits of one handhold as if it had been damaged by a whittler (fig. 1). He wanted to avoid gratuitous damage, trying to simulate only the ravages of natural wear. (But compare his chair to its model: you can see — even in photographs — the crisp edges of the genuine and the excessive wear of the fake.)

LaMontagne dismantled the chair and delicately burned each part to imitate wear. He removed the char and then bleached all the wood to remove every trace of carbon. He cut dowels by hand, reassembled the chair, and gave it a thin coat of black paint.

Then he gave the chair a thin coat of water and white glue and dusted it while still damp with all the dust he could vacuum up in his house. When it was dry, he waxed it and then prepared to smoke it. He borrowed an open-ended steel drum and, raising it off the ground, built a fire below. The chair was suspended in the drum. The operation, aimed at drying the wood and browning it, was tricky, and LaMontagne "had to experiment for quite a while."

Next, to rid the chair of the smell of smoke, he had to bathe it several times, including immersions in salt water and bleach baths. This was an arduous, trial-and-error procedure because the smell of smoke was tenacious. Feeling he had then inflicted about one hundred years of history onto his fake, LaMontagne repeated the entire finishing process two more times, ad-libbing damage, painting the chair red at one point and coating it with gray enamel afterward.

Then, he imposed "major damage." After giving it much thought, he removed two spindles so a sitter could rest his heels on the lower stretcher. Only after being dunked in the sea and pounded by the surf for a while was the chair deemed ready.

Faking is not an easy business. And what did this faker profit from his labors? He gave his fake away — to a friend, a dealer in on the deception, who sold it to another dealer for "a few hundred dollars," which, even had the sculptor received it, would hardly have been fair recompense for his efforts. His real reaping was in the revenge.

The "few hundred" really was a few, for the chair went through two more dealer sales and arrived in a prestigious shop still priced under $1000. Roger Bacon, a well-known and respected New Hampshire dealer, then sold the chair (which by this time had been stripped of its ugly gray paint) to the Henry Ford Museum in Michigan for more than $9000. Robert Bishop, museum editor and consulting curator of furniture at the Ford, included the "antique" chair in his book *How to Know American Antique Furniture*, and the fake was proudly illustrated on the cover of a Ford Museum collection brochure.

Even after Roger Bacon learned the story of LaMontagne's hoax and told the museum to reexamine the chair, offering to buy it back, the museum staff refused to question its own expertise. The "wonderful seventeenth-century" chair remained on display, as genuine, for another four years. Finally, coverage in *The Detroit Free Press* moved the museum to reassess the chair and then, when X rays revealed modern drill-bit holes, to acknowledge the fake. (The museum announced that it would keep its $9000 purchase.)

LaMontagne had reached his goal. To do so, he had labored hard for two months without compensation. Had he sold the chair for what his labor was worth, it would have had another history. An-

FIGURE 2:
Spinning wheel, a fine
source of material for
"repairers."

tiques dealers, like everyone else, are less wary of cheap finds and can be encouraged by very low prices to delude themselves into thinking the "antique" is a steal. All buyers should be wary of the enticement of the obviously underpriced. The first rule of sound antique shopping: *Beware of the "it's-a-steal" impulse.* Someone else is doing the stealing.

The market value of antique furniture generally does not allow fair payment for such talent, time, skill, imagination, and perseverance as LaMontagne expended to settle his grudge. Unless a faker has a grudge against you, you probably are not endangered by a new fake.

But how about an old fake? If "by a new fake" in the paragraph above did not prompt you to that question, you need work both on skepticism and on attention to detail, and this book will provide it. If you *did* wonder about the old, you will surely make a fine member of the furniture fraud squad.

Fifty to seventy-five years ago, making fakes was economically worthwhile; fortunately, the old fake usually suffers from its age, and you benefit. As the years pass, LaMontagne's hoaxing will become more apparent. The ravages of time after a premature aging reveal rather than conceal. The effort expended to make a fake look right in 1920 has, by the 1980s, made it look more and more like 1920. As the wood shrinks and moves, as the finish changes, and as more is learned about genuine antiques, the fake comes to look more "antiqued" than "antique."

OLD PARTS/NEW OBJECT

The preface tells of a Chippendale double chairback settee made up principally of parts of old armchairs, because a rare settee is worth far more than two chairs. Combining elements from one form to create another is a common fraud. Spinning wheels (fig. 2), for example, were once commonplace; many survived in attics and barns, and they were often picturesque accouterments in Colonial Revival interiors in the late nineteenth century. Few people, however, want spinning wheels today, and the handsome turnings from three-legged spinning wheels can be found reassembled into folksy tripod candlestands of a common fraudulent type (fig. 198). Turned banisters from eighteenth-century staircases have been reborn as legs on "quaint" tables. Floor or wall boards — architectural elements are irresistible to furniture fakers — can provide the tabletop and other elements. The beautiful wooden boards that were leaves for nine-

teenth-century dining tables, which expanded to lengths seldom required today, are routinely reborn as tabletops, drawer fronts, case sides — you name it.

Spurred to reuse extant parts by the desire to save time and the need to avoid the laborious faking of age on new wood, fakers devise wondrous ways of remaking old parts into "antiques." Their imaginations are bound only by the availability of old wood. The disastrous World War II bombings of Britain proved to be a boon to English craftsmen engaged in the old parts/new objects trade.

MADE-UP SET

A variation of the old parts/new object is the made-up set. Some sets of chairs are assembled — that is, composed of chairs from two or more sets. If you want the number of chairs in the assembled set, this may not be a bad thing, for to begin assembling a set yourself is a difficult task. But you should be apprised of the assembled nature of the set and see how many variations appear. The more variations, the less valuable the assemblage.

Another type of made-up set is the enlarged set. Often a set of chairs was enlarged with new reproductions, copied directly from one of the old chairs. This too may be a felicitous arrangement if the set is of the size desired. If such a set was enlarged recently, the added members will be easy to spot. But many sets were enlarged long ago. The additions may have been made not to deceive but to

FIGURE 4:
High chest; mahogany (primary wood), 1765–1785, lower Housatonic River valley, Connecticut. H. 87⅝; W. 43⅞; D. 22⅝. (Society for the Preservation of New England Antiquities.)

FIGURE 5:
Detail of figure 4. The upper shell drawer was originally uncarved and had a central brass handle. A pair of small plugged holes flanked by larger holes attest to an original handle and at least one replacement. The enhancement probably dates to about the turn of this century.

accommodate more dinner guests, but don't let that deceive you today. Every chair must be examined, for enlarging sets was common practice.

The longer ago a set was enlarged, the more valuable the added members. Two copies added in 1780 to ten Chippendale chairs made in 1760 will probably go unnoticed, and that is just fine. All are period chairs. If the chairs were added a century later, the new ones are nineteenth-century reproductions and should be evaluated as such. When all of the set but one seem to be of one age, make sure that the several are the old chairs. The antique may be the single.

REMADE OBJECT

In this category we find the lower part of a high chest that passes as a dressing table; a high chest reconstituted from a remnant (fig. 3, a remnant needing cabriole legs and an upper case); the high-chest top that became a chest of drawers (fig. 109); and the flat-top high chest that gained a pediment because pedimented high chests bring higher prices. We may even find a new case built around four old legs (fig. 103). And that's just high chests.

In some shops not very long ago, a bustling business was done in slenderizing. Bureaus were made narrower because narrow cases sold better than wide ones. Although everything about the chest is old, and every part original to it, the chest remade to suit a taste for slender cases has little value now as an antique.

Antique furniture has been enhanced in many ways, some almost commonplace. A plethora of objects sporting freshly painted "original grained surfaces" appeared in recent years because old painted finishes became fashionable and handsome "folk" graining won favor. The adding of new inlay and reveneering are other favorite embellishments.

Probably the most common way to enhance old furniture has been to add carving, and the most commonly added carving has been the shell or fan (figs. 4 and 5). A newly carved fan on a plain case can quickly move it out of the shop in which it had become a fixture.

Forged or misread inscriptions, added labels, and the like have been used to enhance the value of an antique by bestowing upon it a history it never had. The otherwise genuine antique becomes a fraud when labeled with a lie.

MARRIED PIECE WITH TWO OLD SPOUSES

Married pieces are double-cased objects — a chest-on-chest, a desk and bookcase — that did not start out together but have been joined in matrimony for monetary gain. Some marriages took place long ago. Though they may have lived together for years, the partners will have aged unequally, and you can quite easily spot the matchmaking. Other marriages are fresh from the alter. You can recognize these too.

When a bookcase — the top of what was once a desk and bookcase — survives without its desk, it is of comparatively little value. Immediately a search begins for a suitable desk (and there are so many desks). "Suitable" entails correct dimensions (shallow or deep waist moldings can compensate for a slight mismatch), compatible if not identical wood (stain is a boon to the fraudulent-minded), preferably — but not always — the same style (the customer may not know any better), and ideally the same area of manufacture. (But matchmakers seldom, as we shall see, wait for the ideal.)

Innumerable upper cases of high chests have become separated from their bases over the years, and the two parts have since gone different ways. Matchmaking dealers fervently seek a spouse for each separate case that comes into their hands, but inconsistency of construction gives new unions away (figs. 11 and 12). A marriage broker may put a high-chest top on what is really a chest of four drawers. The resulting chest-on-chest, a new arrangement for both pieces and thus actually an instance of old parts/new object, can be exposed in the same way as a married piece with two old spouses.

MARRIED PIECE OF THE MAY–DECEMBER SORT

Not every dealer has the patience to wait for an old mate for the old better half in his shop. Sometimes a desk will elicit no interest while a desk and bookcase of the same period attracts buyers. To hasten the turnover of stock and to accommodate customer tastes, many a new bookcase has been made for what was originally simply a desk. The top board of the desk can testify to its single past. The top board of a desk intended as the bottom half of a secretary will be covered by the bookcase and is left unfinished; the top board of a desk made as a desk is finished, for it will show.

In considering the worthiness of any married piece, evaluate it as two separate entities, for that's what it really is. A May–December marriage is usually less desirable than the marriage of two old spouses, because one half is really only a new reproduction.

ENGLISHMAN WITH AN AMERICAN ADDRESS

The Englishmen who busied themselves making antique furniture with wood salvaged from bombed-out buildings after World War II were not new to the trade. In the early twentieth century, American tourists seeking their ancestral roots in Britain brought home boat-loads of "seventeenth-century" English fakes (see fig. 149). Today some of these are passed off as American seventeenth-century furniture, although they are neither American nor seventeenth-century. Americans were not the only ones taken in by English fakers: one wag claims that the survival rate for "eighteenth-century" easy chairs in Britain is so high that there are more of them today than there were in the eighteenth century.

Many American shops sell English furniture as such, but others dub a Briton "American" or fail to mention the country of origin while placing English among American pieces. With American furniture priced much higher, with English fakers superb at their work, and with rural English and Irish furniture displaying some of the provincial quality seen in American design, much British furniture passes as American. The converse is rare because American pieces command higher prices. Wood is one clue to origin; style is another; construction also helps.

A reproduction is an object made in an old style, in admiration and honor of that old style, and never intended to be presented to a buyer as an antique. Some reproductions (fig. 6) are copied from antique examples (fig. 101); others are based on antique styles, with the craftsmen using varying amounts of imagination (as we shall soon see).

Old reproductions cause concern lest the age they have acquired make them appear antique. In dealer's language, the honest presentation of an old reproduction is, "It has some age." This is not mispresentation unless the reproduction is completely new. New reproductions, of course, look new and cannot pass as "having some age" unless the buyer fails to examine the furniture. You, however, will *never fail to examine the furniture.*

Most old reproductions (like the marked Wallace Nutting, fig. 6) were made with modern methods in shops equipped with modern tools. The techniques of construction are clear and obvious evidence that the reproductions are just that. These were never intended as fakes; the wood was finished in the manner, with the materials, and to the sheen that was popular at the time. The age of such finishes is so evident today that our chief concern is that we might overlook a good antique hidden under a 1920s refinishing.

Some reproductions are labeled (fig. 129) or branded by the maker; others are not. Some makers' labels and brands have been obliterated in an attempt to pass off an old reproduction as an

FIGURE 6:
Reproduction kneehole bureau table on the auction block; early twentieth century. Made by Wallace Nutting. (Photograph courtesy Maine Antique Digest.)

antique. That's a shame — not because the object cannot then be recognized as a reproduction (it can), but because the mark of the reproducer can add to the value of the furniture. Wallace Nutting reproductions bring extraordinary prices, almost rivaling those of the antiques they emulate.

If the reproduction has been made by hand with antique tools, or if the furniture is a fake created long ago, there will be no evidence of machine construction to give it away. These objects then offer a challenge to the fraud detective who is beginning to find other fakes and frauds easy to spot and for this must pull out most of the tricks of the trade. Most old fakes and handmade old reproductions were not copied line for line, measure for measure, tool for tool, piece for small piece from an original. Something of the taste of the time in which it was made almost always creeps into the product.

You can search for telltale signs of the time of production in the places they are likely to frequent:

* in the proportions,
* in the finish,
* in the materials, and
* in the design details.

Usually the proportions of the reproduction as a whole or of its several parts are not consistent with those of period pieces, so you need to know the proportional relationships found on genuine examples.

Most often the finish applied to a reproduction is whatever type was commonly used at the time the furniture was made, not the sort used in the period being simulated. The faked "antique" finish has since aged; having a different past than the genuine, it now has a different appearance. So you need to be familiar with finishes.

The breach of authenticity may be a blatant mishandling of the materials, such as making a reproduction Chippendale chair of oak (fig. 160) because, at the time, oak was the preferred wood — although it was not used for such chairs in the eighteenth century. You must learn which woods were used when and how if you don't already know.

Look at the changes of design details over time and in different regions, and find out where to see — in the wood or on paper — genuine examples for comparison. Until recent years, the diversity and various characteristics of regional styles were not well appreciated or understood. Out of ignorance, a craftsman in 1920 might have placed a Boston-style high chest on New York–style legs and furnished it with a Philadelphia-style pediment. In creating reproductions, in making fakes, and in remaking or repairing antiques (as

FIGURE 7:
Desk and bookcase, Lancaster County, Pennsylvania, with pediment restored by Alan Miller in 1984.
H. 105½; W. 45; D. 22½.
(The Heritage Center of Lancaster County.)

we shall soon see), lack of knowledge of regional design variations was a common cause of error and is now a giveaway.

Although it is most unlikely, the possibility does exist that a fake or reproduction was copied exactly from a model, was constructed by hand in the old ways (even using old finishing techniques), has aged so that it now looks old enough to be of the period, and has escaped all the influences of its time of manufacture that might reveal its true nature. It is possible for you to be fooled. Though it is unlikely, so can all of posterity. You would enjoy your "antique" as an antique, and so would all who followed you as its owners. In a way, it would be as wonderful a creation as what it copied.

TWO NON-VILLAINS OF SUSPICIOUS APPEARANCE

It is important to be aware of and to recognize two genuine types that can be confused with frauds. They compose the Wanted (If Not Most Wanted) List.

REPRODUCTION RECOGNIZED AS WHAT IT IS

The honest reproduction is, to an extent, marred by the pitfalls of inaccuracy in reproduction mentioned above. Some odd quirk in proportions spoils its appearance; the several elements of its design do not really belong together because it is trying to be all things at once. Often the quality of the wood is not so fine as in a period antique. The finish does not look old. To find the really slick reproduction — and there are some — can take longer than to find the antique.

HONEST REPAIRS ON A GENUINE OBJECT

Antique furniture deteriorates with use and just with time. Repairs are needed, sometimes frequently and repeatedly. Discerning repairs and recognizing them as such (not mistaking them for enhancements or remakes) is not always easy. And all repairs are not equal. Some are fatal, others are easily accepted, and some are even welcomed.

Take the case of a William and Mary chest (figs. 92 and 100) that, after standing on turned ball feet for three hundred years, has developed severe foot problems. Feet — there to keep the bottom board safe from the floor and its dangers — are vulnerable to moisture, vermin, decay, breakage, and loss. You have to scrutinize all

FIGURE 8:
Pediment of the bookcase in figure 7 before the recent Miller restoration. It was easy to distinguish the repair made early in this century from the few remaining inches of original pediment, which had faded.

FIGURE 9:
Detail of a pediment of a privately owned desk and bookcase, Lancaster County. (Photograph courtesy Israel Sack, Inc.) This and similar pediments served as models for Miller's restoration, figure 7.

feet, but especially those that were originally discrete parts, such as ball feet.

If the case stands on four new feet, you should question whether the replacements are accurate replicas. If the case has only one new foot, and the three originals show it to be an exact duplicate, your problem has vanished. The repair — one new matching replacement foot — is legitimate. In fact, if three of the feet are exact replicas and only one foot is original, the situation and value are not very different than with three old feet and one new one. The propriety of a repair can be validated by just one original foot that assures that the replacements are proper copies.

Let's return to the first instance, that of four new feet. Let us say that one of the original feet has been stored in a drawer; the authenticity of the repair can be established. Such a repaired chest may actually be more valuable to you than one with four decayed feet that need immediate replacement, in which instance you would have to find a turner, make sure he copied the originals exactly, and pay his bill.

Completely accurate and documentable restoration, then, is the best of all types of repair. Also desirable are fine repairs based on scholarly extrapolation (figs. 7–9). A desk and bookcase, its pediment cut probably to fit in a room with a rather low ceiling, was well-meaningly but inauthentically repaired early in this century. The repaired pediment (fig. 8) distorted the appearance of the case, making it look dumpy by Lancaster County, Pennsylvania, standards. Now a new pediment based on other furniture from the same locale and era (fig. 9) restores the case to proper height. The current design (fig. 7) is scholarly extrapolation; the old repair was a detriment.

Many repairs are not accurate restoration and may not be acceptable. At some point a repaired genuine antique mutates into a remade object. Is a chest with four new feet and no documentation for their size or shape merely repaired? Is it as much a remade object as a high chest with four new cabrioles?

A genuine antique with minor losses is a desirable and rather common find. Learning from the case of the Lancaster pediments, try to get antiques accurately restored the first time. When you have repairs made, beware if the well-meaning craftsman says, "It'll be so much more usable." He can unintentionally move your antique from the Wanted List to the Unwanted.

And so, provided with a list of characters to look out for, you will want to know the two characteristics to look for.

Equipment for Sleuths

2

WHAT is it you look for in your pursuit of the genuine? Two things — economy of labor and consistency in construction.

Time was precious in the seventeenth and eighteenth centuries, much more so than in our day of labor savers. Men and women worked far more hours each week than we do. In fact, the assigning of different tasks to men and women was an attempt to make more efficient use of the family's labor. We know that Puritans spent long hours of their Sundays, morning and afternoon, listening to sermons, and we may imagine that they had little else to do. But the Puritan paid dearly for the blessing of a day without labor. It cost him twenty-four hours' worth of productivity. Throughout the preindustrial era, time was tied to productivity. No craftsman wasted his efforts or time at unproductive tasks, and, in his one-room shop, he could make sure an apprentice or journeyman didn't either.

A furniture maker, frugal with his labor, did not paint or stain any wood that did not show. For example, staining the underside of a chest was a waste of labor, time, and materials. Painting and staining, however, are not a waste of labor for a faker wanting to cover up his handiwork.

The original maker of an antique did not smooth any surfaces that did not require smoothing. The back of the chest, the bottom of the drawer, the insides of seat rails — all areas that are generally not seen — were left rough, with the visible marks of the wood-

FIGURE 10:
Underside of a drawer (detail of chest shown in plate 6). The joiner, making no effort to neaten the underside of the drawer, left plane marks, saw marks (at the back), and tears in the wood. A raking light makes the marks more visible. See the nail hole at the back close up, figure 37.

worker's plane (fig. 10) or even those of the sawmill's blade (fig. 53). If you see a backboard that has been finished (i.e., sanded smooth and waxed, shellacked, or varnished), you know that it is not original to an antique. You benefit from the craftsman's need to do everything as expeditiously as possible, to do nothing the hard way, because you can examine his product for his hallmark: *economy of labor.*

The faker — making an "antique" and not just a piece of furniture — could always afford to expend the extra time and effort on what the period craftsman had to do as efficiently as possible. The evidence of this extra expenditure testifies to post-period work.

As you examine an antique, mentally reconstruct the object (Chapters 5–9 will show you how). As you do so, you will figure out how the craftsman used his time and why. For example, although the underside of the drawer is rough, the interior of the drawer is smooth. Why? So the fabric stored inside and the hands of users would be protected from splinters. If you are examining a non-tilting table and find that the underside of the top is painted, you again ask why. Since no one needed this unseen and unused area to be painted, the paint is evidence of wasted time and effort. You have found a repair, a fake, a reproduction, or a fraud; you will discover which during the rest of your investigation.

Consistency is related to economy of labor. If a man made drawers a certain way, it would have been an uneconomical use of his labor to vary his technique — if he could. When furniture was being produced in a shop with a few craftsmen, the man who made one drawer for a Chippendale chest of drawers made them all. He may

FIGURE 11:
Detail of the high chest in
figure 12. The dovetailing in
the upper case differs from
that in the lower.

not have been the same man who carved the claw feet, but he made all the drawers.

Throughout each piece or set, you will look for consistency of construction. The dovetails in an upper case should correspond to those in the drawers of the lower case; if they don't (fig. 11), you are looking at a married piece (fig. 12). If the plane marks inside the seat rails of one chair are unlike those inside the rails of others in the set, it's not because the chairmaker changed tools — another chairmaker made the chair. You are examining a made-up set.

Looking for consistency is not enough; feel for it. *Pass your hand lightly over every surface.* All the finished, or primary, surfaces should feel the same. All comparable surfaces — the several parts of all the drawer interiors, all the drawer bottoms — should feel alike. Touch is a keen sense for detecting variations. Use it.

An exception to the consistency rule can be seen in the carved elements of some English William and Mary cane chairs that were imported into America in the late seventeenth and early eighteenth centuries. When you know how such chairs (fig. 140) were made, the apparent inconsistency makes sense. Sets of cane chairs were made in large London shops that employed various specialists. Sometimes one carver produced only crest rails, while another cut out front stretchers. Within a genuine set, all the front stretchers should be consistent, and all the crest rails too, but on any one chair the carving on the crest rail may not match that on the stretcher.

Variations in contour may give the appearance of inconsistency: the thicknesses of the several turned spindles on an antique chair do vary (fig. 133); the left silhouette of an eighteenth-century chair splat may not be identical to the right (fig. 157; even photographed at an angle, the asymmetry is obvious). These variations are not, however, evidence of inconsistency. Instead, they indicate a lack of — to use a twentieth-century term — quality control. The varied spindles and unmirrored outlines are not the result of inconsistent workmanship but rather of speedy, casual craftsmanship. It may be an expensive antique to you, but it was just furniture to the man who produced it and to his client, who, not bred in a world of machine-made identical products, was not accustomed to identical, interchangeable parts.

You will have no trouble distinguishing between the irregularity of casual craftsmanship and inconsistency. And, having made that distinction, you will search for the productive craftsman's signature — *consistency in construction.*

To look for consistency, to see the methods of the craftsman, you have to be able to see. The furniture detective must be properly equipped so that no clue is missed. Standard supplies for antiques

FIGURE 12:
Married high chest; maple (primary wood), most of the chest 1790–1815, southern New Hampshire. H. 82; W. 40⅞; D. 20⅜. (Yale University Art Gallery Study Collection.) Even the photograph shows a difference in color between the two cases (the dark-shaded cornice is new).

sleuths include a magnifying lens (a lightweight plastic Fresnel lens will do) and two photographic flood lamps on tripods, with a 500-watt bulb in each (one floodlight creates the shadows in which problems can hide). If at all possible, examine every antique in bright sunlight. Only when this is not possible (if, for example, the case is too heavy to carry outside) should you resort to the bare 500-watt bulbs. Don't examine an antique in ordinary interior lighting; too many important clues can go undetected.

The lamps go with you, of course, if you antique by car. If you visit city shops by foot, train, or bus, the lamps are left at home. Then, after an examination in the shop, you buy only on condition that the antique can be returned in a few days, and you put it under the big lamps at home. (Chapter 11 will cover purchase agreements for savvy collectors.)

Even in city shops, your compact tool kit (fig. 13) goes along. In addition to the magnifying lens, the kit contains your tape measure; a twelve-inch ruler will not do. You may want to measure a square tabletop to see if it shrank out of square (it should have). Or you may want to measure the height of a table to see whether the feet have been cut (it should be about twenty-eight inches high if it is for dining). Measuring also helps in comparing the several chairs of a set. To measure for shrinkage or machine duplication of turned parts (chair banisters and table balusters), include calipers.

Carry a stubby screwdriver, a ripping tool (a tack-lifter that is gentler than it sounds), long-nosed pliers, and a small sharp knife. Not every antiques dealer will let you unscrew the top from a tilt-top candlestand, lift an upholstery tack, pull out a nail, or cut a small sample of wood for microanalysis, but some will. Be equipped so that if you need tools, you only have to ask to use them.

Bring pencils and a five-by-seven or larger pad of paper or spiral notebook, choosing one with a sturdy cardboard edge that will double as a seven-inch or longer straightedge. You will be writing down more than the price. Take a few small envelopes in case you take a wood sample. A small magnet of the type that holds messages to a refrigerator door may come in handy as well.

Come equipped with time. You will have to examine every surface (plates 1 and 2), every part of the furniture, and that takes time. If snacking on an apple or sipping from a thermos will free you to pursue a problematic point longer, come supplied or go to lunch and continue the investigation on your return. One piece of equipment you do not need is a watch. If you must wear one, don't look at it while solving a mystery.

FIGURE 13:
Kit for a member of the
fakes-and-fraud squad.

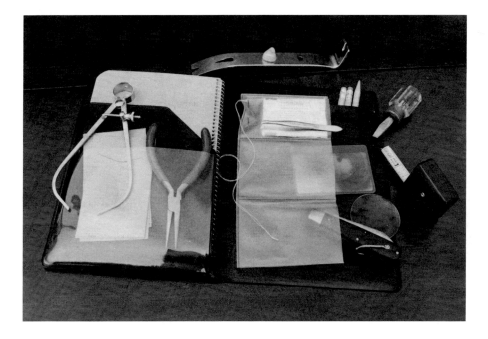

Remember that your hands are going to feel for what your eyes cannot see, so bring moistened towelettes by the bundle, tweezers, and a needle (with thread in it so you can find it and because the thread itself can be useful). Although the tweezers do occasionally extract important clues and the needle frequently probes for fraud, the two are most often used for splinters. Detective work is dirty, at times dangerous, business.

False Identities

<table>
<tr><td>

3

</td><td>

WILLIAM Saxton, who lived in Boston in the late eighteenth century, became a cabinetmaker in 1930. Saxton's post-mortem furniture career was started by a zealous history-citing antiques dealer — Warren Weston Creamer, of Waldoboro, Maine — and abetted by apparent innocents, including the author of "Historical and Documented Antiques from Maine," an article in the May 1930 issue of *Antiquarian* that reported on "the Creamer collection" then on the auction block.[1] ("The Creamer Collection" consisted of the goods from Creamer's shop.)

</td></tr>
</table>

A Federal desk of Creamer's (fig. 14), the article said, "bears the original salesbill stating its purchase from William Saxton, of Boston." Actually, the illustrated bill was only the top part, or billhead, which was printed:

BOSTON,   178

Bought of William Saxton

No. 85,

Newbury Street, directly opposite the Sign of the White Horse,

and inscribed with the date, the year (1785), and the buyer's name, but which made no mention of Saxton's business. Boston directories of the time show that he was a grocer and seller of crockery.[2]

The crockery vendor could have sold a desk he owned and written up the transaction on his business stationery, but it is also possible that someone, in more recent years, used part of a Saxton bill — a

document of little interest or value — to upgrade a rather ordinary piece of antique furniture. The latter possibility begins to look like a Creamer *modus operandi*, for the same collection and auction featured a Federal secretary bearing an Enoch Brown billhead (fig. 15) similarly devoid of any citation of the cabinet trade or of the nature of the goods sold in Brown's store. Brown, the Boston Directory tells us, actually sold dry goods.[3] The date inked onto his billhead is 1783; the secretary it accompanied is of a style that was first made at least a decade later.

W. W. Creamer, the furniture-documenting antiques dealer, also started Andrew Brimmer on his way to a career in cabinetmaking, a position Brimmer reached in 1957 when Ethel Bjerkoe included him in her book listing the cabinetmakers of America. The Brimmer label, though illustrated in *Antiquarian*, was not pictured or mentioned in the auction catalogue itself. Probably the auction house was leery of it; it looks and reads like a newspaper advertisement:

ANDREW BRIMMER,
No. 52, Cornhill, Boston,
has for sale,
A general Assortment of
GOODS.

By Wholesale and Retail,
Exceeding Cheep for Cash.

Cabinetmaking is not mentioned. Shopkeeper Brimmer may have sold furniture among his "general Assortment of Goods," but that doesn't mean he made it.

Ebenezer Knowlton, according to the Boston Directory, did make furniture.[4] Creamer acquired a bill signed "Eben Knowlton" and listing a table worth four dollars. He was not sure what table the bill was for — he misread Knowlton as "Knewstead" — and he

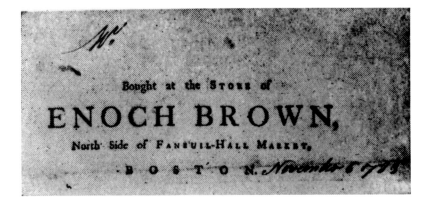

FIGURES 16, 17:
Creamer's "billed" and
"labeled" table and detail.
(The Henry Ford Museum
and Greenfield Village.) The
"label" is somewhat lifted
at the center top, and the
color of the wood beneath
is uniform.

certainly was not aware that Knowlton made furniture. So Creamer
suggested that the bill belonged with a table he owned (fig. 16) —
a table with what he called "the maker's label of Andrew Homer"
(fig. 17). The bill supposedly proved "its purchase by Captain
Smouse, of Waldoboro, for four dollars." Tying the Knowlton bill
to the Homer-labeled table was symptomatic of Creamer's affliction.
He had an especially virulent strain of a malady then current among
some of his fellow antiques dealers — an overactive drive for documentation.

Aware of Creamer's malady, one might easily be led to wonder
about the Homer label. It indeed looks like a genuine label (fig. 18).
Labels, meant to be glued to furniture, are rarely dated and usually
have a decorative border on all sides. Billheads are not labels. Designed as the top part of a sales receipt, they were not meant to be
glued to furniture; they are dated; and as a billhead is only part of
a bill, they have no decorative border. The cautious collector does
not accept a billhead as a label.

Though it truly looked like a label, coming from Creamer's shop,
the Homer document still raised a question. Why not wonder all the
way to the pages of the Boston Directory, that fine source in checking
the other Creamer wares? There, in fact, is Andrew Homer, a shopkeeper, not a cabinetmaker. He had a shop from at least 1803 until
1821, and in it sold English goods.

Staff members at the Ford Museum, owner of the table, did not
know Homer's trade, but in 1983 they became suspicious of the
Homer label because it looked "new." They quickly discovered (we
will see later in this chapter how easily, in "Labels That Lie") that
the labeling was a relatively recent job.

Then, in 1984, on learning of the other "label" problems at the
Creamer sale, the staff examined the table that had passed
inspection — or escaped it — for over half a century. They found
that machine tools had been used and that the screws securing the

FIGURE 18:
A good label. (Society for
the Preservation of New
England Antiquities.) The
Haskell label is torn at the
top edge, and the wood
beneath is of a paler color.

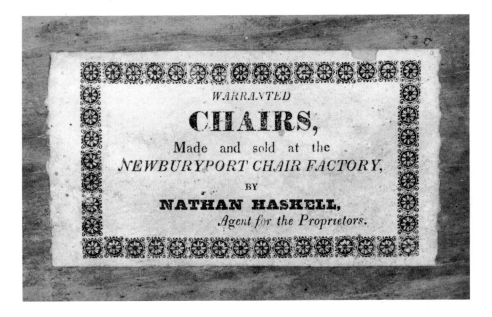

top — the only fasteners the table ever had — were modern. The labeling was but one problem; the table itself — a reproduction or a fake — was the other.

There is probably nothing as effective as a bill, brand, label, or inscription in distracting a buyer from further inspection of the furniture itself. ALL-POINTS BULLETIN: *Never be distracted from a thorough inspection by anything, including documentation.*

For savvy customers in the antique furniture market, an identifying mark or document, rather than solving a mystery, adds to the detective work. It doubles the doubts, broadens the investigation, and increases the assignment because both furniture and mark have to pass scrutiny. *Because you pay for both — for the furniture and for its documentation — check both.*

As long as documented objects bring higher prices — as they should and always will — documentation will materialize and adhere to objects. The challenge for the furniture sleuth, then, is to distinguish the honest documentation from the deceptive.

SPOTTING PROBLEMATICAL ATTRIBUTIONS

The most tenuous and by far the most common false identities occur in attribution, usually verbal and made without benefit of any documentation. Attributions may be to a particular craftsman or to a place of origin; of either type, they are routinely and cavalierly offered because they add value. Misattribution is a notorious pitfall, yet fear of it has never daunted the owners of objects (including antiques dealers) or their agents (auctioneers or consignment shop-keepers).

Attributions can be innocently inaccurate. Numerous misattributions are fostered more by a seller's wishes than by deception. Other instances are purposeful and so prevalent that misattribution actually enjoys cycles of fashion. The only-one-man-in-town caper is a good example.

In the early twentieth century, when Federal furniture was especially sought after, emulated, and reproduced, the names of known craftsmen of the Federal era — John and Thomas Seymour, Duncan Phyfe, and Samuel McIntire — became affixed to Boston, New York, and Salem furniture, respectively. The Seymours and Phyfe had large urban shops, but they also had competitors. And McIntire would have needed more hands than the Hindu god Shiva to produce all the carvings attributed to him. But even after 1931, when Mabel Swan published evidence that "Salem" work long called "McIntire" was actually by Boston craftsmen, McIntire's name was still on the tip of many a tongue.[5] The best carved work done in Federal Salem was probably not even by McIntire.[6]

Regional attributions are more accurate but lack the appeal of the personalization that comes from a maker's name. Antiques dealers are not alone in attributing a regional style to one man or shop. Through publications such as *John and Thomas Seymour: Cabinetmakers in Boston, 1794–1816*, Vernon C. Stoneman, a collector, proliferated Seymour attributions. Today, his attributions have been reassessed and debunked, but museums continue to display desk after desk attributed to the Seymours, cases so dissimilar in construction (e.g., in their dovetails and drawer construction) that they can in no way be ascribed to one shop. With some museums still guilty of Seymourizing, many antiques dealers have no qualms about doing the same. As long as a desk looks vaguely like Boston work of the Federal era, it is in danger of being dubbed Seymour; if it has painted interiors of a certain shade of blue very popular with Federal Bostonians, it will surely be called Seymour; and it it has lunette inlays (fig. 58) — available to any cabinetmaker in the area at the time — "Seymour" will be named with authority.

The eagerness for documentation is especially strong today, spawning a plethora of attributions. Publication of a craftsman's name leads to examples of his work being "discovered" in hither attic, thither shop, and yon museum. So strong is the penchant for affixing a name that it is barely stayed by the presentation of contrary facts, such as proof that a name is not that of a craftsman or even not a name at all (meet Walter on pages 28–29).

An antique should properly be attributed to a craftsman or his shop only after careful comparison has shown it to be closely related to a documented object. The documented antique must have a genuine maker's signature, brand, label, or bill of sale, or be unambiguously cited in other papers, such as a journal or family correspondence.

The savvy collector will accept no attribution to a maker for an unmarked piece of furniture unless it can pass three tests: (1) the furniture in question is identical in construction to a documented example; (2) the documented antique has proved to be genuine; and (3) the identified maker has been ascertained to have been a furniture craftsman.

These tests may at first seem intimidating, but soon they will not. Identity of construction is easy to ascertain when you check, for example, dovetail conformation, tool marks, drawer assembly, molding contours, and template pattern. Even when the objects are not in the same place, you can compare contours, templates, or one set of dovetails to another by using your pad of paper and pencil to make rubbings (as a child does with a penny).

In regard to assessing the genuine, most of this book deals with just that. And a little detective work can help you avoid being taken in by such ploys as transforming the man who owned the furniture into a cabinetmaker. Fairly accurate and extensive lists of craftsmen have been published in recent years and are a boon when tracing names. Old newspapers, city directories, and published lists, such as birth, marriage, and death records, are valuable resources. (Saxton's true trade was there in black and white in the Boston Directory.) A town's directory is available in its own library, if not in others, and librarians welcome serious inquiries by mail or phone.

Casual attributions are so prevalent that the three-part rule is worth repeating. *For an attribution of an unmarked piece of furniture to be acceptable, the piece must be identical in construction to a documented one that has proved to be genuine and whose mark has been ascertained to be that of a furniture craftsman.*

Until the very end of the eighteenth century, American furniture craftsmen rarely signed their work. About the time that the colonists became free — and probably not coincidentally — many craftsmen chose to abandon anonymity, and the marking of furniture quickly became a common though not universal practice. With the establishment of the republic, many furniture makers, in a newly ambitious and almost arrogant fashion, vied for trade, proudly signing their work with inscription, label, or brand. All of these types of identification have figured in fraud.

FIGURE 19:
Chest-on-chest; mahogany
and white pine, 1782,
Boston. Made by John
Cogswell. H. 97; W. 44¹/₄;
D. 23¹/₂. (Museum of Fine
Arts, Boston, Warden Fund.)

The most personal (and therefore usually the most exciting) mark on furniture is an inscription. Although there are exceptions, almost all inscriptions are authentic — authentic but not necessarily unambiguous or informative. An inscription penciled under the seat rail of a handsome Chippendale chair reads, "In the year 1849 I will be married."[7] The musings of the future bride or groom reveal nothing, because the style and construction of the chair shows that it was made before that date.

Even an authentic inscription can be a mystery. The most common is a single name or a last name with merely a first initial, a solid but scanty clue. Published lists of craftsmen and city directories may pinpoint the workman. Often the initial is the ubiquitous J (written as I in the Colonial era), which fails to rule out most of a clan well represented with Jameses, Jonathans, Josiahs, Jeremiahs, Josephs, and Johns. When tracking a subject, you will consider yourself blessed to find, for example, an initial Z to point to the one Zachariah in a family.

The standard for an authentic, unambiguous, descriptive inscription — the ideal — is the one on the top of the lower case of a chest-on-chest by the Boston cabinetmaker John Cogswell (fig. 19). "Made By John / Cogswell in middle Street / Boston 1782" gives all the information you could ask for: the man's name in full, the town, the date, and the important "made by" that proves that Cogswell was the craftsman, not the owner.

Owners also signed their furniture. As a result, owners of furniture have frequently been dubbed cabinetmakers, and so advertised and listed. (We will discuss owner/cabinetmaker identity crises later in this chapter, in "Whose Brand Is It?") Desks are especially prone to acquiring their owners' signatures, usually in ink or pencil. Tall case clocks, however, are routinely marked on the inside of the case door by repairers. (The clocks themselves are generally marked on their faces by their makers, whereas the men who made the cases usually remain anonymous.)

Cabinetmakers, when inscribing furniture, used ink, or pencil, or the marking chalk that was always on hand. When you find a chalk inscription in old script, make sure you are seeing what is actually there, not what you wish were there. The desire to find a craftsman's name can lead to highly imaginative misreadings. In the 1940s, for example, a cabinetmaker named Walter Edge was discovered. The chalk inscription on the back of a desk (part of a desk and bookcase) read "Gilmanton / June 5 1799," and above it was "a signature" in chalk, "Walter Edge." In 1965, Ada Young looked with clearer eyes at the chalk and saw the craftsman's working notation, "Upper Edge."[8]

"Walter" should never have been conjured up. Gilmanton and the date are excellent documentation. The clarity of "Gilmanton" tended to obscure the fact that "Upper" really did not look like "Walter." *Don't let part of an inscription or other document distract you from carefully reading the whole.*

Cabinetmakers regularly mark their work with notes for themselves, such as "upper," "back," or "left." When a bombé chest of four drawers was auctioned in 1972, it was believed to be marked in chalk "Boston." The name of a town can enhance an antique, although in this instance the appearance of the bombé already said "Boston." In fact, the appearance was the only thing that said it — the chalk inscription under the case said "Bottom."

When deciphering chalk marks, look for cabinetmaking notes and terms first. This method should keep the savvy sleuth from misreading inscriptions as names of towns or men.

The case of Walter Frothingham (plate 2) is a mystery created out of reading, writing, and misreading. Among the large Frothingham family no one was named Walter, yet in 1953 a "Walter" appeared to be part of a signature pictured in an article in *Antiques*.[9] Walter, it was supposed, was related to the illustrious Benjamin Frothingham (1734–1809), a cabinetmaker and son of a cabinetmaker, who ran a shop in Charlestown, Massachusetts, in the late eighteenth century. Benjamin has been the best-known maker of Massachusetts Chippendale furniture, and much Boston furniture of that style has been attributed to him.

Benjamin employed many woodworkers, and among them there arose a penchant for signing the furniture they made in the Frothingham shop. Some inscribed tiny signatures, merely scratching them in the wood. Others, apparently taking the lead from their master — who as early as 1753 signed and dated a desk and bookcase — put large, readable signatures here or there on the unfinished surfaces of their products. One worker, probably an apprentice and a relative, signed Wm *Frothingham* on the bottom of a drawer. Generations later someone, probably mistaking the superscript *m* (which made *William* out of the initial *W*) for a calligraphic flourish, filled out W^m's inscription by writing *alter* after the W. Faking, you see, can stretch so far as to alter a perfectly good signature.

LABELS THAT LIE

The staff at the Ford Museum became suspicious of the Homer label on the Creamer table (figs. 16 and 17) because it looked too new. In investigating it, they lifted a tiny portion of the paper and found that the wood underneath was about the same color as the surrounding wood. (Wood darkens with age when exposed to air; wood protected from air by paper or other materials does not darken.) Because the wood that had supposedly been exposed for a century and a half was not noticeably darker than that covered by the label, the curators decided to lift more of the paper.

They discovered that it was not a label at all. Writing on the obverse showed that it was in fact a bill. Eighteenth-century commercial stationery was sometimes printed with an emblem in the center of the page, and merchants wrote on the obverse side of the sheet. The Homer "label" came from such stationery. The "label" looked rather new because it had evidently not been exposed to air and light until it was glued down on the already darkened wood of the table. Freshly cut out, it showed none of the usual wear. Its four edges were almost intact, its corners sharp and square.

Labels exposed to air and light darken and become brittle. Original paper labels, unless they are in a protected spot, rarely remain intact on furniture that has been in use for over a century. The wood moves, the glue dries, the paper may lift, and the edges become vulnerable to breaking off. When they do, the wood underneath, paler than the surrounding wood because it has been protected from air and light, begins to darken (fig. 18). If bits of paper lift up and break off at different times, wood of various shades may show around the remnant of the label, with the lightest tones in the areas beneath the most recent losses.

WHOSE BRAND IS IT?

Branded furniture, until recent years, was assumed to have been marked by the maker. The M.MACKAY brand on some Boston Chippendale furniture — a brand that furniture scholars ascribe to an owner, Mungo Mackay — was the exception that proved the rule. Common wisdom held that craftsmen, not owners, marked furniture, and Mackay's brand was regarded as an oddity. But the J:LANGDON brand on some Queen Anne chairs could not make a furniture craftsman of Langdon, the Portsmouth merchant and shipowner who became a United States senator and New Hampshire governor. And the C.STORER brand on a set of chairs could not make a cabinetmaker of Portsmouth's Clement Storer, merchant, congressman, senator, and high sheriff.[10]

Nor did the tiny (⅛-inch-high) D.AUSTIN stamped on two different

sets of chairs, the R.HART branded on two tables and a chair, the I.SALTER on an armchair, the C BLUNT (fig. 20) on a candlestand (fig. 21), the L.COTTON on a card table, the S.HAM on a desk and bookcase, or the J.HAVEN on a desk make furniture craftsmen of Portsmouth merchants Daniel Austin, Richard Hart, John Salter, Charles Blunt, Leonard Cotton, Supply Ham, and John, Joseph, James, or Josiah Haven.[11] Instead, these men, who in the late eighteenth and early nineteenth centuries were involved in international shipping, used branding irons (Austin and Haven had iron dies that were hammered, not burned, into the wood) to mark not only shipping crates but their household possessions as well.

In 1978, when *Antiques* published an article, "Marked Portsmouth Furniture," about the furniture and the marks of these merchants, most brands were still assumed to be those of the makers. But the knee-jerk reading of branded furniture as marked by the maker has begun to abate. In 1981, another *Antiques* article, "Branded and Stamped New York Furniture" by Roderic H. Blackburn, cited more owner-marked furniture, much of it branded with initials.[12] Additional merchants' brands have since been identified, among them O.BRIARD for Oliver Briard, another merchant of Portsmouth; TREADWELL, probably for Charles Treadwell, yet another Portsmouth merchant; and I HILL, for either Isaac or one of the five J. Hills of Berwick, Maine.

An owner's name can enhance an antique, sometimes by locating a town and suggesting an approximate date for the furniture; a maker's name surely adds to an object's desirability and increases its price significantly. In some circles, the tendency is still to see a maker's name in each newly discovered mark.

Old mistakes endure. Once an imaginary cabinetmaker has been created out of whole cloth, he clings to life by every thread. Two imaginary cabinetmakers — complete with imagined if not imaginary Massachusetts addresses — are R. Hart of Newburyport and D. Austin of Charlestown. Both materialized several years ago from the brands of two of the aforementioned New Hampshire merchants. The R.HART brand of merchant Richard was said to be — and was for years accepted as — that of a cabinetmaker. Based on the style of the branded wares, this imaginary cabinetmaker was said to be from Newburyport.

A fictitious D. Austin sprang fully formed from the mark of merchant Daniel Austin. D. Austin was said to be from a family of furniture makers in Charlestown, where two Johns, a Richard, and a Josiah of that name actually were a carver, two chairmakers, and a cabinetmaker. D. Austin, however, was one Austin who neither made furniture nor came from Charlestown.

In the nineteenth century, the use of makers' brands as well as stencils (fig. 154) and printed labels became common. Many producers of Windsors and other volume-production chairs branded their work, most using a first initial and a last name. Try to ascertain if a mark is that of a maker or an owner; look for confirming information. If the answer is not in the local library, it may be but a postage stamp away.

Priscilla Sloss, a collector with a hearty skepticism, owned a Windsor rocking chair branded A WETHERBEE. She first looked in books for information on the Wetherbee brand; not finding the name there, she wrote to an authority on Windsors, Nancy Goyne Evans, the registrar at Winterthur, enclosing photographs of the chair and of details, including the mark itself. Mrs. Evans responded that the chair was marked by Abijah Wetherbee (1781–1832) of New Ipswich, New Hampshire, and made between 1830 and 1835. Mrs. Sloss's enjoyment of the chair was enhanced, and when she sells it, so will be the price. Mrs. Evans's book, *American Windsor Furniture*, will soon be published, putting similar information on over three thousand Windsor chairmakers readily at hand in libraries.

If the information you seek is not available in any printed source, write to an expert. There are many, and none is in hiding. To find the name of an expert, place a query in a periodical dealing with antiques, write to the curator of a museum that has American furniture, or ask a knowledgeable antiques dealer. (In requesting the name and address of an expert, you can also learn how knowledgeable the dealer is.)

No doubt in the early twentieth century many an antiques buyer was sold a bill of goods when told that a bill of sale or the upper part of one, a billhead, belonged with the antique being sold. If a bill of sale is presented to you as documentation for an antique, be particular.

One: *Do not accept a scissored-off portion of a larger bill as acceptable documentation.* The bill should be as intact as a document of its age can be expected to be.

Two: *Require that the bill have as solid a history as the furniture.* The latter must be traceable from the date on the bill.

Three: *Accept only a bill that is unambiguous, one that clearly is associated with the furniture it purports to document.* For example, an eighteenth-century bill is found among a family's papers. Is it a valid document for the tea chest known to have been in that family? Yes; the household was unlikely to have had more than one tea chest in the eighteenth century. On the other hand, an eighteenth-century bill for chairs found among family papers is too ambiguous. Households contained several sets of chairs; to which does this bill refer? A brief description, at least, would be needed to make a case for the chair bill. Unfortunately, the common description for chairs referred to the color of the upholstery — as in "12 green chairs" — and usually the original upholstery has long since been removed.

It is so hard to prove that the bill and the furniture have the same history that documentation by bill of sale has not been in fashion in recent years. (For the type of auxiliary information needed to tie a bill to furniture, see "The Case of the Case Piece, Part Two," pages 124–126.) Nevertheless, grocer Saxton did enter cabinetry with a billhead, and other furniture in Creamer's antique shop in the late 1920s also carried such "documentation." Those billheads and bills of sale fraudulently linked to antiques in the past may be with them still.

And, as trends are cyclical, bills as documentation may return to fashion, engendering more doctored bills. *Be on guard against all fraudulent identification, be it in script, label, brand, or bill. Check every ID.*

Checking an ID is more than insurance — it can bring a big reward. When the Society for the Preservation of New England Antiquities discovered a 1759 bill of sale from John Scollay to Jonathan Sayward (1713–1797) among the latter's papers, it was exciting news because the museum owned Sayward's house and furniture. Two of the items referred to were still in the house, a tea chest and an easy chair. Each item was the only one of its kind in the household, so tying the furniture to the bill was uncomplicated.

Scollay was a dockside Boston merchant; he sold Sayward an imported English tea chest. However, the easy chair was made in America — probably, it seemed, in Boston. The museum's curator, Brock Jobe, thought it worth a chance to check the surviving journals of a Boston upholsterer of the era, Samuel Grant. The records showed that Grant had sold Scollay "a Green Easie Cha^r & packing [£]4:18:6," the day before Scollay billed Sayward for "1 Easy Chair & packing £4:18:6."

The documentation for the easy chair pinpointed the identity of the upholsterer (the chair retains some of its original upholstery), narrowed the possibilities to two chairmakers (other Grant papers showed that in 1759 the upholsterer obtained easy-chair frames from only two men — Clement Vincent and George Bright), and proved the price of the item, the city of its origin, and the time of its manufacture. By checking identification, the caring collector can sometimes find an entire biography. *Check out an ID on the chance that it might be good.*

Styles as Clues

4

IN PURSUIT OF THE PRISTINE

THE current antiques market is replete with collectors pursuing not merely antiques but pristine antiques. For the last few years, great value has been placed on the object in the rough, the furniture that has escaped the hands of repairers and restorers — the desk with its original brass handles, even if many of them are broken or missing; the table with its original top, even if that surface is badly warped; the chair with old paint, even if it now wears four additional coats. In such furniture the antique's past remains recorded in the object itself. Although many scholars make much of this inherent history, the greatest appeal such antiques hold for most collectors is that changes and damage are most easily discerned in the unsullied and uncorrupted. *So, pursue the pristine.*

But you need not restrict yourself to the pristine. There are few examples of the truly untouched, and you have to pay a premium for antiques in their original state. Most good furniture has been repaired or restored (often soundly) to a sturdier, more useful state. You may be very willing to accept, for example, new handles, refinishing, and sensitive repair. When you are a savvy sleuth who can discern fakes and frauds, you do not need to rely on a pristine state to prove that an antique is genuine.

Whereas today's collectors search for the pristine, early in this century collectors sought the unusual. Equating the odd with the outstanding, they enthusiastically pursued unique examples and fell prey to altered antiques. Furniture craftsmen, alert to the desires of customers for the eccentric, made an industry of making the irregular.

One, a nine-shelled chest (plate 4; see "The Case of the Case Piece, Part Two," pages 110–112) is a particularly spectacular and ornate oddity. This fraud of the old parts/new object sort would never, as we shall see, pass an examination, but it apparently escaped inspection by hiding behind a cloak of rarity. Richard Goodbar wrote that the chest's rarity is "the first evidence that should have raised questions" because a genuine nine-shelled chest would be "more than enough to give a collector a pounding heart and buzzing in the ears."[1] The onset of these symptoms, especially when accompanied by an affordable price, should chill your spine and raise your eyebrows. *When presented with the unusual, lift the cloak of rarity and look behind it.*

In antique furniture, rare birds are usually birds that never were. Genuine pieces of furniture fall within a style period and a design tradition—each reflects the era and area of its origin. Smart collectors look for the typical and, if they can afford it, for the exemplary (the outstanding object that is the best in example of a design but not a deviant from it). *So, stalk the typical,* or, to state the rule in the converse, *eschew the unusual.*

EDUCATING THE (PRIVATE) EYE

To spot the pristine antique and to eschew the unusual, you need an educated eye that can detect telltale deviations from the norm in style and design. You are probably already familiar with the several styles of furniture; if not, you soon will be. You should also become familiar with the idiosyncratic variations in furniture design that occur in different regions of the country. You can become a specialist by boning up on the regional design characteristics peculiar to the

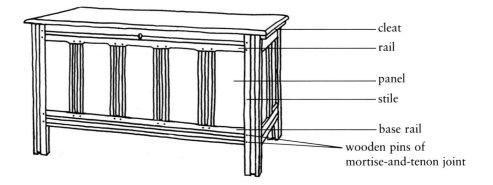

FIGURE 22: Diagram 1, based on figure 74.

cleat
rail
panel
stile
base rail
wooden pins of mortise-and-tenon joint

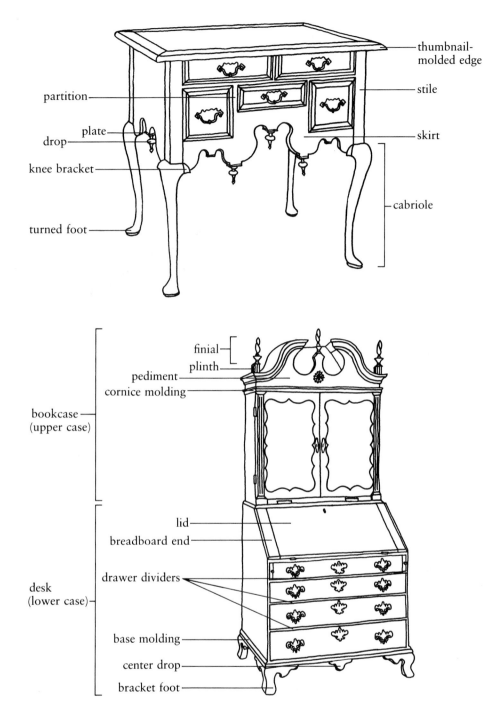

FIGURE 23:
Diagram 2, based on
figure 105.

thumbnail-
molded edge

partition

stile

plate
drop

skirt

knee bracket

cabriole

turned foot

FIGURE 24:
Diagram 3, based on
figure 119.

finial

plinth

pediment

cornice molding

bookcase
(upper case)

lid

breadboard end

drawer dividers

desk
(lower case)

base molding

center drop

bracket foot

areas you live in or are likely to visit regularly — in short, the designs
native to those places where you are apt to be antiquing.

Eye training is rigorous but loads of fun, for it demands looking
at as many examples as possible. Look in museums, including small
historical museums that may contain pristine examples of local origin. Look in antiques stores long before you are prepared to buy.
Look at auction previews before you are skilled enough to tackle
the sales themselves. And look in books, for they offer access to a
multitude of examples.

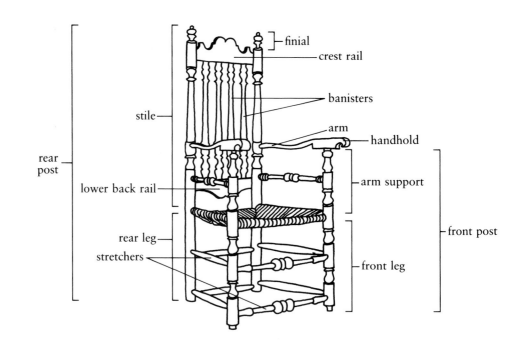

FIGURE 25:
Diagram 4, based on
figure 136.

You can seek out quality when you buy, but while you're training, go for quantity. Quantity will help you to discern the similarities and the distinctions that mark American design. Some fakes and frauds will be hiding among the many, but sheer quantity will help overwhelm the deceptions that you will perforce see.

The following training course has four steps: a quick survey of picture books, a treasure hunt in a museum, a study of regional variations, and a honing of skills in museums, good antiques shops, and auction previews. Rookies should begin at step 1; many trainees are ready to begin at 2; others start at 3. If you are already style-savvy — try your eye on the pictures in figures 33–36 — and well versed in the local design you want to collect, proceed to Chapter 5.

1. The Quick Survey

To study furniture, it is important to become familiar with at least some of the terms for its several parts (figs. 22–26). As you look through picture books, focus on the parts as well as on each piece of furniture as a whole.

Some survey books are recommended in the bibliography. The list is not definitive or all-inclusive; the volumes were chosen for the number of their photographs. Do read John Kirk's *Early American Furniture* — the text is excellent — and perhaps some of the others as well. Choose several books, and look, look, look.

Two outstanding specialized works are Victor Chinnery's *Oak Furniture* and Charles F. Montgomery's *American Furniture, The Federal Period.* The older books on the list are likely to be available

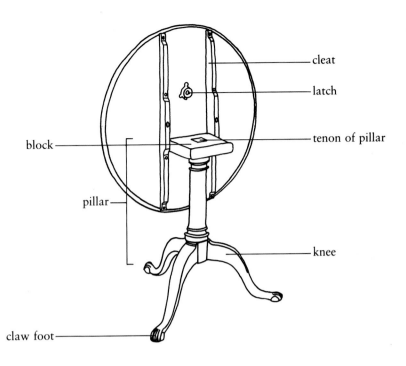

cleat

latch

tenon of pillar

block

knee

pillar

claw foot

in your local library. Unfortunately, most older books — though not only the older ones — contain much that is flawed or fraudulent. Wallace Nutting's *Furniture Treasury*, probably the most frequently perused book on antique furniture, includes the style-confused and misleading table shown here in figure 30.

Look at the object as a whole. Is it generally curvy, or are most of its lines straight and boxy? Is it delicate or hefty, or something in between? *Then look at the several details.* How does each contribute to the general appearance?

Successful designs integrate components so that they enhance the whole. Even unsuccessful designs exhibit some pattern relating parts and whole. For example, on high chests with turned legs, a little surveillance of stretchers — the flat strips running from leg to leg just above the ball feet — shows that the line of the skirt dictated the outline of the stretchers (see figs. 27 and 28). The stretchers not only strengthen the construction of the base but form a reflection of the skirt just above the floor. Yet almost everyone on the squad has seen an old high chest whose stretchers failed to echo the skirt design. The astute detective assumes neither poor skirt/stretcher design nor merely replaced stretchers but instead examines the base carefully, usually discovering that all or most of it is a replacement.

Patterns of designs change over time and over distance. The former are called styles; the latter, regional variations. Old reproductions often mix styles (fig. 196); yesterday's fakes and frauds frequently mix regional characteristics. So furniture sleuths need eyes that are style-wise and can spot mix-ups.

FIGURE 27:
High chest; pine, tulip, and ash, 1710–1727, Saybrook, Connecticut. H. 54⅝; W. 40⅛; D. 21⅛. (Henry Francis du Pont Winterthur Museum.) On this painted high chest, the outline of the stretchers echoes that of the skirt — a good sign.

FIGURE 28:
High chest; 1715–1735, Boston. H. 62½; W. 40½; D. 22. (Photograph courtesy Israel Sack, Inc.) As they should, the stretchers on this veneered high chest echo the skirt.

American furniture is itself a regional variant of European design. To place it in context, leaf through at least one of the many furniture histories that are worldwide in scope (catalogued as 749.2 in the Dewey decimal system). Kirk's *American Furniture and the British Tradition to 1830* is especially good in its illustrations of prototypes for American designs. While you note close relationships, try also to discern differences.

2. The Treasure Hunt

Looking in books, no matter how many, cannot alone suffice, but books prepare you to track down evidence in a museum. If possible, select a museum with a fairly large collection of American furniture. As you have already done in looking at pictures, first view each object in its entirety, then step forward to see each of its several elements at close range. Only then should you consult the label.

In your first, overall view, while gauging the delicacy or heftiness of the design, its curviness or rectilinearity, note how weight and line are combined. A boxy pattern may be broad and ponderous (see fig. 33) or slender and attenuated (see fig. 14). Some rounded shapes — especially spheres and flattened balls — seem heavy; others — vertical ovals in particular — appear light. Some legs appear to bear their load easily; others seem to strain to support great heft (compare two tripod tables, figs. 21 and 201).

Concentrate on distinct elements of the design — the surface decoration, legs, feet, hardware, motifs, shapes, and woods (the museum

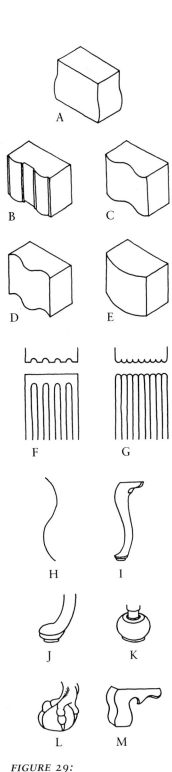

FIGURE 29:
(A) bombé; (B) blockfront;
(C) oxbow facade; (D) serpentine facade; (E) bowed
facade; (F) fluting (top, seen
from above); (G) reeding
(top, seen from above);
(H) cyma curve; (I) cabriole;
(J) turned foot; (K) ball
foot; (L) claw foot;
(M) bracket foot.

labels are helpful here). These design characteristics are the treasures you are hunting. Find an example of each of the following and date the period of its use by consulting the label:

flat facade
bombé (fig. 29, A)
blockfront (fig. 29, B)
oxbow facade (fig. 29, C)
serpentine facade (fig. 29, D)
bowed facade (fig. 29, E)
eagles or other birds
urns
shells or fans
pilasters or columns
fluting (fig. 29, F)
reeding (fig. 29, G)
cyma curves (fig. 29, H)
C curves
cabrioles (fig. 29, I)

straight legs
tapered legs
turned legs
turned feet (fig. 29, J)
ball feet (fig. 29, K)
claw feet (fig. 29, L)
bracket feet (fig. 29, M)
applied turnings
carving
walnut (plate 10, upper right)
mahogany (plate 10, middle left)
oak (plate 8, lower left)
veneer (fig. 58)
inlay (fig. 58)

Some of these characteristics commonly occur together. For example, applied turnings and oak are both featured in seventeenth-century design. Noting such relationships is important in training the eye. Some characteristics that do not occur together in period objects — cabrioles and oak, for example — do make joint appearances in reproductions (fig. 160), where they tip off the detective to trouble.

After completing the treasure hunt, you may want to sort your finds by style, listing all the elements that occur in a certain era and putting the whole in chronological order under these headings:

The several features of seventeenth-century design
The baroque features of William and Mary design
    (ca. 1695–1730)
The curvilinear Queen Anne style (ca. 1730–1750)
The rococo Chippendale style (ca. 1750–1780)
The delicate Federal style (ca. 1785–1810)
The heavier neoclassical style (ca. 1815–1830)
The Machine-Age or Victorian style (ca. 1830–1900)
and, if you can find them:
    The Art Nouveau style (ca. 1900–1920s)
    The Art Deco style (ca. 1925–1950s)

Once you have put together a chronology, look at a few puzzlers. The photograph of a card table (fig. 30) appeared in Nutting's

FIGURE 30:
*Card table with a dual
(neoclassical/Art Deco)
personality.*

FIGURE 31:
*Side chair; maple and oak,
original leather upholstery,
1725–1740, Boston.
H. 43⅞; W. 18⅜; Seat
D. 14¾; Seat H. 18¾.
(Wilton, Richmond, Virginia.)
Chairs with original upholstery are rare and valuable
as proof of what nailing
patterns to expect on a
stripped frame. These Spanish feet were pieced in original construction, and the
added pieces have come off,
a common loss. Not all
Spanish feet are pieced
(fig. 32).*

Furniture Treasury, and he dated it "1810."[2] The only elements of nineteenth-century style on the table are, in the words of the caption, the "Table Frame with a Panel and Rounded Corners" and the "Base with an Irregular Scroll at One End and Brass Feet at the Other." Only these parts are in the neoclassical style. The central pedestal, called by Nutting a "Ring-Shaped Standard Intersected by a Semi-circular Support for the Table" is pure Art Deco design, new at the time the book was published, 1928. The entire table may have been new, its neoclassical elements merely reproductions.

Some chairs (figs. 31 and 32) also mix styles. The bases of both chairs are William and Mary, yet the chairbacks are of later styles. The leather-upholstered chair has the curved back of a Queen Anne chair, and the back of the other is Chippendale. The frame of the leather chair was made by an urban turner; the other chair was made in a more rural setting. Both are authentic antiques. They retain, as eighteenth-century turners' chairs were wont to do, an old-fashioned base while adopting the newer fashion above. When such craftsmen mixed the latest style with earlier design elements, they generally put the new design in the most prominent place.

Your chronology, showing what was stylish when and which design elements go together, is a resource to carry in writing until it is merely redundant with what you carry in your head. *Each time you look at an antique, ask yourself:*

1) "What is its date?" or "What is its style period?" Date an object from its latest feature, not by any older one that may endure and, years after its heyday, be found in combination with newer, more stylish elements. In the instance of the chair with the Chippendale back and the turned legs and Spanish feet (fig. 32), the later, more fashionable back — not the base, popular since the William and Mary period — dates the chair and designates its style.

You must decide on the period in order to answer the next questions:

2) "Do the proportions conform to those of the period?" A common alteration to antique cases early in this century was to diminish their size to make them more suitable for small twentieth-century houses and apartments. How-to literature included instructions for narrowing such typically broad cases as Chippendale chests and Federal sideboards. Many makers of old reproductions copied period details but catered to their contemporaries' taste in scale. Rare proportions are particularly suspect. The "pleasingly petite Chippendale desk" should raise a red flag, because petite and Chippendale do not go together.

3) "Was this form [or type] of furniture made in that era?" Some people want the equivalent of a TV table of the Federal era, so some forms of furniture miraculously appear in a style that predates the form. This question helps you quickly identify some reproductions and a few "antiques" of the old parts/new object type, such as the lower half of a seventeenth-century cupboard posing as a sideboard.

4) "What are the most valuable stylistic details on the antique?" If anything was added after the antique's original production, it is likely to fall into this category. To expedite matters, you can begin your inspection with such high-risk elements and ascertain first that the valuable details are original.

5) "Is the construction consistent with the period?" (Later chapters will help with this question.)

6) "Were the tools used those of the period?" (Chapter 5 starts you on the trail of tool marks.)

So, with style chronology in hand, if not yet in head, you are ready for the next challenge.

3. The Detailed Study of Regional Variations

Books and magazines provide good training in style recognition and regional peculiarities. In the bibliography, regional studies are marked with an asterisk. You should peruse as many as possible of the general works and consult the pertinent starred sources.

It is important (and easier than you may think) to accustom your eye to regional styles, to see the characteristics that objects from one area tend to have in common. Oriental rugs are one example: although all Sarouks are not identical, one can easily learn to recognize a Sarouk as a Sarouk. Like the Persian villagers making wool carpets in their own specific designs, American furniture makers developed patterns distinctive to their locales. A Newport blockfront with

FIGURE 32:
Side chair; maple, 1770–1800, eastern Massachusetts. H. 39¾; W. 18¼; Seat D. 14; Seat H. 17⅜. (Society for the Preservation of New England Antiquities.) The chair is painted black; the front seat corners are painted to match the rush seat.

FIGURE 33:
Cupboard; oak. (Connecti-
cut Historical Society.)

FIGURE 34:
Desk and bookcase. H. 107;
W. 43¹/₈; D. 23. (Yale Uni-
versity Art Gallery Study
Collection.)

FIGURE 35:
Side chair. H. 37¹/₄;
W. 20³/₄; Seat D. 18; Seat
H. 17¹/₄. (Society for the
Preservation of New Eng-
land Antiquities.)

FIGURE 36:
High chest; walnut. (Mu-
seum of Fine Arts, Boston,
Julia Knight Fox Fund.)

Philadelphia carvings is as suspect as a Tabriz with a Bokhara border.

Let's look at a lineup of suspects: a cupboard (fig. 33), a desk and bookcase (fig. 34), a chair (fig. 35), and a high chest (fig. 36). Three of these combine the regional variations of more than one region; one presents a mixture of style periods. An experienced style-wise detective can tell much from just looking at the lineup. Can you see which one mixes time, where and why, and which mix regions, where and why? Tips: one is a reproduction; one is enhanced or incorrectly restored; one is a fraud; and one is a fake. (Answers are below; don't peek.)

4. Honing Skills at Museums, Shops, and Auctions

Patroling museums, good antiques shops, and auction previews will refine your book-learned observational skills. A "hands-off" policy is standard at museums, but in shops and auction houses you can sharpen your skills with stylistic clues and simultaneously put your hands on the material evidence. It's time to get technical.

CONFIDENTIAL: For detectives who have checked out the lineup (figs. 33–36).

The cupboard, desk and bookcase, and high chest combine regional variations; the chair presents a mix of style periods. The wheres and whys, one by one:

The cupboard was made in the spirit of seventeenth-century New England design by Walter Hosmer of Wethersfield, Connecticut, a collector-dealer-restorer-maker-faker in the late nineteenth century. Hosmer's enthusiasm for reviving the old styles is evident in his creation, which once fooled people but today seems a pastiche honoring the past. The general organization and pillars follow eastern Massachusetts cupboards, but the designs on the waist molding emulate New Haven patterns, the flowers on the lower stiles suggest Wethersfield, and the doors are copied from Windsor, Connecticut, boxes. (A style-smart detective need not know all the design sources to discern that a mix is present.)

The desk and bookcase is a fraudulent marriage of a walnut bookcase from Pennsylvania to a mahogany desk from eastern Massachusetts. The culprit who joined the two old spouses carved a shell on the desk-interior door to match that on the pediment.

The side chair, an honest early-twentieth-century "Chippendale" reproduction, mixes eras by featuring neoclassical carvings on the splat. The stylized lyre near the top and the leafy scroll below are neoclassical carvings with Art Deco heft. As is common on some reproductions, the leafage at the knees looks more applied than carved in.

The high chest is a splendid antique made in 1739 in Charlestown, just outside Boston, by Ebenezer Hartshorn (1689–1781), but it has been incorrectly restored, or possibly enhanced, with the addition of flame finials of the Philadelphia type. Urns are missing; the plinths are new; the legs are replacements.

Technology as Evidence

FIXING THE TIME OF THE CRIME

THE furniture detective does not need a scientific mind or a science lab, yet every fakes-and-fraud inspector uses technical facts to pin down the material evidence provided by wood, wood tools, wood fasteners, and wood fastenings. Because the woods, tools, and techniques of furniture-making changed over the years, and because the innovations are datable (e.g., before 1880 there were no wire or round-shanked nails), technology is especially valuable when the assignment is to date the furniture — to recognize its antiquity or spot it as an impostor by fixing the time of the crime.

Knowing only a few dates (and approximate ones at that), you can detect a plethora of clues. Cut nails were first manufactured about 1790, so if cut nails were found in a "Queen Anne" desk, they would identify it as suspect. Because oak was split rather than sawn during the seventeenth century, sawn oak panels would finger a "Pilgrim" chest as not of the period.

However, the technological route to dating an antique is a one-way street. You can date the start of a new technology but not the end of an old one. Old technology is seldom lost. Woodworkers can still split wood. Wrought nails identical to those used before the advent of the cheaper cut nails are still made. Some old technologies are expensive to reproduce, but fakers are not put off by the cost of, let's say, wrought nails. Such nails in a "Bible box" do not establish its age. *Never use the presence of an old technique as proof of antiquity.*

FIGURE 37:
Detail of a drawer bottom
(fig. 10). Blackened wood
surrounds a hole left by a
wrought nail, whose head
and shank were irregular
in shape.

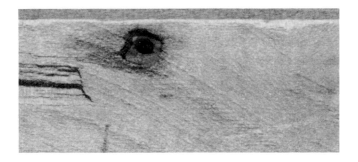

Although old wrought nails themselves do not prove age, they can provide evidence of whether they have been in place for a long time. As the wrought iron corrodes, it blackens the surrounding wood (fig. 37, evidence from a lost nail; and fig. 38, a cotter-pin hinge that has never been moved). Most people expect iron corrosion to be red rust; ferric oxide (Fe_2O_3) is red, but ferrous oxide (FeO) is black. The acids in the wood (oak is especially rich in tannic acid) react with the iron's ferrous oxide, creating a black compound that bleeds into the wood around the nailhead.

So ferrous oxide can help the furniture sleuth, but carbon-14 cannot. Carbon-14 dating — measuring radioactivity to ascertain how long ago organic material was alive — is fine for determining the ages of prehistoric skulls, but, with an error factor of centuries, the technique lacks the precision to authenticate American antique furniture. Carbon dating cannot determine whether a Federal card table was made in 1800 or is a reproduction; it can only prove that the table was not made in ancient Rome.

FIGURE 38:
Iron cotter-pin hinge, detail of box shown in figures 65–67. (Society for the Preservation of New England Antiquities.) The ends of the interlocking cotter pins are splayed on the inside of the box and on the outside of the lid.

Radiography or X ray lets you see inside the wood to spot an otherwise invisible joint. Ultraviolet or black light can reveal paint that is no longer visible to the unaided eye and show restorations in a painted finish. More on these techniques under "The Joints" and "A Painted Past"; first, some less exotic technologies that are more accessible and more valuable in sleuthing.

MATERIAL EVIDENCE: WOOD

Every successful furniture detective has as an ace in the hole a sound understanding of wood. The nature of this collection of cellulose cells is dictated by its original function as the supporting structure and the conduit for fluid in a tree.

Wood in its original state can be envisioned as a handful of parallel sipping straws. Both are largely hollow. The bundle of straws is mostly air; the wood, when alive with activity, was over eighty percent water. Like the bunch of straws, wood has a direction, known as its "grain," and appears very different in cross section (end grain) than it does sideways or in longitudinal section (straight grain). Like the bunch of straws, it offers significant sturdiness for a lightweight material.

The straw analogy can make evident the limited adhesive abilities of wood. Imagine two bunches of straws placed end to end — a honeycomb of openings against a honeycomb of openings — and you'll have a good idea of why end grain cannot be glued to end grain. Envision the straws at right angles to one another, and the image shows why gluing end grain even to straight grain is futile. But place the straws side by side, with straight grain against straight grain, and the glue holds.

Knowing how wood can and cannot be glued enables you to understand the limitations governing the work of cabinetmakers and the similar constraints on repairers, enhancers, and overrestorers. For example, to glue a new foot to the bottom of a sawed-off leg — both surfaces end grain — one must introduce a dowel or spline into both pieces (a doweled joint, fig. 49), or make an oblique saw cut for a long, angled glue surface (a spliced joint, fig. 103). Wood technology controlled the operations in furniture shops of the seventeenth, eighteenth, and nineteenth centuries. The sleuth who understands wood appreciates furniture more and can separate the antique from the fraud more readily.

The principal cells of wood are long, slender, tubelike tracheids, squarish in cross section and with minute openings at each end to allow the sap to rise. The tree grows stouter from a layer — the

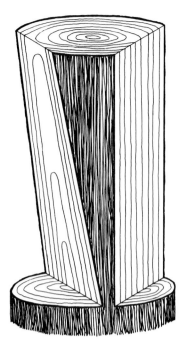

FIGURE 39:
Annual rings in cross, angled, and longitudinal section.

cambium — not far beneath the bark. During each growing season, the cambium lays down a new layer of tracheids, first a growth of broad tracheids, earlywood, then cells with stronger walls and smaller openings, latewood. Each paired layer of early- and latewood is known as an annual ring; the outermost ring is the newest.

Annual rings are easily seen, not only in cross section, where they can be counted to reveal the age of the tree, but in an angled cut, as arcs, and in a longitudinal section of straight timbers, as bands of contrasting color and density (fig. 39). The pattern or design that the annual rings impart to a wooden board is called "figure." Some people refer to figure as "grain," but "grain" should properly be reserved for its academic meaning: the way the tracheids, or fibers — or, back to our analogy, the sipping straws — line up. Grain is a characteristic of wood's structure; figure is a quality of its beauty.

Rays run at right angles to the annual rings, radiating out from the center of the tree. Although the rays on softwood trees — the conifers or needle-leaved evergreens — are barely visible, those on hardwoods — broad-leaved trees — are large and readily seen and often impart an important feature to the wood. The silvery slivers that distinguish the appearance of oak (plate 8, lower left) are rays.

Softwoods have resins and tiny canals in which the resins run; hardwoods have large conduits called vessels that run parallel to the tracheids. Resin canals are invisible to the naked eye, but vessels appear as tiny striations on many hardwood boards. The dark dashes on American black walnut (plate 10, upper right) are vessel lines.

Every wood, whether a softwood or a hardwood, has its own distinctive cellular characteristics and distinctive appearance to the unaided eye. Furniture inspectors who can identify furniture woods may solve a case more quickly than others, because the wood can be a strong lead in establishing the time and place of origin for the furniture and may indicate repair, reworking, or worse. For example, La Montagne's hoax (fig. 1) is oak; the genuine Governor Bradford (fig. 131) is ash.

With the aid of some close-ups (plates 7–10), your eye probably can learn to distinguish oak from ash and walnut from mahogany. (If not, microanalysis can, but more on that below.) Such distinctions are most helpful with repairs, enhancements, marriages, and remade objects. Repairers, restorers, and improvers, working in a shop full of old parts, often used an available mahogany splat on an otherwise walnut Chippendale chair. Or they turned a handy piece of oak, substituting it for ash when filling out a seventeenth-century chair.

Your eye can become adept at distinguishing at least some woods from others. With over 100,000 species, identification problems are inevitable. An experienced furniture detective, unable to identify a

wood, is not defeated, humbled, or coaxed into a wild guess.

When you are doubtful about a wood's identity, a professionally trained eye, a microscope, and a government lab will assist you for the price of a postage stamp. Microanalysis is especially important in differentiating the real puzzlers — a sliver of wood on a microscope slide can be identified as being either American black walnut, *Juglans nigra*, or English walnut, *Juglans regia*; either white pine or pitch pine; and either red oak, *Quercus rubra* (an American wood), or white oak, *Q. alba* (also from America), or white oak, *Q. robur* (from Europe). All you need to do is to cut a small sample of wood to send to the lab.

Many a furniture owner is willing to have his furniture wood analyzed, so ask. He may be as curious as you are. Explain the procedure you will follow. You may need to strike a deal, saying, "I will buy this if it's American. If the sample proves that the wood is American, it's mine; if it's a European wood, it's still yours."

With the owner's assistance, select a hidden part of the piece of wood you want to sample. Don't gouge the wood out of a flat surface, but cut it along a pointed edge — along the inside corner of a leg, just beneath the seat, or at the rear edge of the back of a drawer (fig. 40). You need a sample ⅜ inch long, running with the grain of the wood (in the examples cited, the grain runs with the length of the leg and from side to side on the drawer back).

To get this ⅜-inch sliver, cut down about ⅛ inch on either side of the sample with the sharp knife from your tool kit. As you complete the second cut, rotate your blade so that its upper edge turns away from the sample, driving the bottom of the blade against the sample and causing the wood between the cuts to crack along the grain. Your sample will pop free. Careful: it may pop up and fly away, sending you scouring the floor for a tiny piece of wood with two age-darkened sides and one bright, freshly split surface.

Evidence must always be carefully handled. Immediately place the sliver in a small envelope that you seal and label then and there. When you mark the envelope, be specific: "from the right rear leg of Mr. H's chair." You may want to note your guess: "beech or maple." Beech is common in antique English chairs, maple in American ones. With the cost of an American chair well above that of its English counterpart, your sliver of evidence and a bit of wood technology have great value.

You need only write a short note asking that the wood be microscopically analyzed, enclose your sample, still in its own little envelope (or samples, each in a separate envelope), and mail your letter to: United States Department of Agriculture, Forest Products Laboratory, One Gifford Pinchot, Madison, WI 53705. Your note will be returned, probably in a couple of weeks, with the information you want added. "*Acer* sp., maple," and the chair is yours; "Pine of the white pine group, probably eastern white pine, *Pinus strobus*," and the chest of drawers is also yours.

Although the microscope is in Madison and you probably aren't, other apparatus of wood technology is at your fingertips. Softwoods have that name because most really are soft, and your fingernail is a perfect tool for distinguishing a piece of softwood, such as white pine (or a soft hardwood, such as poplar), from a piece of a similarly colored hard wood. When your fingernail is pressed against a piece of white pine or poplar, you can feel the wood yield beneath it; when your fingernail is lifted, you'll see the arch it indented in the wood. The fibers of woods that are hard do not yield in the slightest to fingernails.

Hardwoods and softwoods play different roles in old cabinetry. Although furniture makers made some common, inexpensive furniture entirely of softwood, they generally combined hardwood and softwood in one object. They chose a hardwood as the primary wood, the wood that everyone sees, the wood that was given a coat of finish. The top of a chest and the fronts of its drawers, for example, were of hardwood.

But for the back of the chest and the bottoms of its drawers cabinetmakers favored local softwoods. The wood that was not seen and consequently was not finished — the secondary wood — was usually soft unless a hardwood scrap was lying around in the shop

Signs of wear. The pine drawer side wore at the bottom, and a new piece of wood was glued on (a pieced repair). The mahogany divider wore, and the places of wear line up. Dividers, too, may have pieced repairs.

or a hardwood would better meet the structural demand. Thus a chairmaker might have used pine, a softwood, for the corner blocks to brace a seat but chosen maple, a hardwood, for the seat rails that were to be upholstered and had to hold rows of nails (fig. 182). Woods that are soft — whether they are from a conifer and thus a true softwood or from a so-called "hardwood" like poplar but nevertheless actually soft — were cheap for the furniture maker to acquire and easy for him to work.

Unlike eighteenth-century cabinetmakers, who did not squander their hardwoods, many nineteenth- and twentieth-century "improvers" and fakers did. The later work may show a profligate use of imported hardwood because such woods became cheaper in the nineteenth century and because a maker or remaker of "antiques" can afford higher shop costs than a maker of household furniture.

Soft woods and hard woods wear differently: the soft wood is less dense and more prone to wear away than hard wood. When used as a secondary wood and unfinished, it can be especially vulnerable to wear. One way to put wood technology to work for you is to check for worn wood, using your eyes, fingers, and ears.

Listen to furniture when you move any of its parts (e.g., pull out drawers). The sound of rubbing tells you that wear is occurring. Whenever you see signs of normal wear (e.g., at the bottom of a drawer), listen to find out if the wood is still being worn. If it is not, look for repairs or replacements. Both are common in the places where wood makes contact with wood.

Check the corresponding point of contact. For example, drawer sides often rub on the drawer divider below as the drawer is pulled out or pushed in (fig. 41). A worn spot on the top of the drawer divider should line up with the worn bottom of the drawer side. The points of wear should correspond; the extent of wear may not. If the depth of wear is not reciprocal, consider the woods. Finished hardwood is likely to rub raw at a point of contact, while unfinished softwood wears away. White pine drawer sides will wear down more than a quarter of an inch while running over a maple divider that is merely rubbed smooth or shiny.

Check points of contact for the possibility of repair. Drawer sides are often pieced out (fig. 41). Badly worn drawer dividers, too, may have been neatly — almost invisibly — pieced. Since wood is easily glued with the grain, it is an excellent material for letting in small replacement pieces. Pieced repairs, whether for appearance' sake or to enable the furniture to function better, may be acceptable or even desirable to the collector, but they indicate hard or extensive use in the past. Other instances of heavy use and laborious restoration should be looked for elsewhere in the furniture. Evidence of consistent wear to the wood will testify to honest repair; inconsistent wear will finger a remade object or a case of old parts/new object.

For example, beware of a pieced repair on a hardwood divider that is not accompanied by a repair on the corresponding softwood drawer side. Because mahogany cannot be worn to the point of needing repair by a white pine drawer side that remains virtually intact, the lack of corresponding wear presents an open-and-shut case of tampering — the drawer may be new to its location, the drawer side may be new to the drawer, or the whole drawer may simply be new.

WOOD: WILLING WITNESS REVEALS AGE

Wood charms furniture owners with its varied beauty and its warmth to the touch. Its great appeal to furniture craftsmen is its ability to be easily worked, for even dense woods can be readily shaped. To furniture detectives, wood has yet another valuable asset — it changes as it ages, presenting clear evidence of the passage of time.

The wood that yields cooperatively to the craftsman's tools is also easily marred. Normal household use works as time's sidekick to wear down furniture woods, supplying the antiquer with proof of age. As you examine the different furniture forms (in Chapters 6–9), you will come to differentiate between the wear of normal use and the intentional marring of fakers.

Even if the furniture was not used and the wood never handled, evidence of age appears on wood. The principal testimony is color change: unfinished wood darkens with age (plate 2). Darkened secondary woods are hallmarks of time and can be read as clearly as a label. *Learn to recognize the color of new wood, the color of old wood, and the appearance of deceptive stain.*

New wood is surprisingly light in color. The many facets of the empty cells on the wood's surface reflect the light, making raw wood bright to the eye. Wet or finished wood is not as pale because the moisture or clear finish fills the pores.

The empty pores of unfinished wood are exposed to air and all that travels in it and get amazingly dark with time. Unless one hermetically seals furniture, the color of secondary woods changes to the darkened, mellow hues that collectors look for as they examine the backs, undersides, and insides of furniture.

The shades of aging vary with the wood. Unfinished white pine turns a reddish brown; unfinished yellow poplar turns gray. On one piece of furniture, a single secondary wood can darken to several shades if the amount of air reaching the various parts of the furniture differs. The white pine bottom of a desk may be darker than the back of the case because the back stood against a wall while the feet lifted the case bottom seven inches above the floor; the case back is darker than the underside of a large drawer because the drawer was enclosed in the case; the underside of the tiny desk drawers are lightest of all because the tiny drawers, each in its own small cubby, are exposed to the least air. Similarly, in a chest of drawers without a case bottom, the underside of the lowest drawer is far darker than the undersides of the drawers above. (The lowest drawer bottom was exposed to air while the drawer itself served to close off the air from the drawers above.) Natural discoloring is uniform only where exposure to air has been uniform. Artificial coloring, however, tends to be uniform throughout. *When checking the darkness of woods, ask yourself, "Where's the air?" and look there for the darkest surfaces.*

Finished surfaces, those whose wood pores are filled with clear finish, immediately become somewhat darker than raw wood and then, sealed from the air, do not age in the same way exposed wood does. With time and exposure to sunlight, a finished rich mahogany can fade to gold, and, in a century, finished black walnut, really a dark brown color in spite of its name, becomes the color of honey.

Because a sealant prevents the darkening of aging wood, the inadvertent presence of a sealant on an unfinished surface, a common

PLATE 1. *Looking under a seat with original leather upholstery. Detail of a black walnut side chair, 1735–1760, Boston. The knee brackets are glued and nailed to the bottom edge of the seat rail and to the side of the knee, characteristic American construction. On many English chairs, the rails extend down behind the knee brackets.*

PLATE 2. *Drawer bottom with a Frothingham signature (see page 29). The pine drawer bottom has darkened considerably; the side strips, abraded in use, are a lighter color.*

PLATE 3. *High chest; black walnut, elm, white pine, birch rear legs, and sumac skirt inlay, 1745–1760, York, Maine. Attributed to Samuel Sewall. H. 74¼; W. 40⁷⁄₁₆; D. 21¾. (Society for the Preservation of New England Antiquities.) Like most nonurban furniture, the case is made of several woods. It retains its original and only finish, a waxed finish.*

PLATE 4. *Chest of drawers; cherry and pine. H. 33; W. 36; D. 19. (Henry Francis du Pont Winterthur Museum, Study Collection.) See "The Shell Game," pages 110–112.*

PLATE 5. *Desk-on-frame; hard maple, soft maple, and butternut, 1735–1760, Essex County, Massachusetts. H. 40¾; W. 33⅝; D. 20. (Society for the Preservation of New England Antiquities.) This desk (see details, figs. 121 and 122, and page 128) gives clear evidence of earlier finishes. The original reddish-brown finish was stripped off before the clear cover was applied.*

PLATE 6. *Chest; oak, tulip, pine, chestnut, and yellow poplar, 1710–1730, Guilford-Saybrook area, Connecticut. H. 43½; W. 44½; D. 19½. (Historic Deerfield.) The paint is original.*

7. Upper left. *Maple: a very hard, heavy, whitish wood with distinct annual rings, distinct rays, and obscure vessel lines.*

Lower left. *Ash: a hard and heavy, whitish wood with distinct annual rings, a strong pattern of vessel lines, and obscure rays.*

Upper right. *Aspen/poplar: a soft, lightweight, whitish wood that is almost featureless, having obscure rings, vessel lines, and rays. For positive identification, rely on microanalysis.*

Lower right. *Bird's-eye maple: a very hard, heavy, whitish wood with a peculiar figure of circles around small dark knots, distinct annual rings, distinct rays, and obscure vessel lines.*

8. Upper left. *Birch: a hard and heavy, pale brown wood with slightly visible annual rings and obscure vessel lines and rays.*

Lower left. *Oak: a hard and heavy wood with distinct annual rings, distinct vessel lines, and unusually distinct pale-colored rays. The rays on red oak (red-brown wood) are short (3/4"–1"); those on white oak (brownish-yellow wood) are very long (3"–4" or more). To distinguish English oak from American white oak, rely on microanalysis.*

Upper right. *Satinwood: a hard and very heavy, yellowish wood with a lustrous surface, faint annual rings, and obscure vessel lines and rays.*

Lower right. *Beech: a hard and heavy, pinkish-white wood with distinct chocolate-brown rays, faint annual rings, and obscure vessel lines.*

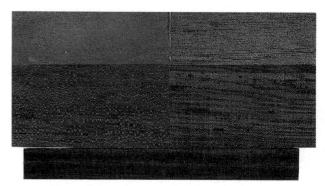

9. Upper left. *Yellow poplar (tulipwood, white-wood): a soft, lightweight, yellow-brown to brownish-purple wood, with rings marked by a thin whitish or pale yellow line, diffuse and very fine vessel lines, and nearly obscure rays.*

Lower left. *Pitch pine: a soft, lightweight, two-colored wood of yellow and deep yellow with pronounced annual rings and obscure rays, and without vessels.*

Upper right. *White pine: a soft, lightweight wood with creamy white earlywood shading to yellow or pale brown latewood in usually distinct annual rings, with obscure rays, and without vessel lines.*

Lower right. *Southern yellow pine: a fairly heavy two-colored wood, with soft, yellowish earlywood and very hard, red-brown latewood in distinct annual rings, with obscure rays, and without vessel lines.*

10. Upper left. *Cherry: a hard, lightweight, red-brown wood with a sheen, rather distinct annual rings, fine vessel lines, and occasionally distinct rays that are flecks of light on dark.*

Lower left. *Mahogany: a dark coppery-red wood ranging from moderately soft and lightweight to hard and heavy, with faint annual rings marked by a thin yellow line and with distinct dark vessel lines and sometimes distinct rays.*

Upper right. *Black walnut: a hard and heavy, uniformly colored wood that is chocolate- to purple-brown, with distinct annual rings, coarse vessel lines, and obscure rays. Distinguish American from English walnut by microanalysis.*

Lower right. *Rosewood: a hard, very heavy, two-colored wood with distinct rings, black streaks on red-brown, and obscure vessel lines and rays.*

Bottom. *Ebony: an extremely hard, very heavy wood that is black or black with brown streaks, having obscure rings, rays, and vessel lines.*

occurrence, can offer proof of age. A drop of varnish that fell on an otherwise unfinished backboard would seal the wood, preventing the usual darkening. Similarly, glue that oozed from a joint would seal the adjacent unfinished wood, keeping it from darkening. If the finish dripped or if the glue oozed in original construction, it would do so onto fresh young wood, and what you would see now beneath dried glue or finish would be far paler than the unglued or unfinished surface beside it. Such two-tone evidence is a welcome sight. If, on the other hand, the wood beneath the drip or glue is dark, the finishing or gluing was done on an already old object.

When wood darkens, it does so only on the surface; the wood beneath remains protected from the air. Newly exposed wood — freshly sawn, cut, or abraded — is light, almost bright, with much of the look of timber fresh from the mill. Scratch even a very old piece of wood, and you'll create a new surface of porous cells that reflect the light. Fakers, restorers, repairers, and improvers may use old wood, but they must cut it here and there to size, introducing new surfaces of fresh wood.

To mask the bright new wood, most defrauders turn to stain, sometimes coffee or tea. Any staining of an unfinished surface (or finishing of a secondary surface) is a sign of trouble. Such work is uneconomical. *Remember: period craftsmen were economical. They did not waste either their time or their materials to stain or finish secondary surfaces.*

The stain that a faker once added to cover his tracks may, today, stand out more than it blends in. In the years since the work was done, the stained surface has aged differently from the surface it was intended to match. Under bright sunlight or your 500-watt bulbs, new stain is usually discernible too. Stain produces a duller, grayer, more opaque hue than natural aging. Fortunately, the faker does not hire the same pigment-blending artist who restores Botticellis.

Israel Sack, the founder of the famous antiques firm, said that the Boston cabinetmaker who employed him on his arrival in America just after the turn of the century (a heyday for fakers) used ammonia fumes and drilled wormholes to "age" wood.[1] Ammonia darkens wood but doesn't really imitate the shades of the naturally aged stuff, and drilled wormholes are the easiest phonies to spot.

WOODWORM

The faker's "wormholes" are drilled in, whereas the woodworm chews its way out. A female wood-boring beetle alights on the wood to inject a microscopic egg in a tiny crevice, and the larva that hatches burrows about in the wood, generally along the grain, creating extensive tunneling. Only when it has matured to a beetle does it eat its way out, and only then does a hole appear on the wood's surface.

The woodworm does not eat a path out of the wood in a straight line or make holes that are perfectly round; only drills make straight, exactly round holes. Use your needle — the one you carry in your tool kit for splinter removal — to probe wormholes. (If you are likely to forget to clean it thoroughly before going after a splinter, consider adding a two-inch length of thin copper wire to your tool kit for checking wormholes.) With your needle or wire, probe the nature of the hole. Your probe will proceed straight into a drilled hole, possibly going completely through or penetrating deeply before coming to an abrupt stop. If your needle barely enters the wood or your wire probe starts to curl, you know a worm was once there.

But when? Woodworm, a.k.a. powder post beetle, has not died out or even faded. In the British Isles especially, it is still a scourge. Wormholes are not unique to antiques. In only a short time, the critters can do their thing to a fake made of a wood they like, such as maple, beech, or walnut (they have no appetite for mahogany). In one house on the Atlantic seashore, for example, infested woodwork turns nineteenth-century reproductions into worm-wracked antiques in short order.

The defrauding crowd has been known to reuse old wood and, in reworking wormy wood, to expose lengthwise stretches of woodworm tunnel (fig. 90). Since borers never eat along the surface, finding a surface full of such exposed tunnels suggests a new use of old wood, a practice that is always suspect. Colonial craftsman occasionally exposed a wormhole tunnel in their work, but they avoided using wood that was heavily infested.

New wormholes are, of course, light and may still contain a soft powder, like face powder in color and consistency. Old holes are dark and sometimes filled with dirt and wax. Inside, however, the tunneling is empty. For every pinprick surface hole, there is a spacious channel.

The wormholes scattered on the surface give a misleading impression, for the shell is far more intact than the wood within. Novice collectors may deem woodworm holes evidence of antiquity; savvy collectors see no proof of age but, instead, a probability of structural weakness. A modest blow can crumble affected wood. In addition, woodworm infestation is hard to eradicate even with the help of a professional exterminator, a fumigation chamber, and lethal chemicals.

TESTIMONY FROM THE SHRINK

The wood in furniture presents proof of the passage of time by changing its size; having been composed originally mostly of water, wood dries out over the years and shrinks. Though the wood had started to dry before the furniture maker worked it, such a porous material does not lose all its moisture for many years. And in a sense it never does. On a damp August day or with a steamy shower running in an adjacent room, the wood absorbs moisture from the air, swelling a bit. On a dry day or with a crackling fire on the hearth, the wood dries and shrinks again.

This movement, the shrinking and swelling, occurs across the grain. As the tracheids give up their moisture, they slenderize but retain their length. In a damp environment, they swell but get no longer. So the length of a piece of wood measured with the grain remains virtually the same over centuries, while the same piece measured across the grain shrinks perceptibly in its first century and thereafter expands and contracts according to environmental conditions. Expand though it may, however, it never regains its original dimensions (fig. 10, a drawer bottom that has pulled completely away from the drawer front into which it was fitted).

The evidence of shrinkage remains and can be measured. For example, the tops of antique tables have slenderized. If a tabletop

was originally round or square, you can make sure it shrank by comparing a measurement taken with the grain to one taken across the grain. A 32″ × 31⅝″ mahogany top on a Chippendale table shows normal shrinkage. With your calipers you can measure turned posts or ball feet and detect the slight flattening out of round that comes with age.

Some tabletops and many desk lids have strips at both ends of the main board that run in the opposite direction — so-called bread-board ends (figs. 42 and 184). Normal shrinkage is apparent because the large board has contracted, leaving the ends, which were origi-nally cut to match, still full-length and now protruding. If you cannot see the difference, you should be able to feel it. If not, the piece is either reworked or new.

Shrinkage often loosens the several parts of wooden furniture. The panels of joined chests loosen and move in their frames, sometimes leaving strips of unfinished surfaces peeking out from the frame. Chair splats loosen because they were merely set in slots in the crest rails above and in the splat shoes below. In veneered work, the veneer shrinks at one rate and the core wood to which it is glued at another, so the glue gives out and the veneer loosens.

The wooden pins that hold some joints together, though they may not actually become loose, are often dislodged by the movement and shrinking of the wood around them. Although still tight and functioning, many a pin protrudes above the surface of the wood with which it originally was flush (fig. 43). Such pins are said, for alliterative more than technical reasons, to have popped. Savvy furniture inspectors run their hands over pinned joints to be assured by the popped pins.

WHEN CROOKED IS WELCOME

Warping, a form of shrinking, occurs because a wood log contracts differently in different directions. While the timber does not lose any perceptible length, it shrinks significantly around the circumference of the log (following the annual rings) and rather less along a radius (across the annual rings) (fig. 44).

By losing more around the periphery than in a radius, a halved log develops a convex face where it was sawn flat. "Plain sawn" boards develop one convex and one concave surface, curling away from the center of the tree. Only a "radially cut" board — a board that includes the center of the tree or radiates out from the center of a tree — will not warp; it develops two convex surfaces. Logs are generally sawn to get the greatest number of radially (or close to radially) cut boards.

Wood shrinks or warps most when it is green, so boards sawn from newly felled timber are seasoned before they are worked. Although Colonial cabinetmakers generally used boards that had seasoned for a year or more, the wood continued to shrink and warp to some extent. Warping is most noticeable in wood that is worked green (sometimes advantageous, as we shall see), in extensive lengths of wood (e.g., the tall back posts of high-backed chairs, fig. 140), and in wide boards, especially those held in place at one end only, such as table leafs.

Many tabletops have warped so much that they have become unsightly or even unusable. Over the years, they have invited repair and encouraged replacement (as we will see in Chapter 9, "Topless Tables . . ."). A repaired top may not adversely affect the value of an antique; however, for the collector, a crooked top is certainly preferable to a replaced one. Though crooked is sometimes welcome, be forewarned: warped boards are not necessarily original; replaced parts are also likely to warp.

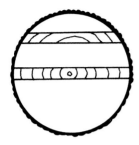

FIGURE 44:
The shrinking ways of wood.

HOW THE CASE IS CRACKED

When wood has to shrink it shrinks, even if it must tear itself apart. If the structure of the furniture prevents the wood from moving, the wood will split, ripping along the grain (fig. 38; plate 2).

Repeated contracting, expanding, and contracting encourages cracks of all sizes. Minor cracks can occur anywhere, and some become filled with wax, more frequently in the course of routine maintenance than as a result of restoration. Major shrinkage cracks, too wide to be filled with wax, are common in the wide boards that form case sides or tops of chests or tables.

Such major cracks seem to have invited repair. Sometimes restorers added thin strips of wood (splines) to fill broad cracks. In other instances, workmen removed a top or took the case apart to pull the split board together again. The disassembling of a case, even if it was just to reunite a split board, constituted extensive repair and was often accompanied by undesirable reworking.

Inspect wide boards for shrinkage cracks, for filled cracks, and for evidence of reunification. Splitting can be expected wherever furniture boards are twenty or more inches wide. An open crack is more appealing than a repaired one to the furniture purist. A spline-filled crack is desirable to those seeking a less aged appearance. A reunited board is usually regarded as a sound repair for a tabletop but can be detrimental if an entire case was disassembled and reassembled to close the gap in the board. Least acceptable — and unfortunately all too common — is the replacement of a cracked or warped wide board, often with several narrower ones. Hundreds of boards that were originally the leaves of nineteenth-century dining tables have been reborn as the sides and tops of older furniture.

MORE EVIDENCE FROM OLD CABINET WOODS

Although wide boards warp and crack, they appealed to the makers of period furniture because working the single board was easier and faster than having to put several boards together to form a surface. Colonial cabinetmakers, ever economical with their labor, preferred wide boards, and, to their good fortune, broad timbers were plentiful. Twenty- to thirty-inch-wide boards were common products of the New World's forests in the eighteenth century. Occasionally cabinetmakers used two boards for a tabletop or case top, or for the side of a desk or chest, but they preferred a single wide board. *Expect one-piece tabletops, case tops, and case sides; accept two-piece surfaces; suspect three or more boards.*

Not only the size of the boards but the quality and nature of the wood are important clues to the age of the furniture. As the forests were depleted in the nineteenth century, men cut younger and younger trees; narrower timbers are standard today. Two, three, or more pieces may be glued together to form a broad composite board, which is as likely to separate as a one-piece wide board is to crack. Plywood was not used until the late nineteenth century; composition board (chips of wood held together by glue) is a twentieth-century aberration.

The most valuable part of a new chest of drawers in the eighteenth century was the material itself. Because the wood was of such importance and because superb timber supplies allowed for selectivity well into the nineteenth century, high-quality woods were often used for antique furniture. Cabinetmakers avoided pieces with knots or worm damage. On finding an occasional woodworm tunnel as he worked the wood, a craftsman was likely to fill it with wax rather than discard the already worked piece; however, worm-riddled wood (fig. 90) was never his selection. Restorers and fakers are much more likely to use inferior wood, having fewer forestry products to choose from and being constrained by the need to match old woods.

THE JOINTS

Every piece of wood in furniture meets another at a joint. In some joints, two pieces of wood simply meet and need a fastener, an adhesive, or an enclosing framework of other joints to keep them together (fig. 45, A, B, simple joints). Other joints slide together in a more secure relationship, also depending on the larger framework

FIGURE 45:
Simple joints in antique furniture (here and overleaf) do many jobs.
(A) Butt-jointed boards sometimes form the bottom of a seventeenth-century chest. The (B) miter may be apparent at the corner of decorative molding or invisible at the corner of a bracket foot. The (C) spline joint, used on a chest bottom, is an improvement on the butt joint; as the boards shrink, the chest remains closed to air and insects. The spline, or slat of wood, is usually left loose in the two grooves. (Glued splines reinforce miter joints in mirror frames.) The (D) tongue-and-groove joint works like the splined butt joint and was the common closing between table leaf and tabletop in the early eighteenth century.
(continued)

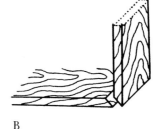

A

B

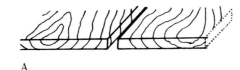

C

D

(FIGURE 45, continued)
More simple joints:
The (E) rule joint, by the
mid–eighteenth century,
supplanted the tongue-
and-groove as the stylish
tabletop-to-leaf joint. The
(F) lap joint, used at the center
of the crossed stretchers on
a William and Mary dress-
ing table, was cut across
the grain with a saw and
chiseled out with the grain.
(G) Rabbeted boards (cut along
the edge by a rabbet plane)
were sometimes nailed to-
gether to form the sides of
board chests. (H) Double-
rabbeted boards are often
stacked one above the other
to create the backs for case
furniture.

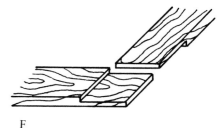
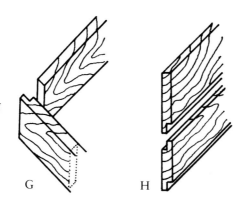
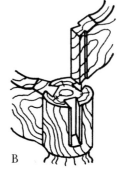

FIGURE 46:
Sliding joints. These joints
(a.k.a. housed joints) include the (A) dado, often
used to hold a drawer bottom in place; (B) the single
dovetail, relied upon to join
the legs to the pillar of a table; and (C) the shouldered
dovetail, which often binds
the horizontal drawer di-
vider to the case side.

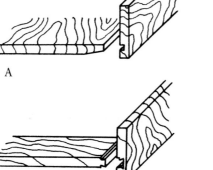

FIGURE 47:
Locking joints. The two
basic ones are (A) the mortise-and-tenon and (C) the
dovetail. A variation of the
former is (B) the round
mortise-and-tenon; of the
latter, (D) the mitered
dovetail.

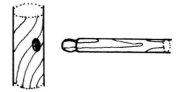
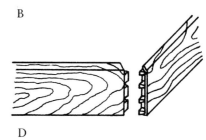

FIGURE 48:
Scalloped "dovetails." Pegged scallops were used instead of dovetails on some late-nineteenth-century drawers. (Photograph courtesy Maine Antique Digest.)

to hold them (fig. 46, sliding joints). The larger framework is a result of the most sophisticated joints, those that lock themselves together (fig. 47, locking joints).

The simple, sliding, and locking joints are identified in the drawings so that when you are on duty you can check them out. In different eras and for different forms and styles, craftsmen used different joints; for specific construction purposes, they selected specific joints. So the rookie should learn which joint to expect in which period and which place.

While looking for the right joints, be on the lookout for modern joints, those never used in antique furniture. Pegged scallops, a much later invention, take the place of hand-cut dovetails and are easy to spot (fig. 48). Even rookie investigators have no trouble identifying the exact and uniform machine-cut dovetails, a late-nineteenth-century innovation. The doweled butt joint (fig. 49) substitutes for the mortise-and-tenon (fig. 50) in late-nineteenth and twentieth-century reproductions and is such a poor joint that many have loosened or come apart. To inspect a slender opening at a joint for a dowel, aim your light at the joint, place a white sheet of paper behind it, and peer through the crack to look for a round dowel less than a half-inch thick. You can also insert your needle into the opening to ascertain that what you see or think is there is in fact a dowel. Machine-made dowels are truly round.

FIGURE 49:
Doweled joints; in repair (a pieced-out leg) and in original construction. A dowel, inserted and glued into two butting pieces of wood, forms a poor joint, but it is common in repairs and nineteenth-century work. Defrauders commonly hide a doweled end-grain-to-end-grain joint at a crease in a turning.

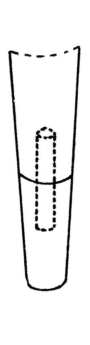

Double mortise-and-tenon joint at the front seat corner of a neoclassical chair. (Photograph courtesy Israel Sack, Inc.) This, rather than a doweled joint, is the joint that the squad expects on period antiques.

The preindustrial practitioners of the three furniture-making crafts — joinery, cabinetry, and turning — specialized in three different locking joints: the joiner in the mortise-and-tenon, the cabinetmaker in the dovetail, and the turner in the round mortise-and-tenon. Every joint that has come apart — as well as any exposed evidence of a joint — warrants a search.

Though you cannot disassemble joints, you can look into some with the aid of X ray (fig. 51). X ray can also reveal the shape of screws that are still in place. Radiology is one modern technology that can help you uncover the craftsman's techniques and identify them as eighteenth- or nineteenth-century.

Merely speak to a radiologist, your dentist, or someone on the staff of your local hospital. Don't be surprised if medical people welcome a respite from tooth decay and broken bones and enjoy the foray into fakes-and-fraud detection. Some may not even charge for their services, but you should expect to be on call the next time your dentist or radiologist discovers an antique.

TOOLS OF THE TRADES

The tools of furniture making — all the artful devices used by joiners, cabinetmakers, and turners — were of only a few basic types.

X ray of a Queen Anne chair showing the joint of the side and medial stretchers. An eighteenth-century brad-pointed bit made the flat-bottomed mortise in the side stretcher.

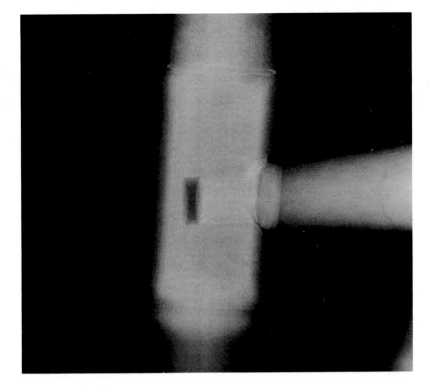

Several tools fully equipped a joiner's shop (fig. 52). Holdfasts held the work to the joiner's bench. Squares, rules, gauges, and compasses helped him lay out his designs. Saws cut; augers and bits drilled holes. Planes (hands behind the blade) and shaves (one hand on either side of the blade) pared the wood down. Shaves came in several sizes, planes in many sizes and with various contours, each plane designed for a specific task for which it usually was named: jointer and smoothing planes flattened; molding or creasing planes formed moldings; plow planes and rabbet planes prepared wood to be joined together by cutting grooves and forming rabbets. Gouges and chisels of various shapes and sizes were driven into wood by mallets in decorating as well as in constructing.

To the joiner's tools, cabinetmakers added the equipment they needed for dovetail joints and for veneering: fine saws, toothed planes (to rough up surfaces for gluing), glue pots, and veneering hammers and clamps. They worked with the joiner's measuring tools when laying out and copying some designs but also replicated their work by using patterns.

Turners were so called because they used lathes to spin the work. The turner's numerous chisels and gouges cut and shaped the spinning wood. Shaves, rasps, and files refined shapes.

The marks of some craftsmen's tools remain on furniture surfaces, even those smoothed by sandpaper, sand leather, pumice, or sharkskin, and, subsequently, by the hands of generations of touchers.

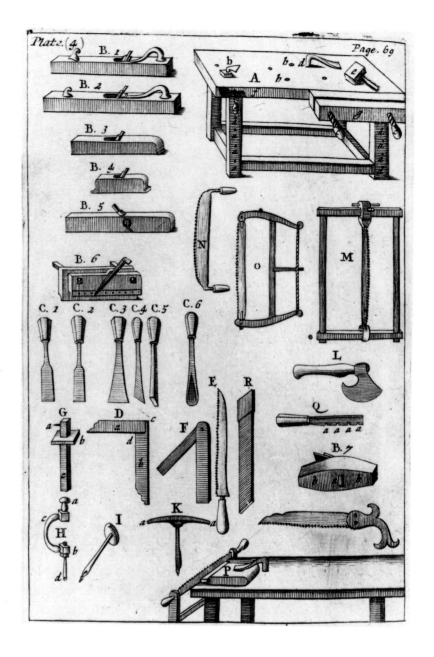

When no tool marks can be found, the savvy collector suspects the work of the faker, who has everything to gain by removing all traces of his modern tools. On the other hand, the craftsman of the period, ever economical with his labor, had no reason or inclination to cover his tool tracks.

THE PLANE FACTS AND WHERE TO FIND THEM

The furniture detective who understands a tool's function can recognize its tracks. Planes work down the surface of wood. The craftsman planed, or dressed, the work by running a plane over the wood, following the grain. He did not remove the traces left by the plane, and the gentle furrows formed by the slightly convex blade remain (fig. 10). The furrows run, of course, as the plane did — with the grain. *Feel across the grain for the ridges between the furrows. Use a raking light — a single source shining obliquely on the wood — to look for the revealing highlights and shadows of a planed surface.* You can augment a skimming hand and an observant gaze with a straightedge (the cardboard cover of the notebook in your kit will do) held against the surface.

Tools driven by hand across wood, a material that itself is uneven in texture, produce surfaces that are neither perfectly flat nor absolutely uniform. Even on a "flat" primary surface that was worked with sandpaper and other abrasives, you can often detect wavy irregularities. *Look at every surface from an oblique angle.* On some primary surfaces, the time-frugal cabinetmaker flattened only well enough to satisfy the casual observer; even moldings can reveal handwork to the careful inspector. If you sight across a flat surface or along a molding, you may well see the irregularities.

Unfinished surfaces and secondary woods, more often than primary surfaces, retain the broad with-the-grain ruts that are clear evidence of hand-planing. The sleuth inspecting secondary surfaces looks for evidence of the joiner's plane and looks out for the marks that should never be on furniture made before the nineteenth century.

Mechanical planers were introduced after 1800. Their rapidly rotating blades leave tiny ridges that are close together (not more than 1/8 inch apart), uniformly parallel, and hard to see without a strong or raking light. Unlike the marks of the hand-powered joiner's plane, the mechanical-plane marks run across the grain. Uniformity and parallel marking usually suggest modern power tools. A drum sander makes parallel scratches; a power-driven bandsaw, uniformly parallel cuts.

THE WAY THEY SAW IT

Saw marks are sometimes found on undressed surfaces, including backboards, the undersides of drawers, or the insides of cases. You can distinguish between modern saw marks and those of the several old types of saws.

Most saw marks that are visible were created by the sawyer and left untouched by the Colonial furniture maker, who did not always plane the marks away. Pit saws (see "M" in fig. 52) — worked by two men, one guiding and pushing on the downstroke, the other assisting in the pit below — left pronounced lines that are straight and only approximately parallel; they are not exact, and they slant. Rarely does furniture bear pit-saw marks.

FIGURE 53:
*Mill-saw marks on the back
of a drawer. Detail of
the joined chest in
figures 76–83.*

Mill-saw marks, however, are often seen on furniture (fig. 53). The vertical blades of mill saws — whose teeth ripped boards on the downstroke — left coarse parallel lines that are more uniformly spaced (¼ inch to ½ inch apart) than the marks of pit saws, and usually perpendicular to the grain. Water-powered sawmills and pit sawyers both processed timber in eighteenth-century America. In the 1840s, circular saws became common in sawmills; the distinct arcs (fig. 54) they leave on wood are proof of post-eighteenth-century manufacture.

The cuts that the cabinetmaker himself made with his framesaw are more irregular than those made in the sawmill pit. They may cut in any direction, often going this way and that (figs. 37 and 56).

If the wood was not sawn but split, as was common in the seventeenth century with oak, a raw, torn surface resulted. With-the-grain roughness is distinctive of riven, or split, wood.

EASY MARKS AND THE TOOLS THAT MADE THEM

When furniture makers planned their designs and made measurements for fitting parts together, they had to mark the wood precisely. Their favored mark was a scored, scribed, or scratched line, because such a line is both clear and narrow, truly precise.

The wood was scored according to the measurements made by squares, rules, compasses, or gauges. Compasses scored circles and

FIGURE 54:
Circular-saw marks on a drawer back from a large mahogany and white pine neoclassical chest of about 1840. (Society for the Preservation of New England Antiquities.) Even in a small area — the drawer is 3½ inches high — the curve of the saw marks is evident.

arcs. Gauges measured breadth and scratched their measured marks on the wood. Awls, omnipresent scribing tools, scored these lines not drawn with a measuring tool itself.

One wonderful thing about score marks is that many remained visible in the completed furniture and today enable the investigator to trace the steps made by the craftsman. Scored lines are likely to be found at joints. At mortises, for instance, some lines define the rim or edge of the mortise itself; others mark the center of the joint (fig. 133).

A cabinetmaker making dovetails scored the breadth of the mating board on its companion so that the line could serve as a guide for the depth of the dovetails (fig. 55). A scored line appears along the edge of the row of dovetails on all dovetailed boards that were hand-cut. A similar technique of measuring and scoring assured the mating of wooden hinges; lines remain there as well.

FIGURE 55:
Dovetails and score marks at the corners of two drawers from one chest. The several drawers in a case show that the hand of the craftsman is consistent throughout.

On turned work, lines incised with the corner of the chisel blade guided the turner in two ways. Many lines marked the positions of joints, usually scribing either the top or the bottom of the mortise. Other scored lines delineated the broadest part of a bulbous turning (see the finials in fig. 131). Having marked the spot that would retain the greatest breadth, the turner used that guide as a starting point from which to move away as he cut deeply into nearby areas.

Some remaining craftsmen's marks are dots rather than lines. The center prick from a compass is a common residual of planning a design. Compasses scribed circular designs and the many arcs of a circle that laid out various outlines and contours. Lathes, too, left pointed marks on wood; the underside of a turned foot may retain the point that reveals where the lathe held the wood. This is also true of a claw-and-ball, which, though no longer round, began by being turned on a lathe. In rare instances, you may even see the score marks with which the craftsman located the central spot for placing the work in the lathe (fig. 56). The wear that comes from years of being dragged across a floor has usually left, at best, only a small dot. A hole made by the shank of some old metal glide (glides were frequently added to chair feet) is much deeper than a lathe mark. Turned posts, such as those on the fronts and backs of ladderback chairs, may have a lathe mark visible on the very top.

FIGURE 56:
An unusually well-preserved claw foot, showing the saw marks and scored lines for centering the work.

BITS OF EVIDENCE

Round mortises offer evidence of how and when they were drilled. Until about the mid–nineteenth century, most turners used spoon bits, or pod augers, to make such holes. The round-ended bits created holes such as only they could make — holes that are rounded at the end (fig. 57). Since the era of the spoon bit, mortises have been drilled by augers of a distinctly different design. Their central gimlet point and an otherwise flat face produced holes with flat ends and a small central pit. However, not all flat-bottomed, centrally pitted holes are nineteenth or twentieth century. Similar mortises were formed by eighteenth-century brad-pointed bits, used by joiners and cabinetmakers for making stretcher joints in Queen Anne and Chippendale chairs (fig. 51).

When examining a turner's chair, where the use of a spoon bit is expected, you may find chair stretchers loose or missing, opening their mortises to investigation. If you cannot see inside, your pinky can probably probe the end of an empty mortise. If not, the moistened towelettes and the tweezers in your tool kit can. Make a loose wad of several towelettes, insert it in the mortise, and jam it in. Then

FIGURE 57:
Round mortises and the
tools that made them. From
top to bottom: a spoon bit;
an early brad-pointed bit;
and a modern gimlet-
pointed bit.

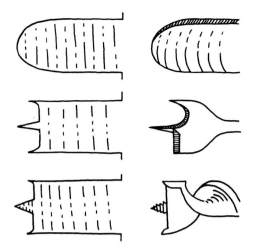

extract the wad (the tweezers may be needed here); the wet fibers
will have taken an impression of the far end of the mortise, leaving
no doubt about what type of drill bit was used. When stretchers are
in place, X ray can reveal the shape of the hole.

THE CHISELERS AND GOUGERS

Furniture makers used chisels to shape and decoratively carve their
wares. Chisels cut along the grain so neatly that often the new surface
needed no further smoothing. The turner's chisel, however, left faint,
narrow ridges because the blade cut pliant green wood being turned
at the slow speed of a hand- or foot-powered lathe. Modern high-
speed lathes rotate the work so quickly that such slight ridges are
not formed. The craftsman seldom smoothed away the tracks of the
chisel, so if they are not worn away or covered by layers of paint
you may see and feel them still.

Cabinetmakers carved so quickly and easily with a gouge (often
in green — therefore soft — wood) that they could scallop the bottom edge of a shell drop (fig. 94) with merely a few blows of the
mallet against a gouge. Plymouth Colony joiners created a serrated
molding (figs. 43 and 74) by cutting a series of V's with a flat chisel.
A single strike formed each side of the upside-down V to be removed,
and a third strike on the edge of the board chipped out the waste
wood. Working quickly, the cabinetmaker or joiner sometimes drove
the chisel deeper than the design called for and often placed or
angled the chisel imprecisely. *Turn your lights on chisel-carved details, and look for the irregularities that are the hallmarks of handwork.* Allan Breed, a master of the techniques of seventeeth- and
eighteenth-century furniture craftsmen, says, "Your eye wants each

detail to look the same, so each one looks the same. But really they are all different."

You can detect inexactness in chisel carvings by measuring duplicated or multiple design details. *Measure chisel carvings with your calipers. (They make this assignment easier than does your ruler.)*

Turners did not make regular use of calipers. To stop the lathe, put down the chisel, and pick up calipers just to measure the work being turned was a waste of time. They let their eyes measure by comparing the turning being worked to a model. This resulted in different widths on the several turnings on one antique.

On close inspection of a turned chair, a furniture detective can usually see the variations without the aid of calipers. The differences may be so apparent close up that it seems amazing that such irregularities were not evident from afar. The turnings appear identical only because we expect to see identical parts. As Breed says, "The old boys took advantage of the human eye."

VENEER: MORE THAN A COVER-UP

Veneer has a bad rep that it doesn't deserve. Collectors have condemned veneer as a faker's cover-up, overlooking the fact that fakers abuse all decorative techniques, misusing carving much more. Veneer is not an accomplice of poor craftsmanship, a disguise for an inferior object, or a cheap way out. "Slipshod methods appeared when it became clear that thin veneers could cover a multitude of sins," says one judge, mistakenly attributing nineteenth-century changes in furniture production to veneering.[2] Others equate applying veneer with economizing on decorative wood figure, thus perpetuating the myth that the technique was designed for economy. Veneering, which became fashionable in America in the early eighteenth century, was neither an easy out for slipshod workmen nor economical; it was a skill-demanding, time-consuming technique.

In recent years, in our age of plywoods and composition boards that flaunt facades of handsome woods, veneer has been misjudged as merely a cover-up for trouble underneath. This century's fashion of "honesty" in the arts and crafts encourages us to view veneer as an impostor. Yet the decorative technique does exactly what it was supposed to do: make the furniture look spectacular.

Veneering embellishes furniture with splendid patterns that are the natural wood figure of some timbers. Let's imagine a block of wood that displays a particularly attractive figure. It may be from a species with pronounced annual rings, cut neither across those rings nor with the wood grain but at an angle that has caused a pattern

FIGURE 58:
Detail of a Boston-area Federal card table. The demilune design is laid into the edge of the folded top board, but on the skirt it is applied onto the core wood in one layer with the veneer, which has a decorative feather figure.

of distinct arches to be formed (fig. 39, left). Or it may be a block from a part of the tree likely to produce flamboyant figure — for example, the juncture of two main branches where the parting has distorted the wood grain, creating a flashy figure.

The desired figure appears on two faces of the six sides of our imaginary block and changes slightly as it moves through the block, appearing somewhat different on each end. If we now imagine slicing our block of wood, we get from a single cut two identical but mirrored images of the figure. Each pair of slices yields identical mirrored figure, which varies slightly from the figure on the preceding pair. By cutting very thin slices, we can get enough material to create wonderful designs of repeated mirrored images (as did eighteenth-century cabinetmakers, using four slices per wide drawer, plate 3 and fig. 36). The cabinetmaker reversed every other slice for a mirrored effect. Creating patterns of identical and nearly identical images and displaying them on flat surfaces is what veneering is all about. The core wood to which the slices of veneer are glued is a mere mounting for the glorious design.

Furniture makers also used veneer from some wood species that produce a handsome allover figure — a wavy grain, a circular pattern, or a splatter of tiny dots. It is not necessary to alternately reverse such veneers as bird's-eye maple or burl walnut (fig. 110).

Once the cabinetmaker decided to apply veneer, he was able to add much to his design by mixing veneers of several different woods, creating borders and highlights, adding contrasts and geometric patterns (fig. 58). So he cut and assembled designs in jigsaw-puzzle fashion and then affixed his mosaic to the core wood. This technique, an almost constant companion of veneer, is called inlay in America, although it is actually marquetry; purists reserve the term "inlay" for a technique of cutting into the core wood to actually *lay in* the contrasting woods. Such inlay is also a component of American veneered furniture (fig. 58).

Metal, especially strips of brass, was often inlaid in solid wood in Europe. Seldom incorporated in American work, metal inlay is limited to some ornate objects of neoclassical design from stylish cities like New York and Philadelphia. But it is common in English Regency furniture.

By 1825, veneers were made by a new rotary process. The earliest veneers are thick, sawn from blocks much like our imagined one, but because sawing produced as much waste as it did veneer, craftsmen soon began to steam the wood and slice it with a blade. In the nineteenth century, the rotary process sliced a steamed and spinning log, making larger sheets of veneer available. Many rotary-sawn veneers are bland because they did not begin as a block specially selected for its remarkable figure. By the end of the nineteenth century, veneers were notably thinner than they had been when the century began.

Furniture detectives who appreciate the charms of veneer and inlay and understand their appropriate use know where and when to expect the elegant enhancers. A laborious and expensive decoration, veneering was done only to principal surfaces, and its patterns were commensurate with the importance of that surface.

For example, a William and Mary chest of drawers at the Museum of Fine Arts, Boston (similar to the example at Yale, fig. 110), looks as if it might originally have been the top of a high chest, and the veneer on top of the chest is the conclusive evidence of later reworking. A tabletop was an important surface in the early eighteenth century, and the table-high surface of a case was only somewhat less important than its facade. On the chest top in question, the veneer is plain-grained, running front to back, and thus completely out of character with the herringbone-bordered burl on the drawer fronts. Verdict: The chest of drawers is a remade high-chest top (more on this MO in "Case of the Case Piece, Part Two," pages 116–120).

To recognize veneer and distinguish it from solid wood, look for the edge of the veneer on the side of the surface in question. In good light, the thin line shows clearly. Veneers have been applied to curved as well as flat surfaces, so look for them there too. In some designs, the edge of the veneer is covered by an applied wooden bead (visible on the skirt of the dressing table in fig. 117). The bead was applied not to hide the edge of the veneer but to protect it from chipping. If an applied bead surrounds a facade, you can assume that it surrounds veneer.

Sometimes an inappropriate mix of inlay designs — for example, an amalgam of inlays from several geographic areas — gives away a reproduction. In the Federal era, most inlay was made by urban craftsmen who specialized in that work and whose distinctive patterns became fashionable in their own communities. Despite touts' claims that they can name the specific cabinetmaker's shop, it is probably only accurate to say that a particular inlay pattern indicates a particular city or region. (For example, the lunette inlay, fig. 58, long attributed to the Seymour shop, is best attributed to coastal Massachusetts, to the area served by some unknown Boston inlay maker.) The border inlays known as stringing (a.k.a. banding) are most noticeably distinctive and peculiar to a certain place and time.[3] Look at stringing for regional facts; look at all veneer for clues to authenticity or duplicity.

ADHESIVES, OR STICKING TO THE STORY

Veneer problems (lost, loose, and bubbled up) are also glue problems, so the detective needs a little inside information on old furniture adhesives.

Until the middle of this century, furniture glues were made from the hides and bones of animals and fish, and all such glues had to be applied while hot. White glue, a twentieth-century development, is much easier to use. The old furniture glues gave way as the woods they held moved and shifted; white glue, a much stronger adhesive, does not. White-glue repairs are permanent, and this alarms the cognoscenti on the antiques patrol.

You are not going to be able to see the difference between hide or white glue once it has been applied. (White glue is colorless when dry.) But you can ask the dealer if he has repaired the object you are examining, and ask what glue he used.

One dealer, who is careful to do the right thing with the objects that he regards as being only temporarily in his care, tried to reassure a customer that the repairs he had made were properly done. He reported that he had reglued some veneer and repeatedly mentioned the glue, but the baffled patron wasn't sure if he said "hide glue" or "hot glue." Whichever. Old glues were both hide and hot.

Repairs should be made with hide glue. Woods are going to shrink and shift, and it is better that the glue give than that the wood split. If a repair needs to be redone — for example, if a replacement piece of veneer fades — it would be nice to be able to remove it (the cognoscenti say "reverse the repair") and do the job over. An application of hot water, often by injection, makes a hide glue repair reversible.

"It'll never come apart again," proclaims a well-meaning but not well-informed dealer who routinely uses white glue. He is right, unfortunately. If the natural movement of wood caused the crack, and the movement continues, the repaired break will not separate and a new crack will form.

White glue should be used on antiques only to rejoin a clean break of a single piece of wood, caused, for example, by a fall. In such cases, the natural movement of wood is not a factor, so additional breaking is not likely; no new elements are being added, so no one will ever need to reverse the repair.

When adhesives arrived on the antique furniture scene, their job was to attach veneer, not to hold the structure together. Glue was used sparingly in furniture construction; glued support strips or blocks, for instance, reinforced some joinings (and any glue that has oozed sends signals about how long the wood has been sealed from air). Cabinetmakers, however, did not glue their principal joint, the dovetail, nor joiners their mainstay, the mortise-and-tenon. Such joints needed no adhesive when the craftsmen made them, and glue around them today indicates repair.

NAILING THE CULPRIT: A LINEUP OF FASTENERS

Nails, screws, hinges, handles, and locks — whether original and in place or, as is often the case with old furniture, replaced or missing — provide the furniture detective with solid facts. By their appearance or by the shadows and marks they leave behind, these informants can date a work, can reveal repairs, reworkings, and reused elements, and can convict the fake. First, the facts about nails and nail holes.

Until about 1800, all nails were wrought by hand. The blacksmith or specialist nailmaker forged nails in several sizes (fig. 59, A) and for various purposes, following essentially the same steps. He made his nails from nailer's rod, a length of iron, square in cross section, that he bought from an ironworks. He heated the rod and hammered it on all four sides to draw it longer, thinner, and to a point. He broke off a length and dropped it, point first, into a hole or clamp, leaving a bit of the thick part protruding. Then he hammered the thicker end, spreading the iron to form a head. The common rose-headed nails have "petals" formed by the hammer blows. Finishing nails (fig. 59, B), designed for those surfaces where roseheads would be too obvious, and small sprigs or brads either have no head at all or small heads that form an L or T with the shank of the nail.

The profile of wrought nails is distinctive and recognizable even

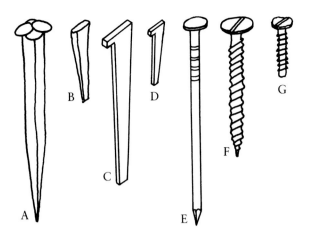

FIGURE 59:
Two wrought nails — (A) a rosehead and (B) a finishing nail — (C) a cut nail, (D) a cut brad, and (E) a wire nail; (F) a machine-made screw and (G) a hand-cut one.

when the shank has bent out of shape. Because of the way they were made, from square stock hammered on four sides, the shanks of all hand-forged nails are irregularly square in cross section. The heads mushroom and are also irregular.

At the end of the eighteenth century, nail-making machines revolutionized production by cutting nails out of flat metal (fig. 59, C and D). The machines sheared off tapered pieces of metal plate (one nail tapering to the right, the next to the left, alternately, across the plate). The shanks of these nails may have burrs from the cutter; they always have two merging faces (cut by the machine) and two parallel faces (the top and bottom of the metal sheet). Cut nails quickly supplanted wrought nails.

Cut finishing nails have either L heads or no heads at all. Cut common nails made in the first years of the nineteenth century have hand-hammered heads that resemble but are thinner than those on wrought nails. By about 1820, nail-making machines formed the heads as well, and their products are uniform in appearance.

In the 1880s, cut nails were superseded by wire nails, machine-made from round stock. Only wire nails have round shanks and flat, perfectly round heads (fig. 59, E).

The one part of any nail that is sure to tip off the investigator is the top of the shank. Just below the head, the three types of nails (wrought, cut, and wire) have three different shapes — squarish, rectangular, and perfectly round, respectively — based on their origins as square rod, flat sheet, or round stock. The top of the shank is sometimes visible because the movement of the wood can loosen nails, popping them a bit from their holes.

If a nail is loose, draw it from its hole with your fingernails, take a look, and reinsert it. Beware of nails with rusty shanks in rust-free wood. Remember, fakers not only use new wrought nails but are also quick to reuse old hardware when and where they can (thus the rusty nail). Reused and new nails usually will not have had time to blacken the surrounding wood (as in fig. 37).

A nail hole is as informative as the nail itself because the part you see was formed by the telltale top of the shank. *Inspect for nail holes wherever you expect nails* (e.g., where the backboard is fastened to a case, along a seat rail stripped of its upholstery) *and answer a simple geometry quiz: square, rectangular, round?* The round holes are modern (or worm or drill holes); the rectangular ones date from between the early 1800s and about 1880; the square holes are original to seventeenth- and eighteenth-century furniture.

A neoclassical chest that is of the period will have cut nails; one that has only wire nails and nothing but round nail holes is a late-nineteenth- or twentieth-century reproduction. You may find squarish, rectangular, and perfectly round holes all in one antique. An eighteenth-century desk may have square holes that are original, rectangular holes from the cut nails used in an 1850s repair, and round holes from the wire nails that hold a brass plaque saying, "At this ancient desk, my great-grandfather, J . . ."

The dating of screws (fig. 59 F and G, a modern and a handmade screw respectively) is mostly a pre-1850/post-1850 sorting. Post-1850 screws have pointed gimlet ends because the gimlet-ended screws, patented in 1848, went so easily into the wood that they quickly replaced those made earlier. Pre-1850 screws do not have pointed ends. Some pre-1850 screws are distinguishable in place because on handmade screws the slot for the screwdriver is sometimes off-center, but often you have to remove the screw to determine its age.

If the end of the screw is flat, examine the shaft. A modern screw may have had its point filed off to shorten it. The threads of handmade old screws have flat edges formed by the flat files that made them, and the shafts of the screws barely taper at all. Sometimes the hand-cut threads look irregular even to the unaided eye. Screws made by machines in the first half of the nineteenth century have regular threads and truly round shanks, but, until 1850, blunt ends.

Old screws can help prove that the top now fastened to a Chippendale tip-top table is original. Even a tabletop with added or replacement gimlet screws can be shown to be original to its base by, perhaps, a single remaining original screw and clear screw-hole evidence (in the right places) of the other early screws.

New screws in an antique require new or enlarged or lengthened screw holes. If a repairer wanted to retain an old hinge, he had to reuse the old screw holes. Sometimes, therefore, a long replacement screw holds a desk-leaf hinge to the body of the desk. But long replacements could not be used in the leaf (they would go straight through) and wider screws would not fit through the holes in the hinge. Hinges often had to be replaced because the screw holes could not be reused. Check the hinges of table leaves and the fold-out tops of desks for replaced hinges or for old screws (fig. 60).

Use your screwdriver in shops (only with permission, of course). At home, carefully select a screwdriver of proper size to avoid damaging the slot of the screw. When removing more than one screw at a time, label or place each as you unscrew it so that you are certain to return it to its correct hole. Every old screw is different; every hole made by an old screw is different, too. A good investigator is cautious and caring. For example, some screws in the underside of tabletops go deeply into the wood. In examining a table, be exceedingly careful when reinserting the screws. As you start to turn the screwdriver, place your other hand on the primary surface, putting the ball of a finger firmly against the wood opposite the screw hole. Keep your finger there until you put the screwdriver down. Turn the screw slowly; your finger can feel the point of the screw approaching the surface, and you can stop turning before it pierces the top and mars the table.

COMING UNHINGED

Cotter pins fastened wooden lids and early brass handles (fig. 38). Two interlocked cotter pins make a strong, serviceable hinge — the primary hinge of the seventeenth century. Most seventeenth-century cotter-pin hinges have broken. The marks left on wood by a cotter pin are an irregular hole large enough for both branches of the pin to go through and, radiating out from the hole in approximately opposite directions, two linear indentations formed as the two splayed branches of the pin were hammered down into the wood almost flush with the surface. Frequently an original hinge is gone, leaving behind aligned cotter-pin marks. Finding an intact cotter-pin hinge on a chest and lid is proof that the lid is original — but not necessarily old. Fakers make cotter pins, too.

Cotter-pin hinges were used on rude furniture throughout the eighteenth century, but on most furniture, from the early eighteenth century on, hinges were of the iron or brass butt variety (fig. 60, or fig. 126, an early example of a square hinge with leather washers under the nail heads). All those decorative iron hinges that look so "Colonial" — the L, HL, butterfly, and long strap types — are more often architectural than furniture hardware. In the late nineteenth and early twentieth centuries, the "antique" quality of such iron hinges commended them to fakers, restorers, and makers of repro-

ductions, and the decorative iron hinges became omnipresent on repairs (fig. 190) as well as on fakes and frauds.

Handsomely worked hinges can be seen *inside* some period furniture: incised and imaginatively outlined hinges were located under the lid of decorative Pennsylvania chests, to be enjoyed when the lid was raised. However, most old hinges are butt hinges and look much like modern ones, with two rectangular plates, each with three (or two, on smaller hinges) holes for screws. Cast brass butt hinges were imported from England for bookcase doors in the mid–eighteenth century, and iron and brass butt hinges were the standard hardware on desk lids and table leaves from the beginning of the century. Many still remain in place. Hinges that were set flush with the wood were sometimes replaced with smaller flush hinges; look for rectangular pieced repairs that fill the recesses left by the original hinges (fig. 60).

GETTING A HANDLE ON THE CASE

Few old cotter-pin hinges are still on the job, and even fewer old cotter pins still hold drawer handles. Finding a cotter pin still filling its original hole on the inside of a drawer front proves that the drop pull is original, but surviving early handles are so rare that an investigator is often more comfortable with a number of holes in a

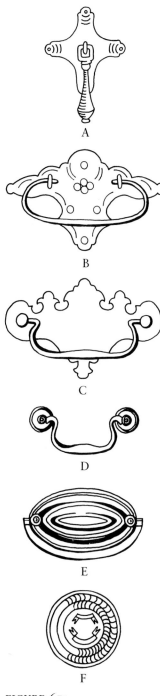

FIGURE 61:
Hardware designs of the eighteenth and nineteenth centuries: (A) a William and Mary drop pull and its plate, (B) an early Queen Anne bail with punchwork plate, (C) a Chippendale brass handle, (D) a Federal bail with two small plates, (E) a Federal oval handle, and (F) a neoclassical brass knob.

drawer front — indicating a series of brasses — than with an "original" set still in place.

The handle history of a piece — any evidence of a series of hardware — is usually more informative than the existing pulls. When the handle-hole history of the upper case of a "Dunlap" high chest (fig. 12) was found to be clearly different from the series of handles on the lower case, the marriage was indisputable.

Become familiar with the styles of handles and key escutcheons, because they clue you in on the spacing of the holes they required and left behind. Knowing the patterns of furniture hardware (fig. 61) will not so much affirm the authenticity of existing brasses (they may be of the appropriate style but not original) as it will confirm that the series of holes and marks remaining on an old piece (fig. 62) conforms to a logical history of old hardware.

Wooden knobs were standard on drawers and doors of seventeenth-century furniture and continued as common pulls for rude furniture and on the intentionally simple cases made by the Shakers. The back of such a knob formed a dowel to go through the drawer front (fig. 81, at left). It left a large hole, sometimes with a circle rubbed about it made by a pin that went through the dowel to keep it in place.

At the end of the seventeenth century and through the first quarter of the eighteenth, cotter pins fastened stylish brass drop pulls with small plates to drawer fronts (figs. 61, A, and 27). These cotter pins, spread out and hammered into the wood, left marks similar to those made by cotter-pin hinges but less coarse, for the metal was of thinner gauge. The bail (or loop) pulls of the Queen Anne style (figs. 61, B, and 28) required two cotter pins and had a wider plate behind the bail. On the earliest of these, the bail curled inward, like a C lying on its back, and the holes are not far apart. Toward the middle of the eighteenth century, the style called for the bail to curl outward (fig. 36) at the ends, putting the two holes farther apart.

During the first half of the eighteenth century, the cast brass plate (between the handle and the wood of the drawer front), which was usually hammered with punchwork for a decorative engraved appearance, grew from a small brass that did little more than surround the hole for a drop handle (fig. 61, A) to a large one that covered two holes and extended down to protect the wood from the hanging bail (fig. 61, B). The larger plates and bail handles prevented the type of damage to facades of drawer fronts that had become the legacy of swinging drops — arcs of scarring on the finished wood. On a genuine old piece with its original handles in place, the scar will line up with the drop. If the two do not line up, don't be surprised — few drop pulls are original hardware.

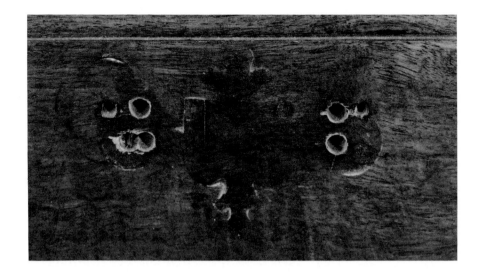

If no old scars are present on a drawer with drop pulls, check inside the drawer for proof that this case originally had them — look for a single central hole with cotter-pin marks. Early collectors coveted the wares of the first century of Colonial life, and restorers and dealers, catering to their tastes, aged many Queen Anne cases by giving them William and Mary brasses. (Another possibility, a mainstay of the skeptical detective: there is no scar because the case is not old.)

Most often you will find that a genuine William and Mary case was scarred by its first brasses, that the holes for those brasses were filled and new holes drilled for updated handles, and that over the generations several sets of brasses were used on the case. Don't be made overconfident, however, by the presence of many holes or get overwhelmed by the evidence of a long history of brasses. Take the time to make sense of it all. *Remember that one of the easiest and surest ways to discover a married piece is to find that the history of the brasses on one case is different from that on the other.* Random holes may indicate a reused piece of wood; extra holes may be from gratuitous drilling done for felonious distraction.

When hardware of the mid– and late eighteenth century replaced earlier brasses, hole-concealment was usually unnecessary. The bails and plates of the rococo brasses of Chippendale design (fig. 61, C) were larger than those on Queen Anne cases and covered the old holes. These larger brasses had no punchwork engraving, although some very elegant ones were pierced. The openings on brasses from the last half of the eighteenth century are much further apart than those on earlier brasses, and sometimes one of the old holes in the wood left by the smaller brass was reused and only one new hole made.

These holes accommodated bolts, not cotter pins. Often the back of the drawer front was gouged so the bolt and nut would be depressed into the wood and would not be a menace to those using the drawer.

The early bolts and their nuts are irregular. Early bolts are usually square at the top of the shank; modern ones are round. Modern nuts are usually square; old ones tend to be round. Because each old nut probably fits only its own bolt, you must be careful to replace them properly if you remove a handle to look for evidence of other hardware, to find signs of refinishing or wood bleaching, or to examine the back of the brass plate to determine its age.

If the plate looks thick — as old plates of this period should — and if the edges appear to have been hand-filed — as period rococo brasses were — you may want to look at the back of the plate to see if the brass was cast in sand, leaving the customary grainy appearance and texture. Reproduction brasses are cut from sheet brass and are smooth in back. You can learn all you need to know by unscrewing a handle; don't remove a key escutcheon, which is held in place by nails.

Of all the hardware, the old escutcheons are the most likely to survive. Sometimes the plates behind the handles (or some of them) are old, and the bails are replacements. Modern bails are rounded at the ends; handmade bails end sharply and are rough to the touch.

On Federal-era furniture, bolts with decorated heads are common, as are bails with a decorative design. A short-lived fashion for two small round or oval plates at the two holes (fig. 61, D), instead of one larger plate, left the bulbous center of the bail free to mark the wood as it fell back down after use. Look for such bail marks where two-plate brasses are used, and expect such brasses where bail marks are found.

Most Federal brasses feature plates that protect the wood from the bail (figs. 61, E, and 127). Many plates are oval; some are round. Most were stamped from thin metal plate and curved back toward the wood at the edge, often cutting a thin, deep oval or circle into the facade of the drawer. Some brass plates were filled with plaster to prevent such marring. Over time, the holes these Federal brasses required in the drawer front tended to get closer and closer until, around 1830, the pull was again a knob requiring but one hole (fig. 61, F).

Nineteenth-century knob handles were of brass, glass, or wood. The knob screwed onto a threaded shaft, and inside the drawer a nut screwed onto the other end, which was also threaded. The era of revival styles revived all types of hardware, in assorted shapes

FIGURE 63:
Lock inside a drawer of a
neoclassical chest. The
screw at upper left has an
off-center slot. The saw cuts
outline the hole for the lock
itself, which is narrower
than its covering plate.

and "appropriate" sizes. Then the modern bolt bolted. It turned around, its head on the inside of the drawer, with the nut, posing as a knob, on the outside.

THE LOCK-UP

The *raison d'être* of a chest or a drawer was to provide safe storage for valuables, and, until the mid–nineteenth century, chests and drawers were usually meant to be locked. Although locks were expensive, they were almost essential. Except for the drawers in tables and an occasional small drawer in a large case, expect chests and most drawers to be equipped with locks.

Metal locks were screwed (or sometimes nailed) into notches individually chiseled in the chest or drawer fronts. Furniture inspectors can see, extending down from the wide back plate of the lock, the flanking saw cuts with which the cabinetmaker began making the notch (fig. 63). Replacement locks rarely fill old holes exactly and do not themselves adversely affect the value of antiques. Neither do missing locks, because the old idea of locking every drawer no longer prevails. But at times (see pages 87–90) a lock is the key to solving a case.

All but the simplest furniture had escutcheons surrounding the keyhole to protect the wood and decorate the facade. In the early eighteenth century, the escutcheons did not necessarily match the handle hardware, but with the advent of the Queen Anne style and bail handles, they generally were made *en suite*. On occasion, a small drawer that was given no lock was, for aesthetic reasons, provided with an escutcheon to achieve a pleasant arrangement of brasses.

THE CASTER CAPER

Casters, those swiveling wheels set under furniture, were often original equipment and probably just as often were added to older furniture.

Wooden and leather wheels, although worthy adjuncts for heavy cases and beds, were rare fittings on American Chippendale furniture. Beginning in the Federal era, however, a fashion for brass-wheeled casters lifted many feet off the floor, making even light-weight furniture rollable. Most casters fitted into holes under the feet; some surrounded slender feet with brass cuffs.

When casters were the rage (that is, for most of the nineteenth century), many people added the wheels to older furniture. Some put them into feet that had lost height, thus restoring a few inches; some drilled holes for the casters that dangerously weakened the old feet. Many people cut feet — sometimes even taking off half of a claw-and-ball — so they could install casters and still maintain a proper height. Such mayhem devalued many objects.

So, although casters are seldom original to pre-1785 American furniture, many antiques of that era have or had them. Casters are appropriate to nineteenth-century styles, yet were not on all nineteenth-century furniture. The design of the feet is a solid clue as to whether casters were originally present. Filled holes underneath the feet of cases, tables, or chairs are sure evidence that casters were once present.

GLASS, THE CRYSTAL-CLEAR GIVEAWAY

Few furniture sleuths get an opportunity to examine an antique bookcase — the top section of secretary — that is, or was, glazed. Although fakers make reproduction roseheaded nails and reuse old screws, few make reproduction glass or reuse old panes. So old glass is usually good evidence of age and authenticity.

Whether blown or cast, old glass is slightly tinted and perceptibly uneven (fig. 64). Perfectly smooth glass was not produced until the late nineteenth century. Look through the panes at a printed page, run your fingers across the surface — old glass readily identifies itself by its imperfections.

Mirrored old glass is also irregular. Never gauge the age of the glass by the condition of the silvering. Feel the front surface, and check the mirrored image. Hold up a white page to see the color of the reflection. Old glass is exceedingly thin, so put your fingernail

FIGURE 64:
Old glass. Detail from the
inside of a door on a Fed-
eral bookcase (window sash
beyond). The panes are not
broken or cracked; the im-
perfections are original to
the glass.

against the mirror to see its depth. (Learn the thickness of modern plate glass by doing the same with a modern mirror.)

Furniture glass is set into the wooden muntins the way window-panes are, and is held fast with glazier's putty. One difference between windows and furniture: window glass is puttied on the outside; the secretary door, on the inside.

Old glass is extremely brittle. Some or most of it often is replaced. Even if all the glass is modern, the furniture may be old. The glass is but one of the hard facts.

The Case of the Case Piece, Part One: Joinery

IT is time to crack our first case. We start with the cases (furniture made for storing and containing) made by joiners, and put each joined case individually under a strong light. To uncover the repairs and restorations, the fakes and frauds, or the charm of the genuine antique, we will follow a skeptic's line of questioning each time.

LEARNING TO UNLOCK A MYSTERY

If "every piece of furniture is a walking encyclopedia of how it was made," as furniture craftsman Allan Breed says, then a box is a small volume.

The oak box (figs. 65–67) was made by a joiner using simple board construction. For such a small structure — this box stands a mere 7³⁄₁₆ inches high — the joiner did not need to frame with mortises and tenons; he just nailed or wood-pinned boards together at simple joints.

The box, purchased in the 1880s from an Ipswich, Massachusetts, family, features carving that closely resembles other furniture from Ipswich. For almost a century after its purchase, it appeared in decorative arts publications, regarded as a Bible box, of which there were many in the early colonies and maybe more in the 1880s, when such boxes were favored by collectors enchanted with seventeenth-century design.

As seen from the outside, the front, sides, top, and back of the

FIGURES 65–67:
Box; red oak, 1663–1680, Ipswich, Massachusetts; three views. Attributed to William Searle or Thomas Dennis. H. 7³/₁₆; W. 25⁵/₈; D. 16⁷/₈. (Society for the Preservation of New England Antiquities.) On the carved facade, scored lines (across the middle, down the center and flanking verticals) form a grid for the design. The finishing nails on the facade and back are original; the nails seen on the underside are roseheaded.

nailed oak box pass the first test. The oak is suitably old (the boards are all the same color); the nails look good (finishing nails, instead of conspicuous roseheads, secure the front board). The form makes sense: nailed oak boxes made of rabbeted boards (fig. 65; looking inside, note that the front and back boards were rabbeted to receive the sides) were common in the seventeenth century. The oak lid is held by its original cotter-pin hinges (fig. 38, the right hinge of this box).

The lid is made of two oak boards, glued together and also unified by two cleats. The left cleat is original (a hole through the lid and cleat remains from a missing original wooden pin); the right one is an old replacement (the hole in the lid for a wooden pin does not extend through the cleat). Cleats are common on lids; some form

88   FAKE, FRAUD, OR GENUINE?

part of the hinge (fig. 68). Lids made of one pine board (wider boards were available in pine than in oak) have cleats that help keep the board from warping. Savvy collectors regard one replaced cleat as a common, acceptable repair.

A till (fig. 65, at left) is unusual in a box but standard in chests of the period. The till, designed to hold small objects, usually has a lid; this box had a till lid that is now missing. Two holes above the till (one is just visible in the corner of the backboard) held protruding pintles on which the till lid hinged (see fig. 80).

All the inside surfaces look equally old and — except for the one cleat and a replaced lock — original. But two holes are visible on the top edge of the front board (fig. 65). *Never let any hole pass unexplained.*

On turning the box over to look at the last remaining surface (fig. 67), the inspector finds that the holes go completely through the front board. Why the holes? Is the front a reused old board? What purpose could such holes serve?

Now is the time for tough detective work. Standing back to think it through, let's look again at the box. Compared to other boxes of the period (fig. 68, a typical example), its proportions are odd, a bit squat. Also, the shape of the base molding is not that usually associated with bases (on an angle, broadest at the bottom). On most old boxes, a one-piece bottom board extends under the front and protrudes so no molding is needed. Here the bottom is composed of several boards and stops short of the front, and the molding looks

as if it has always been there. If it is not a base molding, could it have been a mid molding? What could have been below?

A drawer. If there had been a drawer underneath, the holes could have been used to lock it. The front of the drawer needed only two corresponding holes (that started at the top but did not go all the way to the bottom). Rods dropped through from beneath the lid of the box could extend into the front of the drawer and lock it. Unlocking the lid and pulling up the rods, probably by strings attached to their tops, would release the drawer. With only one expensive iron lock (at the lid), both compartments could be secured.

Although a very similar box (fig. 69) has no such drawer-locking arrangement, it shows clearly what this box originally looked like. Despite minor repairs and major losses (a drawer, the lower part of the case, and feet), the box in question is a genuine and desirable antique.

Case closed (but unlocked).

FIGURE 70:
Chest of four drawers; oak and pine. H. 37; W. 38½; D. 20½. Moldings painted black and red. (Historic Deerfield.)

FIGURE 71:
Chest of four drawers; maple, oak, and pine, 1670–1710, Massachusetts. H. 36⅜; W. 39¾; D. 23⅜. (Yale University Art Gallery, Mabel Brady Garvan Collection.)

TRYING THE CASE, PART BY PART

On the box from Ipswich, locks (metal and wooden locking devices) provided the investigator with the important clues. In our next case, a sophisticated chest of four drawers of late-seventeenth-century style (fig. 70), the drawers are not lockable. The detective notices on first inspecting the facade (after looking at the overall design and then focusing on small details) that although the drawers all have keyhole escutcheons, they have no actual keyholes.

As the examination proceeds, the detective posits possible answers. Perhaps the escutcheons are merely decorative or later additions to a chest that never had locks. In the seventeenth century, some furniture was not given locks, although one expects at least a couple in a chest of drawers of this stylishness and quality.

Perhaps the chest has or had wooden spring locks. In such a lock, a slat-spring attached under the drawer bottom springs open and catches behind the rail below when the drawer is completely closed. A very similar chest at Yale (fig. 71) originally had spring locks under two drawers (the top and third from top), which could be unlocked only from the drawers below. A savvy sleuth recognizes evidence of a spring lock under a drawer (fig. 72).

91 JOINERY

FIGURE 72:
Evidence of a wooden spring lock. Detail of the high chest shown in plate 3. The nail holes show where one end of the slat was attached; the other end sprang away from the drawer bottom and caught behind the rail below.

Perhaps the drawer fronts have new facades. On drawer fronts such as these, all the decorative moldings are applied (glued and nailed), including the flat central piece behind the escutcheon. Perhaps the applied wood behind each escutcheon has been replaced.

One drawer after another reveals that none of the drawer fronts ever had a metal lock, nor any of the drawer bottoms a spring lock. When members of the museum staff at the Wadsworth Atheneum investigated a closely related, nonlockable chest of drawers in that collection, they concluded that all four drawer fronts were replacements. When a chest relies almost entirely on its decorated drawer facades for visual impact, as this one does, four replaced drawer fronts should certainly raise doubts about the whole.

The one theory the fakes-and-fraud squad does not hypothesize is: With other chests like this in museums, this one must be authentic. Museum connections — "There's a closely related piece at the Wadsworth Atheneum," "Yale has a very similar one" — are enticing testimonials, joyously broadcast by sellers and generally warmly received by curators and collectors. However, a museum relationship is no guarantee. The antiquers who amassed the great collections in the late nineteenth and early twentieth centuries, those wealthy collectors whose treasures are now the backbones of museum holdings, were covetous acquirers and easy marks for fakers and defrauders. Francis Patrick Garvan (1875–1937) — whose fine collection, named for his wife, Mabel Brady Garvan, is at Yale — was aware and wary of the con artists. Having worked in a DA's office, Garvan said of antiques, "I try every piece as I would a murderer."[1]

Take a tip from Garvan: sharpen your skepticism. Approach each object as an adversary. The museum connections set aside, let's continue to check out the case at hand with our doubts at the ready. Since the drawers have already captured our attention, let's examine them.

Remove each drawer and examine every surface, ten in all. Check for uniform color, inside and out. If the drawer sides and front are oak and the back and bottom are pine, are the same woods the same shade inside the drawer? In the top drawer of the case in question, the color shows all the wood to be the same age. *Check stains and other damage.* Do they make sense as the result of normal use, or were they deliberately inflicted?

FIGURE 73:
Drawer side and bottom of a hung drawer, rear edge. Detail of the chest shown in figure 70. The needle goes clear through the "wormhole." The drawer bottom is "worn" where it does not rub against anything.

Under examination, the first drawer reveals extensive "woodworm" holes in the drawer sides. The holes do not pass the needle test (fig. 73). As the needle goes completely through the "wormhole," it punctures any theory that the drawer is genuine. All four drawers tell the same story.

The chest already stands condemned, but let's illustrate other evidence of foul play. The sides of the drill hole–ridden drawer were gratuitously worn where they run over drawer supports in the case. Drawers of joined chests are usually hung, grooved on the outside of their sides (fig. 82) to fit and slide over slats in the case (fig. 83). Joiners made such drawer sides of oak because the mighty wood endures a lot of use without wearing away. The grooves on the drawer sides of this fake are worn much more than those on genuinely old drawers. And the underside of the drawer bottom has been "worn" along the sides by the faker. *Beware of gratuitous wear.*

The case itself is stained to look old, with the same red-black color applied to both pine and oak. The forgery may not have looked old enough to its maker, for he added something "new." The "later" front bracket feet (above the "restored" turned ball feet) are red herrings. *Don't be distracted by "later additions" and "repairs."* The smart detective recognizes them for what they are — a con artist's attempt to gain the buyer's confidence. *Examine the entire case, the "old" parts and the "new repairs," and you can catch the faker red-handed.*

So our second case is a fake, and, like many other fakes, it is of a rare form. *Be suspicious of rarity in form as well as design.* Chests of drawers — chests with nothing but drawers — were a new form in the seventeenth century, so joined chests of drawers of this period are not common. The standard joined chest had a lid.

EXAMINING THE BODY

A lid-top chest, whether of board construction or joined, is examined like a box (six exterior surfaces, six interior surfaces) except that the inspector now has to check out feet as well. They require special scrutiny because they are the most vulnerable part of furniture, the most common replacements on antiques. Down on the floor, they are attacked by dampness, mold, vermin, and inadvertent kicking. Supporting the heavy weight above, wooden feet are sorely stressed when the furniture is pushed or pulled without first being lifted free of the floor.

Intact old feet, if not broken or replaced, are usually worn; many sustain considerable loss of height. The feet on the joined case in figure 74, an antique chest in unusually fine condition, have their full height. The astute detective knows that shorter feet have either been well worn or cut down.

The detective inspects the chest from every angle and does not

skip any surface. Inside, the till is intact (fig. 75). The scratched decoration on the till lid, which echoes the serrated chisel carving on the front bottom rail, shows a unity of design and is, therefore, the type of detail the squad welcomes. The chest is a fine example of joinery, and members of the squad, expecting mortise-and-tenon joints at every juncture of rails (horizontal) and stiles (vertical), find the telltale evidence: two wooden pins, holding each tenon fast in its mortise.

Because many old pins no longer lie flush, you can detect them with your hand. *Run your hands over each surface as you look it over.* When Francis Garvan recommended to other collectors "the education of the eye," he added, "or rather of the eye and hand, because the feeling of a piece is as essential as the appearance."[2]

A briefing on another good example of joinery will be useful. Let's direct our attention to an intact and genuine example of a very popular form: the chest with drawers, a.k.a. the blanket chest — a lift-lid chest with a drawer or two beneath.

FIGURES 76–84:
Chest with two drawers; oak and pine, 1680–1700, typical of the Blin workshop, Wethersfield, Connecticut. H. 39¾; W. 46; D. 21. (Historic Deerfield.) A series of identification shots taken during a typical inspection. As first seen, the facade reveals some missing moldings, some broken applied pieces, full-height feet, and handsome carvings and turnings.

FIGURE 77:
The right side of the chest facade. Shrinkage has pulled the panel's molding away from the stile at the right side. Faded remnants of the original paint can be seen on the moldings and applied turnings. The discoloration of the wood reveals the outlines of missing parts. A clinched nail (just to the right of the flower) will be checked out in the interior (where it will prove to secure the till). The wooden pins visible beneath the double applied turnings are far from perfectly round. The uniform color of the wood speaks of a uniform age.

DRAWING ON SOLID EVIDENCE

This extraordinary chest (figs. 76–84) is perfect for training a detective's eye. A picture of the pristine, it is everything today's collector wants and more. It has its full height, original wooden pulls (check the ones inside the drawer, fig. 81), original cotter-pin hinges (seen inside the chest, fig. 80), and original paint. Even the detached

FIGURE 78:
The back of the chest. All the parts seem to have started out together; they share a common color and history of discoloration. (Note the spotting on both panels and on the middle rail.) The feet evince some water damage at the floor, where it is to be expected.

FIGURE 79:
Inside the chest. A rodent has gnawed up from the drawer below. Mouse holes are frequently faked; this one is real (rasp marks don't really look like tooth marks). The lock is missing. On the inside, the panels are roughly riven to fit into the dado joints of the frame.

FIGURE 80:
The right rear corner, inside the chest. The till and its lid are intact. The back panel and lid are pine, the rest is oak — the expected combination of woods. The lid has its original cotter-pin hinge, which has blackened the surrounding wood and has never been disturbed.

moldings are not all missing; most are in a drawer (fig. 81); broken parts frequently are. The wormholes were made by worms (the needle barely enters the hole, fig. 81), and, where the applied turnings have broken off, discolored wood proves their original presence (fig. 77). It was never touched by a restorer, let alone overly restored.

Because the edges of the panels sit in grooves (forming dado joints — see fig. 46, A) in the rails and stiles, an inspector can sometimes see evidence of these joints if a panel has shrunk and pulled out of its groove (fig. 77).

Beneath the case, added proof of the joiner at work is visible near some mortises, where an alert inspector can find plow-plane grooves that extend beyond the mortise. The joiner routinely overshot the area being worked when he cut the long groove that served both as the groove of the dado joint and as a starter for the mortises. (The groove was widened to a mortise with a mortising chisel).

FIGURE 81:
Inside a drawer. Most of the moldings that have fallen off the chest are stored here. The round tenon of the wooden pull and the wood around it look undisturbed; the pull is original. The needle barely enters the real wormhole. As expected, the drawer sides are oak; the bottom, pine.

After he cut out both mortise and tenon, the joiner drilled the mortised piece for each wooden pin. He inserted the tenon, marked the location of each hole, and withdrew the tenon. Then he drilled not where he had scribed the circles but slightly farther from the end and reinserted the tenon. The pins, which had to be forced in, pulled the tenon fast into the mortise. Pinned mortise-and-tenon joints need no adhesive, and the fakes-and-fraud squad suspects any evidence of glue.

The squad also suspects perfectly round wooden pins. They are machine-made and are at best replacements. The irregular shape of the old joinery pins is obvious (fig. 77, just below the applied turnings), especially on the insides of some joined furniture, where pins may be left uncut and may extend beyond the joint.

Joiners notched the case stiles for slats (fig. 83) upon which to hang and slide drawers. They grooved the drawer sides to run over the slats (fig. 82). Some joiners nailed drawers together (fig. 84); others made large dovetails (fig. 85), sometimes augmenting them

FIGURE 82:
Outside the drawer. Outer surfaces of drawers are very revealing; examination of this hung drawer shows the grooves (on the sides) for hanging the drawer, mill-saw marks (on the back), and nailed construction. The drawer is nailed sides to front (see fig. 84), back to sides, and bottom to drawer frame. The very thick drawer bottom was chamfered (beveled) where it was to be nailed. Some water stains are visible.

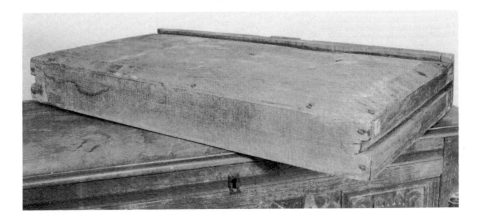

FIGURE 83:
Inside the chest, with drawers removed. The drawers run on slats let into the case stiles. The slats show wear and appear never to have been disturbed. Overcut grooves for the dado joints extend down the rear leg.

FIGURE 84:
Drawer side. Detail of the drawer shown in figure 82. The drawer side is nailed to the drawer front with finishing nails.

with nails. Although joiners constructed the drawers solidly, astute detectives realize that drawers, as separate, movable, and removable parts, are vulnerable to wear, loss, and replacement.

FOUND: A GOOD CASE IN A ROTTEN CROWD

One form favored by fakers in the late nineteenth and early twentieth centuries is essentially a box on a stand (fig. 86; most have a drawer, but the upper "drawers" are merely decorative moldings on the facade of a lift-lid box).

One museum example of the form, apparently called chamber tables in their day (an example very like fig. 86, left, with similar applied turnings and carving of the same design) is, as the curatorial crowd says, "almost entirely made up," a product of the early twentieth century with — if any part is old — possibly old legs.

Another, at the Winterthur Museum, though virtually identical to the made-up case, is a genuine antique that was fixed up to attract a collector's attention. The shelf at its base is replaced (the underside of the wood looks very light and young), and the applied turnings, which are probably related to the originals, are new (the turned wood shows no age or wear to the eye or hand). The drawer bottom and drawer back are replacements made of old wood (holes that make no sense in their present locations bespeak an earlier life).

The underside of the bottom of the Winterthur box — not the bottom of its drawer — is darkened from being exposed to air for many years. Nail holes through the case sides, which line up with

FIGURE 85:
Detail of a dovetailed hung drawer from a Boston chest of the seventeenth century.

others in the drawer sides, explain why. The detective reasons that the drawer was a backless and bottomless remnant when its still-intact front and sides were nailed in place. In that way, the underside of the box, instead of being protected by an intact drawer, was exposed to the air.

Most of the Winterthur case proves to be good, which is rare for this form; many of the frauds began with an old box, to which the defrauder added a base with a drawer to create a rarer, more useful, and more elaborate object.

On one museum example of this type, even the box is not old; the entire object began with a single old board, from which the box front and sides were made (a new board formed the back). The faker dressed up the box front with initials, an easily accomplished, sale-enhancing, common bit of fraud. He did not give the box a lock. Old locks are not cheaply acquired, and faking an old-looking empty recess for a lock is a lot of work. The faker "aged" the bottom of the hung drawer with stain (fig. 87), but he failed to pay attention to what he was doing. The underside of a hung drawer is entirely and evenly exposed to air and ages uniformly (fig. 82). Yet in this case the faker did not stain the entire surface. He omitted the stain at the sides and back of the drawer bottom, emulating the two-tone discoloration of a drawer that is supported all around by a frame. Ironically, no such frame supports the hung drawer. Old faking is often illogical, and the modern investigator spots it at once.

This faker inflicted gratuitous injuries, chipping out large areas of both front-leg balusters. At the base of each injury, the detective can still see the saw marks with which he began his attack of instant aging.

INCOGNITO

A related object, a desk on stand, is our next case. At first glance this one-piece unit (fig. 88), which is merely the width of a chair, seems unusually narrow, with insufficient room on the writing surface. Looking over the facade, the detective finds a heavy concentration of nail holes on the rail above the front stretcher. Alerted to holes, the sleuth discovers similar ones on the corresponding side rails as well — on those rails and, mysteriously, nowhere else. *Remember: Let no holes, including nail holes, go unexplained.*

The holes look like those on an upholstered and reupholstered seat rail. That connection solves the mystery. If it has holes like a chair and it is the width of a chair, it probably is a chair. The base of an old turned chair was fitted with two drawers and a desk and painted "Colonial" blue. Made up early in the twentieth century, this is a splendid example of old parts/new object.

Philip Zea, who features this adaptation of an old chair remnant when he teaches connoisseurship at Historic Deerfield, thinks he can hear the old antiques dealer making the sale: "This good, narrow antique desk will make a perfect telephone stand. And the drawers are the right size for directories." The desire on the part of collectors to give a Colonial appearance to modern equipment or a modern use to an antique (also see pages 134–135) spawned cases of old parts/new object, altered antiques, and amazing adaptations. Such

"useful antiques" sold quickly earlier in this century — this one for just under $2000 in the 1950s — and still do.

OUR FIRST BIG CASE

Our next case (fig. 89) is mostly antique, but one wouldn't know it to look at it. Like many other antiques, it has been stripped down and "refurbished" so that what is new barely differs from what is old but scraped and sanded.

In the 1880s, many collectors wanted either newly made objects in the antique style or antiques that looked newly made. Dealers catered to their tastes. The Metropolitan Museum collection includes a cupboard, dated 1699, that Horace Eugene Bolles (1838–1910) bought "in the rough and defective in 1894." The cupboard was missing its door, columns, top boards, and many moldings. Bolles had it restored by Patrick Stevens, a Hartford cabinetmaker.[3]

Not all collectors liked the "new" look. Dr. Irving W. Lyon complained of objects that "had been planed down & freshened & modernized so as to be painfully noticed."[4] When he saw what was probably this very cupboard (fig. 89) in 1884 in the collection of Henry F. Waters of Salem, Massachusetts, Lyon said that "a cupboard had been spoiled in doing over—scooped or planed down so as to look fresh as new oak — & I think other liberties had been taken with feet & possibly moldings."[5]

Although a cupboard is the hardest furniture form to examine because so many inside surfaces are hard to see, enough is usually visible and touchable to reveal any fake or fraud. The skinned finish of this mostly antique cupboard is visible even in the photograph. Old parts were sanded, including turnings, which were probably done on a lathe; new parts — the top, the dentil molding, some turnings — were added; painted areas were repainted; wear was simulated on new surfaces with smears of black paint. New and reworked moldings and turnings were secured with cut nails. Part of the left stile is a replacement made of old wood that has exposed worm tunnels (fig. 90). The rejuvenation of the cupboard exceeds honest repair, making it more a remade object.

FIGURE 91:
Chest with drawer; oak and pine; ca. 1901, Deerfield, Massachusetts. Made by Edwin C. Thorn and Caleb Allen. H. 36; W. 47; D. 20. (Historic Deerfield.)

COPYCAT CRIME

Our next case (fig. 91) was neither made as a fake nor reworked into a fraud. Nor is it antique, although in 1962 it was for sale in an antiques shop. Nothing about it would worry the veteran detective, and it's a gem to a collector of Colonial Revival furniture. However, any rookie still susceptible to copycat crimes should read on, because this copy is typical of a common breed.

The chest, one of several, was made about 1900 by Dr. Edwin C. Thorn (1874–1920) and Caleb Allen (1861–1927) of Deerfield, Massachusetts, and decorated by Thorn, who based the design for the most part on an antique chest in Memorial Hall, Deerfield.[6] He copied the carving on the panels, but this chest lacks most of the molding-plane work on the stiles and rails of the original. For some evidently "practical" reason, the inside of the chest is lined with zinc. The drawer, instead of hanging in joinery style, stands on runners like a modern one. (Such an anachronism assures that the squad will have no trouble with this case.)

The antique original has a simple, molded drawer front; Thorn "improved" on the design (a common practice of copiers), substituting a more elaborate, carved drawer front that is, in terms of seventeenth-century work, hokum throughout. The carving itself, a sort of adaptation of the Wethersfield, Connecticut, style, is awkwardly — and uncharacteristically — confined between the drawer handles. And those iron handles! Thorn had them made by the local blacksmith, Cornelius Kelly (1874–1954), to go with the iron strap hinges proudly emblazoning the lid.

Thorn displayed this example of his craftsmanship (or, in honor of the times, his Arts-and-Craftsmanship) in 1901 at Old Home Week in Deerfield, when the "bride's chest," whose drawer moved "as though it were on oiled runners" was lauded as "one of the most successful specimens of work in the exhibit."[7] Apparently the chest that would eventually reappear in a Belvidere, New Jersey, antiques shop was originally sold between 1901 and 1920 at a Deerfield crafts display and sale.

Let's move on to other kinds of cases.

The Case of the Case Piece, Part Two: Cabinetry

7

SINCE the early eighteenth century, furniture making has been dominated by cabinetmakers, practitioners of dovetailing. Their special joint locks the end of one board to the end of another by fitting a row of fan-shaped tenons on the one into a row of identical notches on the other. Each row of dovetails is individually made and mated, with the cabinetmaker using his finished dovetail tenons as a model for cutting the matching notches. Dovetails need no glue or nails, though country joiners sometimes reinforced rude dovetails with nails (see fig. 92, a detail of the underside of what will be our first dovetailed case).

THE FRAME-UP

We begin by focusing on a series of frame-ups: the framing of the individual drawers and of the cabinet that contains them. For each drawer, the cabinetmaker created a four-sided frame with dovetails at all four corners. For the cabinet — a larger but similar frame — he dovetailed the case bottom, the two sides, and the top (or bound the sides to the bottom with dovetails and affixed the top in another way).

The squad, looking for the familiar signs of dovetail-making, notes the scribed line that remains at the base of the dovetails, where the cabinetmaker, before he cut the dovetail's tenons, determined their

FIGURE 92:
Bottom corner of a dove-
tailed blanket chest. Re-
inforcing nails secure the
dovetails; the detective also
notes a clenched nail near
each foot. Detail of our first
dovetailed case, figure 100.

FIGURE 93:
Saw overcuts inside a
drawer front. Lining paper
(on this drawer bottom),
unless glued, should be removed during inspection.

depth by marking his work with the thickness of the mating board (e.g., figs. 92 and 55). Detectives also track the craftsman's work in his saw's overcuts, made as he sawed in from the edge (in preparation for chiseling out the waste across the grain at the scribed line).

Inside those drawers whose fronts are made of solid wood there are long and obvious overcuts (fig. 93). To avoid cutting the drawer facade, the cabinetmaker had to saw at a sharp angle; to minimize the more laborious work of cleaning out the notches with the chisel, he sawed as far as he possibly could. On veneered drawer fronts, angled cuts were not needed because the saw cuts would be hidden by the veneer.

Because dovetailing forms a rectangular frame without any protruding parts, a dovetailed case has an inherent weakness: its legs cannot be an integral part of the case; they must be attached. Savvy sleuths know that in antiques the merely attached is the most readily detached (whether broken, lost, or replaced). Determined to scrutinize the feet (and gather other clues), they place the dovetailed case on its back early in the investigatioin and look underneath.

THE UNDERWORLD

*For evidence of wrongdoing, quickly turn to the underworld —
the undersides of cases and the undersides of drawers.* You should remove the drawers before putting a case on its back. And *as you take out each drawer, turn it over.* Undersides reveal a lot because they do not show, hence the wood was left unfinished (figs. 94 and 95). Many fakers and defrauders of the past paid little attention to undersides. Gratuitous staining often sufficed. Restorers, having no need to cover up their legitimate repairs, often leave their work visible on the undersides of things, although some are inclined to stain new wood (see the replaced corner blocks in fig. 95). *Be suspicious of finished undersides; they are at best reworked and may be fraudulently reused boards.*

FIGURE 94:
Under a Boston case. Detail of the chest of drawers shown in figure 107. A row of glue blocks supports the base molding. Additional blocks support the feet and central drop. All the blocks are of one color and show signs of having always been together. The feet once had casters; the left front foot is pieced out at the bottom.

Amid the natural changes in the underworld (e.g., darkening of the unfinished wood), the detective looks out for unnatural alterations, especially replaced feet (fig. 92). Although turned feet are doweled into the bottom of a case, many more feet are merely glued to the undersides. A few bracket feet are an integral part of the base molding (usually in country-made cases), but most are simply glued and nailed to the base molding and rely for stability on wooden blocks, glued and nailed snug up against them (fig. 96). A vertical block behind the bracket may really hold the weight. Claw-and-ball feet, which are usually taller than bracket feet, have a more tenuous stance (fig. 97). Cabinetmakers in various regions and shops worked out different arrangements of supports, yet feet — even broadly bracketed ones — are basically vulnerable.

FIGURE 95:
Under a Rhode Island case. The support blocking for the base molding is inside the case (fig. 115). The left rear foot was pieced out with a 3-inch piece of thinner wood. Six glue blocks at the feet — two vertical corner blocks at the rear, four horizontal blocks in front — are new, and all are stained.

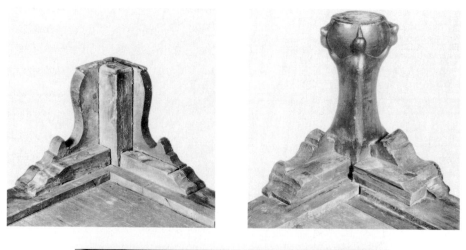

Because the cabinetmaker shaped foot brackets after he put them and their blocking in place, both the bracket and its support block should bear the same saw cuts and rasp marks (figs. 96 and 97). A variation in wood color betrays support blocks of various ages. Stained blocks are replacements. Looking at wood color and at saw and rasp marks, even a rookie spots replaced supports and new feet (fig. 98).

New feet substantially reduce the value of a piece. Two block-fronts, each with identically constructed drawers, each marked with the same initials and year, brought very different results at auction not long ago. The chest with old feet sold for $38,500; the one with new feet (fig. 98) was bought in (that is, it failed to sell) at $18,000.

"Look at these fake feet [fig. 99]!" a rookie called to the experienced detective leading the way on a first patrol of auction previews. "The faker didn't finish carving the rear toes on the claw-and-ball feet!"

"Looks good," the veteran said, pointing out the unity in wood color and the rasp marks on feet and brackets. "Missing toes are a good sign, because eighteenth-century Boston cabinetmakers didn't bother to carve talons to face the wall. On Boston stuff, I expect rear feet with toes only where they'd show."

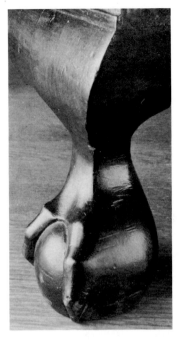

FIGURE 99:
Rear claw foot with
uncarved toes. A sign
of economy.

The realm underneath is so revealing that you can greatly expedite furniture inspection by turning things over early. If a case presents apparently contradictory information, *put more credence in what you gather in the underworld than in what appears on the surface.*

MORE CASE STUDIES

A pine chest with drawers (fig. 100) is our first dovetailed case. Underneath (fig. 92), we discover that the craftsman reinforced his dovetails with nails (sometimes done with early, large dovetails such as these). The rear feet, which are round-tenoned into the case bottom, are clearly modern replacements. (The wormholes on the old feet pass the needle test, suggesting that the other original feet were done in by woodworm.) When compared to the old feet, the replacements prove to be faithful copies.

The undersurface is rough and unfinished; the color under the case (with the exception of the new feet) is uniform. The points of old clinched nails are visible just inside the dovetails and near each foot (fig. 92). The alert inspector checks inside the case to determine the role of these nails, and finds that they secure half-inch-thick strips upon which the bottom drawer rests. The nails, which clearly have never been moved, establish the age of the drawer supports.

FIGURE 100:
Chest with drawers or blanket chest; white pine with maple feet, 1730–1750, coastal Massachusetts. H. 41¾; W. 36; D. 18⅛. (Society for the Preservation of New England Antiquities.)

Base molding usually covers the dovetailing at the lower edge of the case sides. On this chest, the dovetails are exposed, but nail holes prove that there was originally a base molding. Although the molding is missing, its shape is known, because it would have echoed that of the front molding. Old abrasions, extending under the case bottom and front molding (just left of the old foot, fig. 92), prove to the sleuth that the front molding is old. New side moldings replicating the old front molding would be as acceptable a restoration as the authentically copied feet.

This chest with drawers never had a lock, which is not very unusual for an unsophisticated object, but it retains its original brass pulls and escutcheons. The pattern of the hardware suggests to the experienced eye that moldings like those that outline the drawers originally simulated three additional drawers above. Close inspection of the facade reveals old nail holes that mark the right places.

In examining the case back, the chest interior, the drawers, and the lid, we find but one other flaw — nail holes on the edges of the lid indicate that side moldings are missing there too. All the extant parts except the two new feet began life together.

Check the Most UNwanted List. This chest is not a fake (age is evident everywhere); it is not an instance of old parts/new object (its parts started out together); it is not remade (restored does not mean remade); it is not enhanced (restoration is not the same as enhancement); it is not a made-up set, or married, or a misrepresented reproduction. Nor is it English, a likely possibility when genuine woodworm is present — the design is typical of New England, as is the wood, white pine with maple feet. Our first dovetailed case, though it is not without losses, is genuine. The replacement parts are exact copies, and the contours of the missing moldings are known. The case is a smart choice for a collector.

THE SHELL GAME

The nine-shelled chest (plate 4), whose rarity should raise questions (page 36), is not only a fraud but an enhanced fraud, "improved" while its true nature apparently went unrecognized. In its enhanced state, it was presented as genuine in 1952 in a "bible" on antique furniture, Joseph Downs's *American Furniture: Queen Anne and Chippendale Periods in the Henry Francis du Pont Winterthur Museum*. After being displayed in the museum for years as a prized possession, it is now in the Winterthur Study Collection, a tool for educating connoisseurs, curators, and collectors.

If du Pont, Downs, and the Winterthur staff were taken in by the

"nine-shell" (to use its museum moniker), you may wonder how you would unmask it. The answer is, easily. The nine-shell passed when no one was looking. Collecting was different a couple of generations ago; "spectacular" was the goal, not "authentic," and the story of the nine-shell proves it.

Henry Francis du Pont bought the "antique" nine-shell based on a black-and-white photograph, a photograph that remains in the museum's file on the object. In the picture, the chest has wooden knobs, since replaced with brasses, and a simpler, entirely different base — different feet and a different skirt.

Most decorative-arts collections in the first half of the twentieth century, Winterthur's among them, were built amid collecting goals and preservation ethics far different from those we have today. Replacing obviously inappropriate handles with brasses more suitable to the period can be regarded as a sort of restoration and would be done today. But the creation of a new base (whose design suggests Connecticut craftsmanship rather than the Rhode Island work the simpler base implied) is an alteration that would now be frowned upon. The base may have been changed in an attempt to explain away the oddness of the nine-shell form by making the piece attributable to Connecticut rather than to sophisticated Rhode Island. Downs should have known from the museum's records that the base had been changed, yet he did not consider it imperative to mention the reworking.

This epitome of fraud is riddled with many easily detected flaws.

Let's start with the nine shells themselves. If a table-high chest of drawers has shells, it has three, all on the top drawer. This nine-shell chest is a rare, perhaps even unique, example. *Rare* is an offensive four-letter word to sensitive sleuths; *unique* is an abomination. The reason there were no nine-shell chests is that the facade makes no artistic sense. A three-shelled chest of drawers makes sense in eighteenth-century design terms; Newport cabinetmakers used shells like these to crown their blocking. Just as carved capitals finish off columns and pilasters, concave shells complete central recesses and convex shells cap the flanking convex blocks (fig. 101). Thus, considered in eighteenth-century terms, the arrangement of nine shells on three drawers makes the shells look bereft of their columns. *Put style to work by thinking in terms of period design.*

Fakers do not always conform to period taste; they cater to their customers' appetites. If three shells appealed to collectors (as they did and still do), then, a faker could reason, nine shells must be three times as good. Shell-carved objects bring far higher prices than their plainer cousins, and an ever-greedy faker, seeing each shell as money, created the nine-shell, which is, as has been aptly put, "too good to be true."[1]

The fakery is too bad to be believed, and even a rookie will not be fooled by this one. The sides of the case are composed of narrow boards instead of the wide boards that the sleuth expects. Seen close up, carefully stained wooden plugs tip the hand of the faker: the plugs fill holes that held hardware when the boards, in an earlier incarnation, were drawer fronts. *Look inside the case when examining the sides; there, evidence like narrow boards and plugged holes is more apparent.*

If the case sides, so essential and integral to a cabinet, are wrong, what can be right? Not the top; like the sides, it is made of narrow boards. Had the case sides been good, this would have suggested that the top was a replacement. The bottom drawer has unexplained nail holes and traces of earlier, larger blocking above its convex shells. The nine-shell excels not only in the number of its shells but also in the number of its reused drawer fronts.

DON'T RADIO FOR HELP

The attitude prevalent earlier in this century toward authenticity affected not only the newly made but also the genuinely old. In the magazine *Antiques* for May 1943, the author of "Shop Talk" noted that "the introduction of the most modern addition to the domestic interior, the radio, into a room furnished with antique furniture raises a problem."[2] Decrying a radio of simulated period design as "inevitably a mongrel," acknowledging some "protest against tampering with . . . an original early piece of cabinetmaking," and discouraging the use of "a piece of museum quality," the author advised the reader to "conceal the radio in furniture which has its place in the room on its own merits."[3] Instructions for the alterations were accompanied by four drawings (fig. 102, two of them) illustrating "a few of the ways in which both radio and phonograph may be neatly fitted into old pieces."[4]

Today's detective, aware of the crimes of the mid–twentieth century, is alert to two kinds of problem pieces: the antique that underwent such alteration, and the one that was altered and then further abused by having the radio removed and an "old interior" installed.

Nor has the "updating" of antiques ended. On October 25, 1984, the *New York Times* spoke of wardrobes and sideboards being taken apart, "their components recycled into smaller, tidier and more useful forms." The author, Michael Varese, focused on smaller antiques: "Those elegant, sloping knife boxes, their contents dispersed, the knife holes removed, are now fitted with dividers to hold stationery — graceful additions to any writing table."[5]

A focus on the adaptability rather than the integrity of antique objects, although not all-pervasive, is common. One Queen Anne high chest has all new drawers in the upper case. "I had to restore it," the antiques dealer said, pointing out the new drawers, new drawer dividers, and new partition between the two top drawers. "For years it was a curio cabinet with shelves in the upper case."

FIGURE 102:
Two of four suggestions for antique radio cabinets.
(Courtesy Antiques.)

The veteran collector examined the case thoroughly to ascertain whether it had begun as a curio cabinet in the Queen Anne style. It had not; the old parts were eighteenth-century and intact. Someone had made a curio cabinet out of an antique high chest.

EBEN. HARTSHORN'S CASE

The rookie detective can learn about the problems routinely encountered with high chests from the famous, glorious chest Ebenezer Hartshorn made (and signed) in 1739 in Charlestown, Massachusetts (fig. 36). The losses suffered by Hartshorn's chest (aside from the finish, which is almost never original) are the most common ones for high chests. In spite of two inscriptions, "Rep 1808" and "Repaired 1915," the high chest was regarded as essentially intact in 1931, when it entered the collection of the Museum of Fine Arts, Boston. In honor of the chest's two-hundredth birthday, the museum replaced obviously inappropriate hardware with brasses that follow "the indications on the drawer fronts."[6]

The flame finials, however, still do not pass the style test; their design indicates Philadelphia. The lower part of the finials — the urns — are missing; the plinths, which look like mahogany whereas the rest of the case is walnut, are doweled in, and each mortise was made with a modern auger. And John Kirk, a veteran on the squad, didn't like the cabrioles: why would Hartshorn, with all the walnut available to him in the eighteenth century, select a piece of wood with a visible knot for a front leg? The museum followed up on the question scientifically, and recent X rays show that Hartshorn did not, in fact, make the legs. The X rays reveal doweled joints in the top of the legs, whereas eighteenth-century cabrioles are of one piece, extending from the top of the lower case to the floor (see the caseless cabrioles, fig. 103).

This restored antique is an important if imperfect object. Its losses are hardware, finials, plinths, and legs — in that order the most common losses suffered by high chests. Finials can be lifted right out of their sockets, and brass handles, easily replaced, are frequently updated. Such parts disappear in normal circumstances and are also special targets for pilferage. But it's hard to purloin legs!

THE CABRIOLE CONTRABAND AND THE CROOKED CADGE

In 1985, at an August auction in Maine, the summer doldrums seemed to keep bidding sluggish until suddenly a number of bidders

FIGURE 103:
Cabrioles, previewed at auction. The key highlights clues awaiting close examination. (Photograph courtesy Maine Antique Digest.*)*

stirred for four high-chest legs (fig. 103) and raised their hands, if somewhat sheepishly.

Four cabrioles are not a common auction lot. The crowd would not have been surprised at the sight of the reverse — a high chest standing on its cabriole knees as if they were bracket feet. That sight though startling, was quite common in old houses by the end of the nineteenth century. Folklore points to low ceilings and insensitive owners as the culprits, but the old legs often split and broke before the saw could get to them.

Lowered high chests still show up, but today most of them stand once again on full-height legs. Some (like the Hartshorn piece) have doweled additions, some have spliced additions (usually a sound repair, but chancy for the gams beneath a high chest), and some lower cases were taken apart and rebuilt around new legs.

The four old legs at the August auction looked like a rebuilding opportunity. The high bidder paid $110 a leg, $440 as a down payment on a high chest. Before he began to work with the old legs, however, he decided he couldn't go through with the job. It wasn't his conscience, as a usually savvy sleuth soon found out.

The high bidder telephoned Sam Pennington, editor and publisher of the *Maine Antique Digest* (a.k.a. *M.A.D.*), a man charmed by old fragments and prone to display them around his office. Pennington reports on antiques, he doesn't make them, so the high bidder wasn't conceding anything to his competition when he asked, "Want them at the next increment bid?"

Pennington was not about to hand over more than $440, but he was interested. "Stop by. Maybe we can trade."

And trade they did: the cabrioles and other oddments for an antique Chippendale desk on turned Victorian feet. Later Pennington looked closely at his cabrioles for the first time and laughed at himself — "So that was why he didn't build a high chest around these legs." Each of the four cabrioles had been spliced. Pennington found a barely visible diagonal line above the ankles, showing where new feet had been added.

In a catchall section of *M.A.D.* called, ironically, "Fragments," Pennington told the tale of the spliced cabrioles, which had "some black paint mucked around to hide the splicing."[7]

The tale has one moral for each cabriole:

1. There are antique high chests with new legs. Somewhere out there, the old chest that was once supported by these cabrioles probably stands on new legs.

2. There can be a new high chest with antique legs. The high bidder almost built one.

3. *Before you bid, buy, or trade, remember: even a fragment requires inspection.*

4. Most often you win, but even the smart ones lapse and occasionally lose. Like Pennington, *laugh when you lapse.*

THE DOUBLE LIFE

Unlike the caseless cabrioles, which are obviously fragments, two other, common types of fragments are hardly recognizable as such. They are the upper or lower case of a double case, leading a second, single life.

Over the years, the upper and lower cases of many high chests (a.k.a. highboys) have been separated, as have the two cases of some chest-on-chests. Almost every time one of these hits the street, it does so incognito: lower cases of chests-on-chests and upper cases pose as chests of drawers; lower cases of high chests pretend to be dressing tables.

Because dressing tables, a.k.a. lowboys, were made en suite with high chests, they are very much like them, but the dressing tables are narrower, measuring about 32 to 36 inches wide. A "dressing table" that is 41 inches wide is a reborn high-chest base.

In trying to determine whether a case has led a double life, the detective's first impression of the facade is important. For example, the facade of the upper case of a high chest usually looks like what it really is even when the case is posing as a low chest of drawers (compare figs. 110 and 28). Another clear and trustworthy informant in such cases is the top.

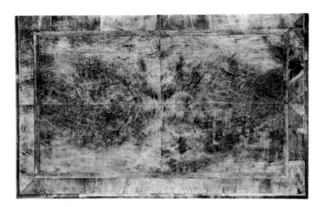

FIGURES 104, 105:
Veneered top of a dressing
table, and the dressing table
itself; black walnut and
white pine, 1730–1740,
Boston area. H. 30¼; W.
34 1/16; D. 20 7/16. (Society for
the Preservation of New
England Antiquities.) For
an interior detail, see
figure 117.

STAYING ON TOP OF THE CASE

Scrutinize the top surface. To pass as a dressing table, the lower case of a high chest needs to be fitted with a top. Most new tops are not up to the job. Eighteenth-century dressing tables typically had tops (fig. 104) finished almost as grandly as their facades (fig. 105). If the drawer fronts are veneered, a smart detective expects to find a veneered top; if a drawer front features an inlay shell, an inlay star may appear in the center of the top. When the front is carved, the top, of course, is not similarly decorated, but an inspection of its underside (see "Questioning the Board Further" and "Favorite Pranks of the Unprincipled," pages 172–173) should settle the question of the top's authenticity.

The flat top of the upper case of a high chest is even more revealing (fig. 106); it closely resembles the bottoms of dovetailed cases. The top of a high chest (or of a chest-on-chest) is well above eye level, so the top board is not of the primary wood and is left unfinished. Because the top was not meant to show, the dovetails binding it to the sides of the upper case are exposed. The cornice moldings surrounding the top are usually flush with the surface of the top.

In contrast, the tops of chests of drawers were table-height or a bit higher and were meant to be seen and used as table surfaces. Such tops are of finished primary wood (fig. 107). The top may overhang the case sides and front, and there may be moldings beneath the overhang, but very rarely are moldings merely attached along the edge without concern for the appearance from above.

When moldings are attached along the edges (figs. 108 and 109)

FIGURE 106:
Top of high chest. The
dovetailed top board is visible because of the facade-
only pediment. The supports
and blocks that back the
pediment are closely related
to rear feet and blocks under cases from the same
area (fig. 94).

and when the top of a chest is of secondary wood and has exposed dovetails, be very skeptical. And watch out for a top veneered in other than period style. Earlier (on page 74) we learned of a chest (much like that in fig. 110 but with ball feet) whose top was veneered without figure or pattern, with all the veneer running in one direction — a stark contrast to the table-high top (fig. 104) on a veneered dressing table of the same style and date. The bland unidirectional veneer covers an unfinished top, exposed dovetails, the crack between the top and the molding, and the top edge of the molding itself. The top here (figs. 108 and 109) has no veneered cover-up and looks just like a high-chest top.

FIGURE 107:
Chest of drawers; mahog-
any and white pine, 1770,
Boston. Made by George
Bright. H. 31; W. 39; D.
20¹¹/₁₆. (Society for the Preservation of New England
Antiquities.) Details of this
chest are pictured in figure
94 (underside) and figure
118 (inside the case).

FIGURE 108:
The corner of a top. Detail of chest shown in figure 109. Many high chests have a drawer at the top whose drawer front, like this one, is the cornice molding.

Once you become skeptical, discovering the true nature of a high-chest top in disguise can be amazingly easy. Sometimes a redone case even has the long drawer hidden in the cornice molding (fig. 108) that was a popular feature of flat-top high chests. Again, any chest that looks like the upper case of a high chest probably is.

The undersides of reborn upper cases reveal little. After all, during the years when the upper case was on its lower case, its bottom board was not exposed to air and did not darken. The board darkened only after the case was placed on feet. Feet added around 1780 to the upper case of a Queen Anne high chest that was only a generation or two old (fig. 109) went onto wood that had barely aged. If the feet have remained intact, the undersides are of one uniform color. *In a chest of drawers that resembles a high-chest upper case, look to the top for the reliable story.*

FIGURE 109:
Chest of drawers (adapted from the top case of a high chest); black walnut and white pine. Made ca. 1750; adapted ca. 1780. H. 39⅝; W. 36⅜; D. 20⅛. (Society for the Preservation of New England Antiquities.) A detail of this case looks behind a brass handle (fig. 62).

FIGURE 110:
Chest of drawers; walnut, maple, and pine, 1700–1735, Massachusetts. H. 37; W. 36⅛; D. 20¼. (Yale University Art Gallery, Mabel Brady Garvan Collection.) Rare example or altered high-chest top; legit conversion (as in fig. 109) or impostor?

A case at Yale (fig. 110) has its original top surface coated with finish. In 1970, John Kirk, that usually skeptical sleuth, threw caution to the wind. Having acknowledged that a high-chest top fitted with feet to pass as a chest was "a standard faker's item" and "a favorite faker's trick," and having stated that every example of the form (which he called "popular in England" but "rarely found in America") is immediately suspect, Kirk wrote that this particular chest "is one of those instances where the near-unique is genuine."[8]

Harold Sack says otherwise. Citing the top — with its exposed dovetails — as proof of its origin, Sack says the Yale case is the upper part of a William and Mary high chest, with bracket feet of a later style.[9] *Where expert testimony is contradictory, side with the skeptic.*

WITHOUT A LEG TO STAND ON

There is a reason why so many William and Mary high-chest upper cases lead a double life: their lower cases were done in by weak underpinnings (fig. 111). This is the way the deck was stacked against them.

The double case stands on a stack of separate elements: ball foot, stretcher, and baluster-turned leg. The turned leg dowels through the stretcher and foot and, above, dowels into the lower case. But not directly: the dowel enters a block glued in the corner of the case.

To understand why blocks are needed, you should know that the lower case of a William and Mary high chest is a dovetailed case; the high chest's matching dressing table is dovetailed too. Four boards — the front skirt, the two sides, and the back — are dovetailed together at the corners. (In front, the dovetails are hidden under veneer.) Since the legs could not be doweled directly into the thin boards of the frame, cabinetmakers set blocks in each corner to receive the dowels.

The series of delicate joints was prone to come apart. Especially under the weight of a high chest, the legs or their blocks gave way. Later in the eighteenth century, cabinetmakers in many areas stopped dovetailing dressing tables and the lower cases of high chests and instead mortise-and-tenoned Queen Anne and Chippendale cases together, using the upper part of the cabrioles as the case posts (fig. 103).

Some William and Mary high chests have been fitted with new legs. Many such restorations were done incorrectly, and a detective with an eye for style can spot the problem. *Look at the stretchers.* The boards that tie the legs together near the feet, stabilizing the

FIGURE 111:
*Inverted high-chest base.
Detail of the case shown in
figure 28. (Photograph courtesy Israel Sack, Inc.) The
feet fit over round tenons.
The undersides are unfin-
ished; their color suggests
that all the many pieces began life together. The
stretchers echo the outline
of the skirt. In back, the
dovetails uniting the case
back to the sides are visible.*

frame, also tie the design together by echoing the line of the skirt, as we saw in Chapter 4, "Styles as Clues" (figs. 27 and 28). You can easily spot unmatched substitutions, and if the stretchers are substitutes, the legs and feet probably are too. Such replacements are major. (An eccentric eighteenth-century cabinetmaker may have been so unattuned to style that his stretchers went their own way, ignoring the skirt; the selective collector will probably ignore his eccentric product.)

FIGURE 112:
*Back of a "Newport"
blockfront. (Photograph
courtesy* Maine Antique
Digest.*)*

In a Boston case (from the back). (Society for the Preservation of New England Antiquities.)

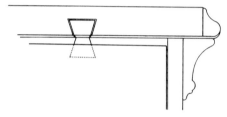

FIGURE 114:
A Newport "butterfly" (seen from the back and partially hidden by the backboard). It locks into the frame-completing top board and into the topmost surface of the frame above.

The back of the chest in figure 112, seen at an auction in 1978, seemed to check out. The wood of the backboard was unfinished and looked old; abrasions that crossed from one board to another showed a unified history; it even had an inscription. Case backs can be rich in evidence (especially on desks, fig. 121) and require surveillance. This back readily revealed a damning detail.

The chest facade was blocked and had "Newport" shells on the top drawer. The "Newport block-and-shell," a form the trade calls "highly desirable," is a favorite of fakers and a regular on the squad's list of suspects. The top of this chest was also typical of Rhode Island fashion, having only a slight overhang beneath which a molding visually united the top to the case side.

However, from the back, an experienced detective could see that the top joined the case sides in "Boston" (fig. 113), not in "Newport" (fig. 114) fashion. Many Boston and Portsmouth blockfronts without shells have been transformed into the more "desirable" Newport block-and-shells, so sleuths on the lookout for enhanced old pieces should be knowledgeable about the different ways of joining a top.

Tops on Boston-area chests join the case sides with a sliding single dovetail visible from the back (fig. 113). A Rhode Island chest, however, really has two tops: a frame-completing top (often of two boards, fig. 115) joined to the sides by locking rows of dovetails, and a topmost surface secured to the case by moldings, glue blocks, and often butterfly-keys (fig. 114).

At the 1978 auction, after intently inspecting the entire "block-and-shell," the investigators had doubts. When the auctioneer announced that it was to be sold without any guarantees, they sat on their hands. The chest didn't sell. (It did two years later. At the Steven Straw bankruptcy-sale auction, Phillips dubbed it "Chippendale Style Block Front Chest of Four Drawers," and it brought $8500 [the 1978 estimate was $100,000].[10] Straw, a gallery owner, had had a "copy" [fig. 116] made; Phillips sold that for $1800. Perhaps as an editorial statement, Phillips illustrated only the "copy" in its literature.)

When investigating the backs of cases, also check the least obvious places. *Look for telltale modern saw marks on the lower edges of a high-chest or dressing-table backboard.* That small and barely visible surface is most likely the one spot the faker neglected. This tip is a standard caution when inspecting table skirts and is useful for long-legged cases as well. It is especially pertinent for dressing tables, a form cherished by collectors as small, cute, and attractive — and thus a type of case that is frequently faked.

FIGURE 115:
A Newport case. (Society
for the Preservation of New
England Antiquities.) The
two boards at the top complete the dovetailed frame.

FIGURE 116:
The not-quite-exact "copy"
that Steven Straw had made
of the "Newport" block-
front (fig. 112). (Photograph
courtesy Maine Antique
Digest.)

THE INSIDE JOB

The insides of cases, which are also unfinished surfaces, also bear informative marks of the craftsman at work and revealing marks of wear. *Feel the inside surfaces. Beware the top, sides, or back whose inner surfaces are smooth and finished.*

Within cases with more than one drawer on a tier, the cabinet-maker inserted vertical partitions, and the scored lines with which he located their mortises are visible on the inside of the back (fig. 117). He may also have scored lines on the back when aligning central drawer-supports. Scored lines that do not pertain to the present partitions and supports probably indicate reused parts or a rebuilt case.

Wherever drawers make contact with the case, the investigator looks for wear. Some drawers run on central supports (fig. 117); most, standing on their edges, slide on support strips that are nailed to the case sides (fig. 118). The bottom drawer may slide directly on the case bottom (as it does in fig. 118) or on supports within the case (fig. 115).

The interior of the case (fig. 118) of the handsome blockfront in figure 107 shows moderate wear; the drawers have corresponding wear beneath their pine sides. With fingers even more than eyes, the sleuth checks for abrasion on drawers and on the corresponding softwood supports. Though the soft pine is worn, the hardwood facade of the drawer divider is merely rubbed. *Always check inside the case for aligned wear.* Replaced drawer supports are a minor

FIGURE 117:
Detail of dressing table shown in figure 105. An applied bead molding surrounds the drawer openings and finishes the skirt edge. Turned drops are often lost, leaving telltale round mortises on the skirt edge. The scored lines on the backboard line up with the partitions and drawer supports. (A central drawer support creates a distinctively marked drawer bottom; see fig. 191, a table drawer.)

loss but may indicate even greater alterations. Fingers can "see" if the original supports have merely been turned upside down, a common and desirable method of repair. Replaced drawer dividers are a major repair.

Looking between a drawer support and the case side (a loose support sometimes affords such an opportunity) can be most revealing. Although the unfinished wood inside antique cases is rather light in color, it has darkened somewhat over the years. Behind an original drawer support, the detective can find its negative shadow on the case sides. Cases made up of old wood exhibit no change of color behind the supports. In the case of the "Dunlap" high chest (fig. 12), proof of a May-December marriage was found when the drawer runners were removed in the upper case, revealing a uniformity of color that showed that the sides of the upper case were not old.

Check drawers for uniformity in wood color and construction and for logical damage. A faker's favorite for suggesting age was random ink stains. Ink stains are logical in a desk but out of place in, for example, a dressing table. And ink may spill inside a desk drawer, but it doesn't easily spill on the drawer's outer surfaces.

When investigators, in the course of the usual "is it what it purports to be" inspection, looked over the blockfront chest (fig. 107), first outside, then in (fig. 118), checking the outside and inside of every drawer, they made a surprising discovery and solved an almost unsolvable mystery. The blockfront, clearly of Boston style, had returned to New England from California. A Boston case in California posed no mystery at all; antique furniture travels far. But the

FIGURE 118:
*Boston blockfront (fig. 107)
with the drawers removed.
The bottom is worn where
the drawer sides rub over it.*

man who returned it to New England did so because he believed he could tie the chest to a bill and prove that it was made in 1770 by Boston's most prestigious cabinetmaker, George Bright.

The bill — for Jonathan Bowman, who had left Colonial Boston for Pownalborough, Maine, to serve as justice of the peace, collector of excise, and other civil posts — referred to chairs of three different sets, several tables, and two mahogany bureau tables (bureaus, or chests, of table height). Was this one of the two bureau tables in the bill? The one descriptive word, *Mahogany*, was no help; most cases made in Boston at that time were of mahogany. The next-to-last item on the bill, however, offered more information: "To Lineing the Buroe Tables Draws with Marble paper."

The insides of drawers of stylish furniture were occasionally lined; plain blue paper was a favorite. Such drawer linings, never common to begin with, have almost always torn and been removed. In this chest too, the drawers were no longer lined.

The man who had located the chest in California had traced it through Bowman's family. The chest, inherited by Bowman's widow and taken to her brother's house in 1809, was left with that house to a nephew, whose widow then took it in 1895 to California, where her daughter inherited it in 1903 and left it to her children in 1909. The chest belonged to one of those children.

With the chest were chairs from two different sets and two tables that matched those in the bill both in description and dimensions.

All the furniture looked like Boston and 1770. Yet a mystery remained: Was this one of the two bureaus in the bill? There was no inscription by Bright, nor do seasoned sleuths expect any on eighteenth-century furniture. One might hope against hope that the drawers might still be lined; too bad they weren't.

Then, inside one drawer, the detective's eye alighted upon a sliver of fiber caught in the crack where the drawer bottom fits into the rabbeted drawer front. The sliver, liberated from the joint by the blade of the wood-sampling knife and the antisplinter tweezers, was a piece of old marbleized paper.

What a joy that bit of paper! The handsome blockfront chest is now acknowledged as the work of George Bright — representing a major discovery in American furniture history, as no other bracket-foot case by Bright was known. The saga of the sliver is the inside story.

The unstained and unfinished surfaces inside a case are good places to check on the woods. To make the grain of unfinished wood more visible, you can wet a bit of the surface. Most urban furniture has only one primary wood and sometimes only one secondary wood; the Bright blockfront, for example, is entirely of mahogany and white pine. In rural furniture, several primary (and secondary) woods may be used (note the many woods in the high chest, plate 3). *If the design suggests an urban origin, expect one primary wood. Question, for example, a dressing table whose top is of a different wood.* When you find a second primary wood on what looks like an urban case, you may have discovered a replaced part or a country case that was enhanced to resemble a city slicker.

On veneered cases, drawer openings and the bottom edge of the veneered skirts usually have an applied bead molding that protects the veneer (fig. 117). On solid-wood cases, like the Bright chest (fig. 118), beaded edges were cut with a molding plane, as were thumbnail-molded edges. Edges often are chipped, and applied bead molding is sometimes missing and very often repaired or replaced. The beaded edges of the Bright blockfront are unusually intact. *Check edges; they are most vulnerable to wear and often have been pieced out.*

SOME COMPLICATED CASES

Desks with loads of drawers on the interior and exterior, desks with bookcase tops (figs. 119 and 120) and all types of double cases require lengthy inspections. *Don't rush a complex case, or you'll*

FIGURES 119, 120:
Desk and bookcase and detail of the interior; cherry, mahogany, and white pine, 1775–1800, Newburyport, Massachusetts, or Portsmouth, New Hampshire. H. 94⅞; W. 43⅜; D. 25³⁄₁₆. (Society for the Preservation of New England Antiquities.)

compound your problems. Nevertheless, a smart sleuth can dispose of some complicated cases quickly by focusing on the most common trouble spots first.

On a desk, the feet and lid are likely to be problems. We have already investigated the underworld, and the routine for desk jobs is no different. And the desk lid (or leaf) is very approachable.

Fold-down desk lids were usually made of one board edged with cleats whose grain runs in the opposite direction from that of the board itself. Desk lids most often break just beyond the hinges. Two-board lids are probably repairs; the new piece, the one at the hinge. To discern replaced lids, check the hinges. At a replaced hinge, the pieced repairs on both sides should show a shared history (fig. 60).

Central doors in desks are especially vulnerable to loss. A few doors, made without hinges, merely fit in a notch, and were locked

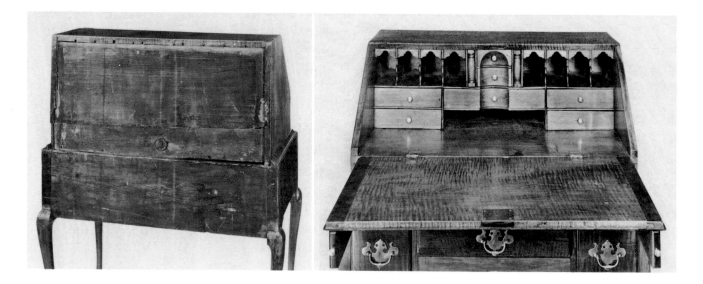

FIGURES 121, 122:
Rear view and desk interior
of desk-on-frame shown in
plate 5.

in place. Central drawers are often missing (some desks never had one), leaving a drawer-size cubby into which the items on the desk can be easily shoved. Frequently a valance (held by tiny glue blocks) above a pigeonhole is missing or broken. Such damage is common and minor. Those desks whose central section pulls out to reveal hidden cubbies and drawers are special favorites with antiquers. The components of such sections are usually well preserved because they were little used.

But desks can have major problems — an enhanced or entirely replaced desk interior, or the marriage of a bookcase to a desk — so check for consistency in wood, color, and craftsmanship. A small desk-on-frame (plate 5), of an attractive form and therefore likely prey for fakers and defrauders, illustrates how easy it is to see consistency. Although the primary wood has been stripped and re-finished, the back has not (fig. 121). The wood and color of the back answer yes to the question, "Do these two cases belong to-gether?" The grooves for the interior partitions are also visible in back; these confirm that the present partition arrangement inside (fig. 122) is original.

The case top of a desk holds much of the answer to another crucial question: "Did this desk originally have a bookcase?" A desk made to have a bookcase has a top board of unfinished wood, exposed dovetails at each end, and nail-hole evidence of a mid molding around the front and side edges. See if the top board is original by comparing it with the sides for consistency in feel and color. And look at its back edge (that view from the back is always revealing).

Sometimes cabinetmakers used an especially time-consuming joint — the mitered dovetail — to fasten a top of a desk to the case sides (fig. 121). The detective who is unable to see how the top of an eighteenth-century desk is joined to the sides suspects invisible mitered dovetails. This uncommon joint was used to join primary wood to primary wood, and no cabinetmaker would have bothered with it on a desk top that was to be covered by a bookcase. But the converse is not so: many desk tops of finished primary wood have exposed dovetails yet were never intended to have bookcases.

Some bookcase tops seems to pass all the "we began life together" tests but exhibit small differences with the desk beneath them. The valances above the pigeonholes, or cubbies, for example, sometimes differ (fig. 120). The wood, however, should always be the same on bookcase and desk, small drawers should be similarly constructed, and the contour of the moldings should match.

MARRIAGE AND THE JUSTICE OF THE PIECE

When Wallace Nutting presented the desk and bookcase shown here in figure 123 in his *Furniture of the Pilgrim Century, Volume I*, he called it a walnut secretary with a detachable top and then noted a "curious feature . . . the top juts back about an inch and a half beyond the back of the base."[11] He related it to brackets on some mahogany secretaries and explained it as "an arrangement designed to accommodate the dado. . . . Thus the desk proper abutted against the dado, and the top also abutted directly against the plaster wall, above the dado."[12]

Nutting also classified as "curious" a lid apparently of yellow pine, whereas the rest of the primary wood on the desk was a completely different wood. *It is not sufficient to justify inconsistencies by merely dubbing them "curious."* Too many people — including just about everyone selling a married piece — justify oddities with ease. The cautious collector views the "curious" skeptically and demands proof of innocence.

Where there is one inconsistency, look for more. Here you quickly find more to call "curious." On this piece, the bookcase is the full width of the desk, whereas most upper cases are narrower and fit within a waist molding. The desk has brass hardware and an iron lock; the bookcase, interlocking wooden knobs.

What about the bookcase is akin to the desk? The wood. Both cases are of yellow poplar. Consistency of wood is an essential factor in establishing a common past for a double case. However, the presence of the same wood does not assure a single date of origin; it is common in marriages of partners coming from the same neighborhood. If an owner other than the first wanted a bookcase added

FIGURE 123:
Desk and bookcase. (Wadsworth Atheneum.)

FIGURE 124:
The wedge (left) and a good corbel.

and had one made, it would be an honestly brokered marriage of the May–December sort. Such marriages are sometimes preferred by collectors to more recent weddings of two old spouses (fig. 34) because the two share some common history. This example (fig. 123), however, is not a May–December wedlock; the design shows that the desk and the bookcase are of about the same age.

The facades of the desk and the bookcase share another feature — the same applied bead molding on the edges. Up close, the detective sees that all of the applied bead is of same type, of the same age, and amazingly free of wear. Alas, every inch of the molding is new. Defrauders commonly apply a unifying molding to married cases.

The accommodating-the-dado story has some basis in fact, although such corbels (fig. 124) reach about twice as far back as these 1⅝-inch-deep wedges, which are too narrow for a dado. Eighteenth-century corbels have a fashionable outline, whereas these are mere wedges — crude details on a desk that, the skeptical inspector notes, is not crudely crafted. The wedges look more like attempts to unify an irregular marriage of a deeper bookcase to a shallow-topped desk.

Inspection of the case sides shows that the desk was originally even shallower; the case sides have been pieced out about one inch at the back, perhaps to compensate for shrinkage. The wedges look newer than the piecing, but could both simply be replacements for original, decorative corbels? The inspection continues.

Although the wood is the same on both bookcase and desk, the woodworm damage is very different on each. The desk sides are riddled with wormholes, whereas the abutting boards of the bookcase are remarkably free of them. Woodworms attack different woods at difference rates, but not different boards of the same wood. When the worms were here, the bookcase wasn't.

From behind, Nutting's "curious secretary" looks like two individuals. The backs of the two cases are both of horizontal boards, but the boards themselves are not akin in color, form, or tool marks. The desk back has been off at some point but may be original; its color matches that of the desk bottom.

This desk and bookcase does not allow for the detective's usual and almost surefire test of unity — drawer dovetail matching. This test, easily administered on a chest-on-chest (fig. 11), can also be decisive in the case of a bookcase that has drawers, which can be compared with similar small drawers in the desk interior. The dovetails in drawers, though not as perfectly individualized as fingerprints, do not fall far short of them as aids in identification. The detective rues the fact that this bookcase has no drawers. The large

dovetails on cases themselves are not so distinctive from one case to another. The case dovetails here are inconclusive.

The interior hardware does not tie the two cases together either. Both the doors and the desk lid have hinges. Although by the second half of the eighteenth century hinges were specialized, with narrow brass butt hinges being used for doors and distinctly different ones for lids, the hinges on this piece date to the first half of the century, when door and lid hinges were often consistent. A closely related desk and bookcase at Yale (fig. 125) has thick iron butt hinges (fig. 126) that are identical on both its lid and its doors. The square-plated hinges on this desk are very similar to those on the Yale piece; however, the thin iron H hinges on the bookcase are completely different.

The intact hinges on the desk and bookcase at Yale retain the old leather washers beneath the nailheads, and all the nails are alike. The hinges on this desk have no leather washers, and — a more damning point — the nails are not all of the same type. These hinges have been off, and why else if not to replace the lid? Nutting's "curious" secretary looks like a bookcase married to a desk with a replaced lid. Nothing "curious" about it. In investigatory algebra, intact old hinges + replaced fasteners = replaced lid.

While examining the bookcase, the determined detective looks under its bottom board and sees that this was neither a very recent marriage nor a very old one. The part of the board that overhangs the desk in back is darker than the part that sits on the desk top and is not exposed to air. But the oxidation is not nearly as great as it would be if the wood had been uncovered since the 1730s. And the board oxidized only where it now overhangs; it never overhung any more than it now does. The wedges are not replacements for earlier corbels; the bookcase married the desk not a moment before the wedges were added.

The top of the desk is a finished board, usually almost as good proof of a marriage as a wedding certificate, since a top intended to carry a bookcase need not be finished. This desk top appears to be original and has, along the back and side edges, informative tack holes and pale areas in the finish. The pale patches (called shadows by the squad) remain from when the finish was protected from light; the tack holes suggest that a wooden gallery once stood around the desk top — a gallery to hold books, but not a bookcase.

Many fixers over many years may have been involved in the changes to this desk. Whoever presided at the marriage, however, added the wedges, the bead molding, and probably the new lid. A lot is involved in some marriages.

As with eighteenth-century examples, smart detectives inspect a nineteenth-century case (fig. 127) for consistency in design, construction, and color. Although expecting to find less wear, they still demand that what wear there is be logical. They also expect a somewhat less economical use of labor.

The dovetailing in nineteenth-century cabinetry is generally more delicate and even than that on most eighteenth-century work. Hidden surfaces are better finished. Drawer bottoms are often secured with a series of small blocks (fig. 128), and are more likely to be neatly cut for the dado joint (as on the small drawer with circular saw marks, fig. 54). The nails are cut nails, and more of them are used.

Dating most Federal, neoclassical, and machine-era cases to the nineteenth century is easy. *Just don't ask* when *in the nineteenth century.* Neoclassical style was in fashion throughout that century and into the first two decades of the twentieth, making possible such crimes of labeling as we will encounter with a sewing table (pages 182–183).

Figure 129, however, shows an honest reproduction. Were it not for its label, "POTTHAST BROS. / ANTIQUE FURNITURE / Artistic Furniture M'f'rs. / 507 N. Howard Street, / 506 & 508 Tyson St. / BALTIMORE. MD." (the firm was founded in 1892), the sideboard might seem to be a product of the 1830s. The figure of the veneer on the sideboard is rich, yet the lack of gilt and inlay and the general simplicity of the decoration suggest a product of machine and factory rather than a work of hand and shop.

FIGURE 127:
Federal chest of drawers; mahogany veneer, mahogany, white pine, and yellow poplar, ca. 1815, Westfield, Massachusetts. Made by Erastus Grant. H. 34¾; W. 42; D. 20½. (Historic Deerfield.)

FIGURE 128:
Drawer bottom. Detail of chest shown in figure 127. The blocks along the sides secure the bottom; the two small blocks behind the drawer front are drawer stops, which meet up with stops on the drawer divider. Tape had once closed the seam between the bottom boards.

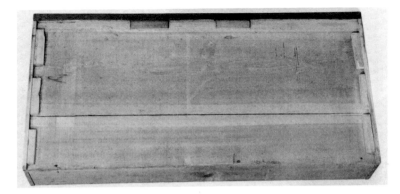

The best clues for determining when in the nineteenth century a piece of neoclassical furniture was made can be found in the joinings. Mortise-and-tenon joints hold early examples of the neoclassical style together (fig. 50); doweled joints (fig. 49) belong to the late nineteenth century, as do wire nails and gimlet-pointed screws. The Potthast sideboard has doweled joints, as well as gimlet-pointed screws, circular saw marks, and thin veneer.

Revival furniture and reproductions appeal to a growing number of decorative-arts collectors. Labeled pieces are particularly popular. The "new" antiques are, as Potthast advertised in 1915, "Hand-made by trained craftsmen with a half-century experience, using precious selected Mahogany and authentic designs. These future antiques will be treasured for generations as prized family heirlooms."[13]

FIGURE 129:
Neoclassical sideboard; mahogany. Made by Potthast Bros. (Collection of Donald L. Fennimore.)

Crimes Done to Chairs

8

LOOK out for seating furniture! Chairs and other types of seats are the defrauders' most frequent victims. Seats are credible witnesses, however, and an investigator needs only to draw out their testimony carefully. The story told by our first witness is clear and concise.

A CASE TO SETTLE

This simple two-seater (fig. 130) is just right for the entry hall of a "Colonial" house. A welcome place to sit while removing one's boots, it even has a drawer for gloves and hats. It is practical for today, yet it looks like yesterday. The skeptical sleuth is always alert lest a bit of today and a bit of yesterday add up to a double deal.

Although it is an antique, this settle is not an antique settle. Its true past becomes clear almost at once. The inspector, spotting pieced repairs on an upper right corner of the back that continue on the right wing, asks why they are there. The filled grooves, set off in a corner, resemble those left by a missing till. A till in a settle? Never. Tills, as every detective knows, are in chests.

Small filled holes along the top edge of the back near each wing remain from hinges that held a lid. The verdict: this was once a blanket chest. With the removal of two boards — the lid and the front board of the chest — the chest bottom became a seat. Some decorative cuts at the back and sides, and an old pine chest began a new life as a settle. This chest-to-bench, an easy adaptation, is so

clever an instance of old parts/new object that it probably is not unique. The adaptation is fun, a bit of whimsy that appeals to those interested in the Colonial Revival, for the settle now bespeaks the era of its alteration rather than the time when it was a pine chest.

Settles were not nearly so numerous in early houses as stools and benches, but while few stools and benches survive, today there is a plethora of "Pilgrim-century" settles. Such anomalies alert the skeptic. A fashion for "antique" settles began in the last quarter of the nineteenth century; fakers, defrauders, and adapters, as they can be relied upon to do, responded to the demands of fashion and obligingly filled collectors' needs. (We will meet another settle, fig. 207, in "Finishing 'Em Off," pages 187–189.) *Beware this form.*

APPEALING TO GOVERNOR BRADFORD

A chair can be even more puzzling than a large cabinet because it has few hidden or unfinished — and thus revealing — surfaces. Chairs are a great challenge and therefore a lot of fun. We will take

testimony from many different types, so let's divide them into two groups based on two joints: round mortises and tenons and rectangular mortises and tenons. Turners and chairmakers specialized in round mortises and tenons, joiners and cabinetmakers in rectangular ones. As the investigators will learn, in certain geographic areas — and only there — and at certain places in a chair — and only at those particular places — a worker in one craft borrowed the other's joint. We will begin with the round-jointed chairs of turners and chairmakers.

The first example is of seventeenth-century turned style (fig. 131). Aware of LaMontagne's successful deception (fig. 1), a detective needs courage to believe this chair. *Hone your skepticism, but be prepared to believe.* This chair, reputed to have belonged to Governor William Bradford (d. 1657) of Plymouth really is old enough to have been the Governor's.

Although not intact, the chair is in an exceptionally fine state for furniture of the second quarter of the seventeenth century. Style-smart detectives spot at once that the knobs, a.k.a. pommels, used as handholds on top of the front posts (see fig. 152) are missing and that the feet have lost some three inches (the bottom stretchers in front and back should be raised off the ground).

The wood of the crest rail seems to be of a slightly different color, and close inspection reveals that it is, in fact, another wood — oak rather than ash. So are two spindles. In general, ash was used by seventeenth-century turners, oak by reproducers. For example, a nineteenth-century reproduction of a chair said to have belonged to Elder Brewster (fig. 132) is of oak.

The replacements on the old Bradford chair are well done: the spindles are accurate copies, and the crest is a repeat of the rail below. (The original crest would have been a more elaborate turning, so the replacement was apparently made after the crest had been lost and could no longer be copied.) The inspector, looking under the chair, sees from its color that the pine plank seat has some age, but not enough — it should be thin, riven oak. The pine seat, too, is a restoration.

For such a repair, the chair had to be taken apart, a drastic event during which any element could have been changed. Here, however, the rest of the chair is original. In places exposed in normal use, the turnings show logical abrasions; the upper surfaces are well worn. In places unlikely to be handled, the turnings are well preserved, and many undersurfaces remain crisp. *Undersurfaces are particularly important; feel and scrutinize them.* Fakers can successfully fake abrasion, but in protected areas their products fail to show edges that, though aged and chipped, are crisp.

This chair is an excellent witness to the art of the turner and to techniques that changed little as chairmaking accommodated evolving styles and new fashions. Inspectors should understand the craft this chair epitomizes, so we will examine it to see how a turned chair was made.

The turner, working on his lathe, formed the parts for this chair and several others at the same time. He turned posts of two lengths, rails of two lengths, and three lengths of spindles. (The spindles beneath the arms are tallest, and those in front and back are taller than those at the side beneath the seat.) As he turned the few long rails (front stretchers) and the many short rails (side stretchers, arms, and chair-back rails), he made a few thicker ones of each length for seat rails.

As the craftsman turned each element, his chisel reducing and rounding the wood, he was guided both by a model and by a measured template (probably consisting of marks on the lathe's tool rest). The two served entirely different functions. The model was for the design, the template for the construction. The model suggested; the template dictated.

FIGURE 132:
Reproduction armchair, oak, and detail. Numerous "Elder Brewster" chairs were made in the late nineteenth century.

FIGURE 133:
Detail of the Governor Bradford chair (fig. 131). The spindles are not identical. On the rails, the scribe lines for the mortises are at measured sites so that the spindles will all be vertical; the decorative ring-turnings, however, were eyeballed and hence are asymmetrically sited.

The turner emulated the model without the constraints of measurement and imparted the designs to the wood with a few chisels. The decoration ranged from simple slender rings (see the front and back posts, above the seat) to complex spindles (fig. 133; the spindles have a central baluster, V-grooved and scribed at its thickest point, and flanking hollowed cones, V-grooved and scribed just beyond their thickest point).

The freely worked turnings reveal that the turner's eye and hand were his only measures. Each turning varies slightly. On the coarse elements, the inspector may need to measure (with calipers) the corresponding patterns to detect the differences, but on the spindles, the variations are obvious. The squad expects variation in turnings and does not confuse it with inconsistency of construction.

Although the turner's embellishments were neither measured nor identical, his construction methods were measured, consistent, and logical. At specific locations taken from the template, he turned incised lines for the later assembly of the chair. These scribed marks are excellent clues for the detective.

The scribed lines dictated the locations of mortises. The chair-maker made round mortises in the posts and rails to receive the somewhat bulbous tenons he turned (and later adjusted with a knife) on the ends of each rail and spindle. On the Bradford chair, the turner centered each mortise for a spindle on a scribed line (fig. 133); the mortises for the rails usually butt against a scribed line (see the line behind the arm in fig. 131).

To assemble a chair, the turner selected parts from the several piles in his shop. With two short posts, a front seat rail, two front stretchers, and eight spindles of correct size, he created a framed chair front. Similarly, he put together the several elements of a back. With a plank for the seat and two assembled sides, he created a chair.

For a plank-seated chair like this, the turner made an exception to his usual reliance on round mortise-and-tenon joints. The weight of a sitter on the plank would rotate round-jointed seat rails inward, so the turner instead put rectangular tenons on the front and back seat rails of such chairs — tenons that go completely through the posts (fig. 131). An investigator finding a rectangular-mortised post on a chair like this knows that the chair originally had a plank seat and seat rails thick enough to be rabbeted for such a plank. The plank may be gone, and rush may have been substituted, a loss of minor import if the thick, decorated, and finished seat rails remain intact under the rush.

For his favorite joint, the turner formed a somewhat oversize round tenon that he forced into the mortise. He used green wood

FIGURE 134:
Armchair with added rockers; ash, poplar posts, and birch rockers, 1670–1690, coastal Massachusetts or New Hampshire. H. 38½; W. 25½; Seat D. 14½; Seat H. 16¾. (Society for the Preservation of New England Antiquities.) The four seat rails are not at the same height, nor are the three upper stretchers.

even though the tenons, because they were thin, were already quite dry. The firm joint would become even tighter as the wood around the mortise shrank, contracting the opening, while the drier tenons swelled, taking moisture from the thick green wood around the mortises.

The joint, though generally not abetted by glue, is aided by wooden pins in a certain few places. On chairs such as the Governor's, the round tenons of the side seat rails are secured with a wooden pin (at the back post just beyond the seat rail), and these joints hold the chair together. On other chairs, pins in the crest rail serve the same function (figs. 149 and 150).

In examining the Bradford chair, the detective picks up a cherished detail with the tape measure, which may be spotted by an experienced eye and confirmed by the ruler: the tier of spindles along each side just beneath the seat is not in a truly rectangular space.

The turner, as turners do, kept the side stretchers parallel to the floor. *Expect stretchers to be parallel to the floor and regard stretchers that are not parallel as indicative of uneven wear to front and back feet.* The seat of this chair, however, is not parallel to the floor. The turner set the back of the seat somewhat lower than the front, creating a more comfortable accommodation for a sitter on an unyielding plank. This type of attention to detail on the part of a craftsman is evident on authentic antiques but is seldom if ever found on fakes or reproductions.

TWO LINEUPS: MORTISES AND DESIGNS

The next witness (fig. 134) makes only a brief appearance. Its handholds are missing, and so are the tops of the finials. The arms are broken old replacements; the upper central spindle is new. The rockers are added. The old rush seat is not original, but the seat rails are.

The scribed lines for the seat rails merit attention. A single line on each post marks two mortises. On the front post, for example, the turner drilled the mortise for the front rail just below and butting against the line, while he put the mortise for the side rail butting against the line from above. In this way, one line served as the guide for two holes, and the two tenons could just pass each other in the dark of the wood (or ever so slightly intersect, thus interlocking). Mortises must not meet head on; round mortises go deeply into posts, and intersecting holes would prevent the use of the long tenons needed for sound joints.

This old chair reveals another telltale trait of antique turned chairs:

the baluster (vase) turnings adorning the posts conform to a pattern. Here the shortest and tallest balusters are on the rear posts and the middle size is on the front post, the pattern thus created being: the farther the baluster is off the floor, the taller it is. The investigator notes the design pattern because it unites the chair front and back (see also fig. 209). *Look for a relationship between the turnings on the front and rear posts.* A lack of unity in design is a good giveaway of chairs made from old parts.

A BANISTER BACK GETS THE BARRISTER'S BACK UP

A banister-back chair standing by an antiques dealer's van at a western New England flea market caught the eye of a particularly savvy sleuth, Robert F. Trent, curator of the Connecticut Historical Society. He was understandably attracted to the Connecticut chair (fig. 135), of mid-eighteenth-century design with a sort of New London County crest (see fig. 136 for a classic example).

FIGURE 135:
Side chair; black walnut.
H. 46; W. 19¾; Seat D.
15⅛; Seat H. 17¼.
(Connecticut Historical
Society.)

FIGURE 136:
Armchair; maple and ash,
1720–1750, New London
County, Connecticut.
H. 47¼; Seat W. 23½; Seat
D. 17½; Seat H. 16¾. (Con-
necticut Historical Society.)
The crest and turnings are
typical of a New London
County chairmaking style
that influenced much of
Connecticut chair design.

But when he reached for the chair, the amazed curator exclaimed, "It's walnut! It's not an eighteenth-century chair."

He bought it anyway.

Why would a curator buy a fake? Well, that's just it. It's not a fake either.

"We'll probably never know who made it," says Trent, who believes he has figured out when and where and why it was made. Let's see how this barrister examined his witness and made his case.

Trent drew out one important fact almost at once. In an antique, he expected maple turnings. These were neither painted nor stained but were actually of black walnut. Trent reasoned that a fake of the 1895–1915 era would probably have been of oak, then the favored wood, and a more recent faker would have used maple or perhaps even an appropriate mix of maple and ash. Walnut, however, was a favorite wood between 1860 and 1890.

Turning the witness around, Trent found that the back rails, which are bowed to give comfort to the sitter, have a lot of gratuitous modeling on their rear surfaces (fig. 137). "Few, if any, eighteenth-century chairs have embowed back rails," Trent noted; and unless the crest was to be pierced — as with a heart (fig. 210) — and so needed to look thinner, "chairmakers never wasted time carving up the back side of anything."

Separating the strands of rush, he found that the seat rails are turned and of walnut (fig. 138). On a genuine antique, they would be roughly formed by a drawshave (see the rear seat rail in fig. 141) from a cheap wood such as ash. Turned seat rails are seen on reproductions and on some fakes. And only fakers, reproducers, and repairers squander primary wood where it can't be seen.

Trent could not believe that this was a new fake, because its maker had omitted the sine qua non of such Connecticut chairs in today's antiques market — a pierced crown crest (figs. 209 and 210). In fact, a common bit of defrauding is the embellishment of a period, yoke-crested chair from Milford or Stratford with a pierced heart.

FIGURES 137, 138: Details of side chair shown in figure 135. 137: rear view of crest. Finials that are sawn or rasped in back to suggest wear are standard on fakes, frauds, and even some reproductions. The modeling on the back of the crest flunks the test for economy of labor. 138: front seat rail.

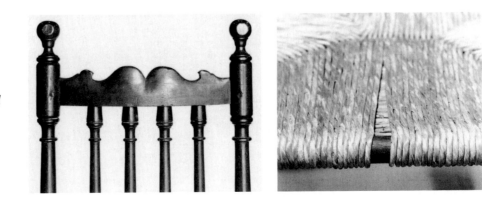

Noticing that the upper front stretcher is a recent replacement, Trent confirmed that the chair is not new.

Focusing on construction details, Trent was able to determine the nontraditional biography of his witness. The turner of this chair, instead of cutting *unseasoned* maple and turning it *slowly* on a foot- or hand-powered lathe, worked *seasoned* walnut on a *fast* motor-powered lathe. The wood fought back, as rapidly spinning seasoned wood will do, and consequently, instead of the gentle grooves left by the old-timer's chisel in the green wood, Trent found turnings full of tears, breakouts, and chips (fig. 139), which, in two places,

FIGURE 139:
Front post of chair shown in figure 135.

the turner had glued back in place. And Trent noticed that the scribed lines, usually fine score marks, were rough and prominent.

The chair's maker didn't understand the function of scribed lines. Unaware of the fact that such marks assured that the mortises did not head straight for each other, the craftsman — if one can call him that — drilled the mortises at the same level (fig. 139). The joints, therefore, are merely ¾ inch deep — not deep enough to be firm without glue, and even their glue doesn't hold them.

And not all the scribed lines line up with actual joints (the scribed lines flanking the crest rail do not line up with the rail itself). Turners goofed on occasion, Trent notes, but he ridicules layout errors as fundamental as this one. He concludes that the maker had not been trained as a turner but had an old chair to copy (the patterns of design are faithful), that he made this one between 1860 and 1890 and did not produce many such chairs, and that he probably did not make this one to fool anyone but rather to celebrate the past, possibly on the occasion of a town's anniversary (e.g., Norwich's two-hun-

FIGURE 140:
Side chair; beech (replaced seat rails, birch), 1700–1720, London. H. 46⅜; W. 17⁹⁄₁₆; Seat D. 14⁵⁄₁₆; Seat H. 18¾. (Society for the Preservation of New England Antiquities.) Note the height of the feet.

dredth in 1860 or Guilford's two-fiftieth in 1889). Although it is not a period chair, Trent respects it as a rare Colonial Revival object.

An accomplished barrister, Trent gets his back up sooner and reaches more detailed conclusions than the average sleuth on the antiques beat. Not many can make as strong a case for the origin of a nonantique; nor do they need to. As with this chair, the relevant facts are numerous, the clues often redundant, and one doesn't need them all.

WITNESS WITH CANE HAS SOUND FEET

Caned chairs were produced in London in the early eighteenth century and exported new to America in large sets. By virtue of the manner in which they were made, and because they did arrive in sets, some of today's caned chairs are no doubt made from the parts of several chairs.

Reassembling began early. In 1725, Thomas Fitch, a Boston upholsterer who imported chairs, had his cargo plundered by pirates. "They took out . . . 2 doz. of the best Chairs wch they abus'd but I found very near all the parts of the whole of them."[1] Fitch reassembled, from parts, the chairs the London chairmaker had so recently assembled. And ever since Fitch's day repairers have done the same. If the various parts all came from broken members of the same set, the loss in value is minimal and reassembly may be virtually undetectable. One of the chairs Fitch reassembled would certainly be a genuine, desirable antique today.

This witness (fig. 140), one of a large set, has been taken apart and repaired. Its restorations are typical; its virtues are special. Its feet retain their full height. Cut or worn feet are a major problem with turners' chairs; one chair in this set has been shortened, the feet cut between the two turnings. The height of the unaltered feet on this chair — the side stretchers are a full five inches above the floor — are a fine guide for detectives.

The other major problem area in turners' chairs is at the seat. Not surprisingly, the caning on this chair has been replaced. At some point in its long history the seat was upholstered. Upholstery tacks have done in many a seat rail and that may have been the case here: when this seat was restored to cane, the front and side rails were replaced. The new rails have atypically flat edges and are so sharp that they are quickly recognized as replacements.

Many rush-seated chairs, too, have been upholstered and reupholstered and often had their seats replaced. Sometimes, even when a seat is rebuilt for upholstering, the original seat rails remain

FIGURE 141:
Seat rails altered for upholstery. Detail of the originally rush-seated chair shown in figure 143. The original rails survive with cleats added in front and at the sides to suggest a stylish rounded seat. The impression of the rush is obvious on the original part of the front seat rail.

in place if not intact (fig. 141). By peeking beneath the rush at the rails themselves, you can see whether the seat rails are old. Insert your pencil between strands of rush (at the inside edge of the rail) and look. The rails should be unfinished, somewhat blade-shaped, and of a strong but cheap wood such as ash. Expect a rushed seat rail to have become slightly fluted from the impression of the rush (the front seat rail, fig. 141). Replaced seat rails are not minor repairs, yet, in many instances, such replacements are acceptable to collectors.

FIGURE 142:
Rush-seated side chair; maple, poplar front legs, and ash seat rails, 1730–1770, eastern Massachusetts. H. 40⅞; W. 18⁵/₁₆; Seat D. 13¹/₁₆; Seat H. 16⅞. (Society for the Preservation of New England Antiquities.)

FIGURE 143:
Side chair; soft maple, 1730–1770, probably Connecticut. H. 41¼; W. 20¹/₁₆; Seat D. 15½; Seat H. 18¼. (Society for the Preservation of New England Antiquities.)

FIGURE 144:
Windsor high chair; maple, pine, and hickory, twentieth century. Made by Wallace Nutting. H. 37¼; W. 19⅜; D. 19. (Henry Francis du Pont Winterthur Museum, Study Collection.)

In some rush- or woven-seated chairs, the seat rails are round-tenoned into the legs (fig. 142). In others, and in cane chairs, the seat rails sit over the legs (fig. 143). Such seat rails are not sufficiently thick for round mortise-and-tenon joints. The turner used the rectangular mortise and tenon to join the side rail to the front seat rail, and to join other unturned elements, including the crest and the lower back rail.

WATCHING OUT FOR WINDSORS

Antique Windsors are popular, numerous, and expensive, and many have problems. A high chair (fig. 144) in the Winterthur collection, regarded for years as an extraordinarily fine Windsor, is actually an example of an honest reproduction that passed as an antique. The chair was number 210 ($28) in the 1928 catalogue of *Wallace Nutting Period Furniture*.

The tipoff to the high chair's age was the fact that it wasn't dirty enough. Even in the cleanest settings dirt accumulates on furniture, in the corners and at the joints. *Look for dirt.* On this Windsor, a lack of dirt in holes where the tenons had loosened led to a quest for evidence of age and for earlier coats of paint, and a member of the Winterthur staff sprung (removed) a leg. There was no earlier paint, the round tenons proved to be perfectly round, just as they had come from the lathe, and the mortises were made with a modern drill bit.

FIGURE 145:
Two Windsor armchairs; twentieth century. Made by Wallace Nutting. (Photograph courtesy Phillips Fine Art Auctioneers.) At auction, each chair was presented as "stamped by Wallace Nutting."

The very gusto of its design is another good clue to the high chair's origins. The work of Wallace Nutting (fig. 145) exhibits exaggerated details; the seats are robustly sculpted, the turnings are delicate yet voluptuous. Nutting stamped much — but not all — of the furniture he made. So many collectors now vie for Nutting furniture that the prices are as impressive as his turnings.

Few reproduction Windsors can pass as period antiques; most don't even try to look old. But hybrid Windsors (old parts/new chair) are a serious menace and a natural consequence of the way Windsors were made. Even more so than other turned chairs, they were made in large volume and sold in sizable sets.

In Windsors, the splay of the legs is highly esteemed. At a 1978 auction, the successful bidder paid $325 for a chair (fig. 146) that he called "a $75 Windsor with $500 worth of splay." The dual identity that the bidder so aptly described alerts the squad to a possible dual history. If the small, handsomely modeled seat on this chair received an intact base from a chair with a wider seat, it would not be the first time this has happened.

Someone need only rotate the round mortise-and-tenon joints at the stretchers to increase splay. Reset into a narrower seat, the rotated legs are more closely spaced at the top and consequently more widely splayed at the feet. The bamboo turnings on this supersplay suggest a base of a later date on a well-shaped seat. *Demand consistency in design; $75 chairs do not have $500 worth of splay.*

Would you believe the next Windsor (fig. 147)? It seems of a whole. As is typical of Windsors, it is made of several woods. Under the pine seat is a brand, "B:GREEN." Maker's brands, not unusual on Windsors, are coveted.

Close up, the inspector sees a characteristic Windsor joint with wedges set in the ends of the spindles to spread the round tenons (a clear example, fig. 212). Wedged joints often protrude like popped wooden pins.

On further scrutiny, the detective spies patches and problems. Angular splices on both arms reveal replacements that begin just about at the hoop of the back. The first back spindle on the right changes direction at arm height.

In a Windsor armchair, the spindles start in the seat, go through the arm rail, and end up coming through the crest. Therefore they should follow a straight, though not necessarily vertical, line. A change of direction indicates a broken and possibly replaced section of spindle.

Each large mortise in the seat — four for legs, two for arm supports in the case of an armchair — should be a single undisturbed

FIGURES 147, 148:
*Windsor armchair, with and
without its added parts.
(Photograph courtesy Maine
Antique Digest.)*

hole (fig. 212). A doubled-up hole for the left arm support of this chair reveals a replacement.

On the maple legs, a change of wood at the scribed line points to legs that have been ended out — that is, added to. Even through the paint, the wood below the line shows the distinct vessel lines of ash or oak, not the closed pores of maple. Repairers do not always use the appropriate wood. When the repair was new, the paint masked the difference; the finish aged, and the old repairs are now visible.

Additional parts become suspect as the detective feels every turning and spindle. The central stretcher and the left arm support fail the touch test.

Looking carefully at chips in the painted finish, the sleuth spots green paint under the present coat of black. A search for parts that never had green paint beneath the chipped black reveals other replacements.

Perhaps the leading question was misleading. "Would you believe this Windsor?" could more fairly have been phrased, "How much of this Windsor do you believe?"

M.A.D.'s Sam Pennington created an illustration (fig. 148) showing those parts of the chair that are original. The little pieced repairs along the hoop are relatively minor and would be acceptable to many collectors. The numerous other replacements, however, place the chair somewhere between an honest repair and an enhanced fragment.

Savvy collectors appraise what is antique and separately evaluate the rest as repair and restoration. For those willing to accept repaired furniture, the Pennington technique is valuable. *Form a mental picture made up of original members only.* An original-only image can prevent the collector from acquiring a chair that is restored to one original spindle.

LAYING ONE'S HANDS ON A FOREIGN FELON

The best way to put the Pennington technique to work on many turned chairs is with hand work. *Clasp each turning lightly and turn your hand to feel the wood.* On this chair (fig. 149), touch easily separates the turnings into two distinct groups — one rough (note the striations in the sheen on the back post, fig. 151), the other smooth (the spindles at the bottom of the same figure).

The two textures have two different dates. When the wormy back posts were ended out with unwormy wood (fig. 150) at a line above the rear stretcher, a rear stretcher of new wood was added. The side stretchers were also added at that time. They feel the same as the new rear stretcher, and the wear behind the front foot (fig. 150) proves that no stretcher was in place when the wear occurred. The inspector's hand discerns that all the spindles in the back, on the seat, and beneath the arm are the same age as the added stretchers. Four wormy old posts and a rail or two hardly make a chair!

So what apparently passed not many years ago as an old American chair is not much of a chair. Nor is it American. Tenons that pass beyond the posts (see the back posts behind the arms in fig. 149) are a European feature.

Nutting included a similar chair in *Furniture of the Pilgrim Century,* where he noted that the unusual turnings on the back raised the question of "whether the chair is American."[2] Some collectors would still answer, as Nutting did, "The wood, however, is ash. . . . While ash construction does not compel our belief in an American origin, it favors that belief."[3]

It should not. The easy equations Ash = American, Oak = English are not correct. English chairs of this period and type — and this is an English chair — are of ash or fruitwood, not oak.[4] Instead of looking to the wood, the detective can look to the "unusual" turnings and the tenons that go through the posts. Style and construction can separate the American from the English.

Several generations ago travelers abroad sought their English roots, searched church records, purchased renderings of their family coats of arms, and bought "English antiques," many in similar condition to the chair we laid our hands on. Importers and dealers

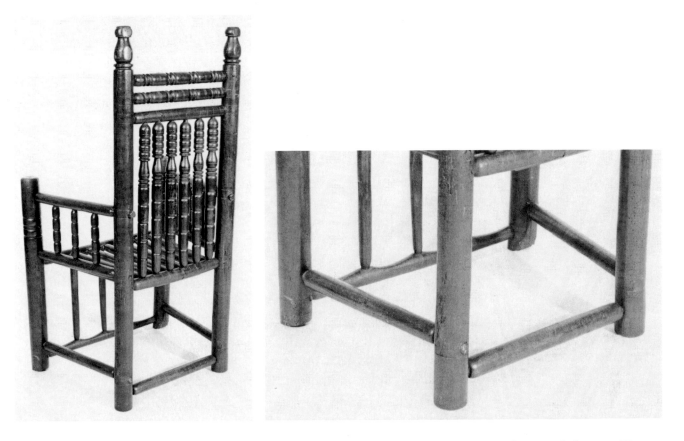

FIGURES 149–151:
Armchair and details; ash,
England. H. 42¾; W. 24;
Seat D. 17½; Seat H. 15⅜.
(Historic Deerfield.)

introduced additional European "antiques." Some of these still pass as American.

The British are still coming. In 1985, a London dealer told the *New York Times* that "the Americans are over here and buying like crazy."[5] He said that a 1760 snake-foot table priced at $19,300 and a pair of George II chairs at $55,200 sold "15 minutes after [an antiques show] opened. . . . The table will go to Montreal and the chairs to the United States." "Eighty percent of our business," said another English furniture dealer, "is with Americans."

WHEEL IN THE WITNESS

The rocking chair, an American form, was invented after we were no longer British. Despite all the examples that seem to be Colonial-era rocking chairs, smart detectives know that every last one was originally just a chair (if it is in fact pre-Revolutionary). The old turned chair (fig. 134) whose brief testimony we have taken is a case in point. Its rocker bends are generations younger than the chair itself.

In the late eighteenth and the nineteenth centuries, many old chairs were outfitted with bends. Often the outsides of the legs were notched, and the rocker bends merely nailed on. Sometimes the legs

FIGURE 152:
Wheelchair; maple, ash, and white oak arms and wheels, 1750–1800, America. H. 37⁵/₁₆; W. (at seat) 21⁵/₁₆; Seat D. 17⁵/₈; Seat H. 17³/₈. (Yale University Art Gallery, Mabel Brady Garvan Collection.) The mid-nineteenth-century paint emulates that on the chair in figure 153.

were cut so that the bends could be let in (fig. 134). A few chairs have successfully passed as genuine Colonial rockers because they have blocks at the feet, blocks that seemed proof that the turner originally fitted the chair with bends.

But it is not so. Turners put block ends on chair legs for wheels, as the witness just wheeled in (fig. 152) testifies. The savvy collector judges a pre-Revolutionary chair that has been made into a rocker as a period chair and not as a Colonial rocker.

CALLING COREY TO THE STAND

The next chair (fig. 153) tells a clear, almost complete story about the chairmaker's products of the mid- and late nineteenth century. Truthful testimony helps a detective to recognize the fraudulent, altered, or repaired.

The chair's back seat rail (fig. 154) has the maker's mark. Nineteenth-century chairmakers were less shy than the furniture makers before them; many signed their products, some with brands, others with stencils like this one.

In Walter Corey's Portland, Maine, chair factory (1836–1875), over one hundred men, housed in a six-story plant, worked with machinery powered by a sixty-horsepower engine. The curved marks of the rotary saw remain on the inside of the seat rails of this chair. Corey's men used machine-cut nails, and just such fasteners hold the flat front stretcher in place.

The cane on mid-nineteenth-century chair seats is seldom original, but this chair has escaped the upholstering that afflicted the seat rails of many earlier caned or rushed seats.

Stenciled maker's marks do not always survive. Corey's mark would have been lost if this chair had shared the sad fate of so many of its ilk and been stripped of its finish. (The Corey testimony continues in "Beware the Biedermeier Blonde," page 189.)

ONE WITNESS AT A TIME, PLEASE

Nineteenth-century chairmakers' products often remain in sets, although attrition has frequently made the sets smaller. Eighteenth-century turners' chairs, however, are less likely to still be in sets and are often brought together by dealers and collectors into pairs or made-up sets. Many made-up sets are sold as what they are and save the collector the chore of assembling a set. But a few made-up

FIGURES 153, 154:
*Side chair and detail of back
seat rail; maple, ca. 1850,
Portland, Maine. Made by
William Corey. H. 33½;
W. 18½; D. 20⅝; Seat H. 17¼.
(Yale University Art Gallery,
gift of Mr. and Mrs. Charles
M. Montgomery.) The chair
retains its original paint; its
crazed original clear finish
was restored.*

FIGURE 155:
*Joined armchair; oak, cedar,
walnut inserts in back.
H. 41⁹/₁₆; W. 23¹³/₁₆; Seat
D. 14¼; Seat H. 18½.
(Yale University Art Gallery
Study Collection.)*

sets are misrepresented. The squad discerns them quickly by calling upon the witnesses one at a time and then comparing their testimony.

Examine each chair of a set individually; then collate the data. Although turners did not even try to make two spindles the same, they did succeed in making all the side chairs in a set consistent in width (armchairs, of course, are wider) and height, including the height of the seat. Individual chairs may wear differently, and comparing the measurements of height can help the squad spot wear at the feet. Ruler in hand, an inspector measures the distances between the lines scribed for joints on one chair and then on another. The ruler quickly divides up the made-up set.

NO. 1678, A FALSE ID

As we begin the cross-examination of our first joiner's chair (turning from the turner's round-tenoned products to the joiner's rectangular ones), it is, ironically, the turnings that mark the chair as completely unbelievable (fig. 155). The exceedingly thin turnings of the front posts are a giveaway. Seventeenth-century turnings are chunky; these are fragile. At best, such front posts would be replacements on a seventeenth-century chair. These are not; all of the chair originated at the same time.

At first glance, the thin chair seems to exemplify the misproportions of much revival furniture. But this is not an honest "Colonial-style" armchair; it is a fake.

It was faked long ago. In 1876, purported to have been "brought over by the first settlers," it was accorded prominence as a pre-Revolutionary relic in a Centennial exhibition and in print (fig. 156). The finials on the crest and the applied heraldic shields on the back panel that it had in those years have since been removed, perhaps because they came to be recognized as blatantly discrediting elements.

Henry Waters, the early collector of antiques, lent the chair to the exhibition. He also owned the genuine but overcleaned and overly restored cupboard now in Yale's Study collection (fig. 89). Waters dealt with James Moulton, an antiques dealer in Lynn, Massachusetts, and may have been one of those collectors Moulton described as preferring the new to the loose-jointed and genuinely old. When Irving W. Lyon, another collector, spotted new objects at Moulton's in 1883, the dealer "would not admit that they were new."[6]

Waters's thin-legged chair passed as an antique into the furniture collection at Yale. There ended its century of fakery. The chair's "antique" finish was found to be a stain. The stiles — "pieced out"

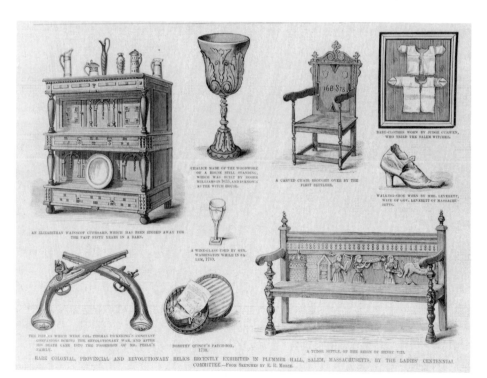

FIGURE 156: "Relics" exhibited in Salem, Massachusetts, January 22, 1876, included a chair (fig. 155) "brought over by the first settlers." (Essex Institute, Salem.)

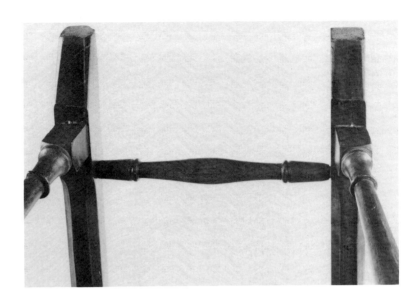

FIGURE 157:
Side chair; black walnut, 1735–1760, Boston. H. 41¾; W. 21⅞; Seat D. 16½; Seat H. 18¹/₁₆. (Society for the Preservation of New England Antiquities.)

FIGURE 158:
Detail of chair shown in figure 157, upside down. The turned rear stretcher is round-tenoned into the legs.

FIGURE 159:
Detail of chair shown in figure 157. A slender rectangular joint is best for the ankle of the cabriole.

behind the arms, seat rails, and one stretcher — were not fixed but rather fixed *up* to emulate repairs.

The "piecing out" dates from the chair's beginnings, closer to 1867 than to the carved date, 1678. The date itself is not a particularly daring bit of fakery. *Remember, dates appealed to collectors and thus were popular with fakers and enhancers.* On this armchair, everything is dishonest, although some sleuths think they see an audacious hint at honesty in the faker's choice of initials — BS.

A YOUTHFUL OFFENDER

Joiners' and cabinetmakers' chairs — chairs with upholstered seats are cabinetmakers' chairs — are assembled with rectangular mortises and tenons at almost every joint (fig. 157). The exceptions: turned parts have round tenons (fig. 158), but even turned stretchers join cabriole legs with rectangular joints (fig. 159). The detective looks carefully at chair joints, demanding pinned rectangular joints at the seat rails of upholstered chairs and around chair backs. The Chapin cabinetmakers of Connecticut, Eliphalet and Aaron, broke this rule, using round mortises and tenons in two unusual places: joining the stile to the crest and the arm support to the arm.[7] Any other sighting of round tenons or dowels is probably a sure sign of a reproduction.

Dowels hold the crest of the Philadelphia-type Chippendale-style chair in figure 160 to the stiles and splat. Doweling is one clue

FIGURE 160:
*Side chair; oak, maple, and
ash. H. 39⅝; W. 22½;
D. 17¾. (Henry Francis du
Pont Winterthur Museum,
Study Collection.)*

attesting to the chair's origin as a nineteenth-century reproduction.

The chair is oak. Were it a period chair, it would be mahogany or walnut, the cheaper alternative in the Chippendale period. A mahogany stain covers the chair, yet through the stain the appearance of oak is discernible.

The chair's design mixes sources. The carved skirt and round back posts imitate Philadelphia forms, while the front legs are squarish in cross section, a shape typical of New England cabrioles.

The carving exhibits two common quirks of late-nineteenth-century reproductions: the knees look applied (see also fig. 35), and the carved feet lack definition. Such crudely formed toes always indicate a repro.

From the toes to the crest, the true nature of this Winterthur Study Collection chair is clear. It is an honest reproduction. The blocks in the corners of the seats are machine-cut and easily recognized as both modern and original. Yet when nobody was looking, a dealer passed this chair off as an authentic eighteenth-century antique.

Unlike turners, who created designs by eye, cabinetmakers used templates to replicate their designs. These templates enabled a cabinetmaker to produce virtually identical copies of each element in a chair. Take a moment to look at a cabriole-legged chair straight on, and compare the front legs (fig. 164). Because templates governed the shape of cabrioles, the front legs should mirror each other. Replaced cabrioles were made without benefit of the original templates and usually go a bit astray in their curves. You can spot a replaced cabriole if you look at it from a distance. *Stand back from cabriole furniture to compare the legs.*

Because of templates, all the splats on the several chairs in a set should match. If one does not, either that splat has been replaced or the set is made up. But the fact that each splat should be the same as the others does not mean that one side of a splat should mirror the other side. The eighteenth century was replete with asymmetrical splats (see fig. 157, the lower third of the splat); on Queen Anne chairs especially, furniture detectives observe innumerable splats that are antique, authentic, but asymmetrical. Asymmetrical templates were the probable cause.

The squad remembers that it is the nature of the observer's eye to see similar details as identical. That tendency, which enabled the original customers to be satisfied with asymmetrical splats, must not govern the eye of the detective. *Do not let your eye infer symmetry or exact replication where the craftsman did not impose it.*

The sleuth — spotting symmetry or asymmetry, exact replication or inexact copies — contemplates templates. *Where templates would impose symmetry and exact replication* (on a cabriole leg and its counterpart, or on the several splats in the same set), *demand mirror images and carbon copies. Where templates tended to allow and to perpetuate asymmetry* (on the opposite sides of one splat), *expect and accept it.*

A CONSISTENT STORY TOLD BY A CONNECTICUT ODDBALL

The two chairs shown in figure 161 are attributed to the Saybrook/ Lyme area at the mouth of the Connecticut River.[8] The chairs are replete with atypical characteristics, which in several places disconcert attentive interrogators. Yet, seeing all the oddities and adding them up, the squad finds that the witness is credible. The consistency of the oddities bespeaks authenticity.

The side seat rails on these chairs are through-tenoned (the tenon

FIGURE 161:
*Two side chairs; maple,
1740–1770, probably Say-
brook, Connecticut.
H. 41½; Seat W. 18⅞; Seat
D. 15⅝; Seat H. 17¾. (Connecticut Historical Society.)*

FIGURE 162:
*Detail of the back of a
Chapin chair. (Yale University Art Gallery, Mabel
Brady Garvan Collection.)
A through-tenon joint —
characteristic of Philadelphia work and some Con-
necticut chairs, including
Chapin's — is readily seen
from the back. Two small
horizontal wedges hold
this tenon. Wooden pins
secure the tenon of the rear
seat rail.*

of the side seat rail passes completely through the back post), a
construction technique characteristic of many Pennsylvania and
some Connecticut joiners' chairs (fig. 162, a chair attributed to the
Chapins). Though Eliphalet Chapin used this joint, not all through-
tenoned Connecticut chairs came from his shop.

Having noted and accepted that feature on the pair of chairs, the
detective focuses on an oddity: the rear seat rail is set high above
the side seat rails (compare the rear seat rails, figs. 161 and 162).
Could the maker, ignoring prevailing design, have placed the rear
rails there to avoid putting a second set of mortises on the same
level as the through tenons? Had he sacrificed design for strength?

The inspector next notices that the joints of the side seat rails are
double-pinned where one pin almost always suffices. An overconcern
with strength was characteristic of some joiners of less-than-sophis-
ticated furniture. The double-pinning looks like overbuilding by a
joiner who was insecure with the usual chair-joining practices. The
splat shoes are part of the rear seat rail, rather uncommon in America
but not in England. But what is this? The splats are double-pinned
at the shoe! And they're pinned at the crest!

Pinning a splat is not merely unnecessary (where's the splat to
go?) but a structural faux pas. As the wood of the splat shrinks and
as the frame of the seat shifts under the weight of the sitter, the splat
needs to be free to move within unpinned housings. Many old splats
are loose, and detectives usually try to (and often can) wiggle them

FIGURE 163:
Balloon seat with horizontal rails. Detail of a walnut Philadelphia Queen Anne chair. (Yale University Art Gallery, gift of Mr. and Mrs. David Stockwell.) A balloon seat made with horizontal rails (typical of Pennsylvania work) needs no corner blocks for stability but requires an applied molding to hold the loose seat. Plate 1 shows a balloon seat with vertical seat rails.

in their crests and shoes. The splats on these chairs, not free to move, cracked instead.

The pin-happy joiner applied moldings around the seat rails to surround the upholstered loose seats. The technique, common on balloon-framed seats constructed of horizontal boards (fig. 163), is not needed on straight, vertical seat rails (fig. 180), which joiners usually cut with rabbets on the inside edge to hold the loose seat and finished on the outside edge with a decorative plane. The applied molding here is another feature that is out of the mainstream of chair construction.

The design is not as peculiar as the construction, but it too is unusual. The bracketless knees of the cabrioles, the slenderness of stiles and splat, and the enthusiastic outline of the seat rails all bespeak a nonsophisticate. The experienced sleuth regards the several features of these chairs as consistent with a not-quite-stylish, over-built product of a not-too-sophisticated, overly cautious eccentric. Some furniture and some furniture makers were oddballs. A consistent oddball is credible.

A BIRD IN THE HAND IS WORTH WATCHING

There is nothing better for most people than a bird in the hand, but not for a member of the fakes-and-fraud squad. *Stay clear of birds.* Flocks of them were carved in the 1920s and 1930s and added to antiques. Most of the several feathered fellows encountered in figures 164–169 are frauds.

One handsome chair (figs. 164 and 165) was a genuine New York antique until the birds arrived and what was once a side chair acquired arms. Neither the arms nor the arm supports are original;

FIGURES 164, 165:
Armchair and detail of an
arm; mahogany, yellow poplar, sweet gum, and white
pine, 1755–1775, New
York. H. 39⅛; W. (at feet)
23; Seat D. 18; Seat
H. 17¼. (The Metro-
politan Museum of Art.)

the supports are screwed to the seat rails with modern screws. Under the supports, the side seat rails retain the old finish necessary when the entire rail was exposed. The wood beneath arm supports should be unfinished; any wood on top of finished wood is a later addition.

A skeptic can determine whether an armchair is really a side chair armed to the hilt. First, the chair will have the proportions of a side chair; armchairs are usually broader (fig. 166). Because decoratively carved arms increase the value of a chair (bird arms make chair prices fly), side-chair-to-armchair conversions have not been infrequent. Be cautious about closing a deal on an armchair with side-chair proportions, and make the price conditional on the arms being original. Have the dealer remove the plugs covering the screws and unscrew an arm support. A dealer who will not, probably has, and has nothing good to show you.

Morrison Heckscher of the Metropolitan Museum, in his fine catalogue, *American Furniture in the Metropolitan Museum of Art, II, Late Colonial Period,* tells all.[9] The Met's side chair with something on the side (fig. 164) came from Harry Flayderman, a Marblehead, Massachusetts, dealer, who said in 1932 that it had belonged to a Van Rensselaer. Heckscher found that two other armchairs (numbered V and VIII) from the same set (the Met's is VII) had entered the White House collections because of a connection with the family of Thomas Jefferson. (The three chairs apparently

FIGURE 166:
*Armchair; mahogany,
1765–1785, New York.
H. 39¼; W. (at arms) 31,
(at crest) 23, (at seat) 23½;
Seat D. 20. (Henry Francis
du Pont Winterthur
Museum.)*

belonged to a Cathalina E. Groot, but nobody mentions her. *Groot* doesn't have the ring of *Van Rensselaer* or *Jefferson*.)

The White House armchairs also have the dimensions of side chairs. The carved birds, with the same stippling behind the neck and the same pupils in the eyes as the birds on the Met's chair, strike a somewhat different pose. Unless the President dislodges an arm of the chair by leaning heavily to the left or right, there seems to be little chance of checking the seat rails as Heckscher did.

An armchair with armchair proportions (fig. 166), said to be from the Stephen Van Rensselaer family, is at the Winterthur Museum. In 1939, Lloyd Hyde, a New York dealer who specialized in ceramics, acquired for du Pont a second armchair, supposedly the mate to this one. The two are clearly not a pair; their measurements are not the same, and neither are their carvings.

A kind thing often said about such chairs as the 1939 addition is that they are copies made to fill out sets. Many sets were broken up over the years, inherited by different people. Chairs broke; sets shrank. Partial sets and old sets that were not large enough acquired additions. Collectors look kindly on such enlarged sets, especially those with old and accurate copies. The armchair in the Winterthur collection, as would be the case when a copy was added to a set, is not stained or otherwise artificially aged. But it shows none of the careful copying associated with an addition ordered by an owner. The crude bird carvings are so inferior that their design may have been taken from a photograph. The chair is a reproduction that was sold to du Pont as something else.

The "enlarged set" story often is a lame excuse for a copycat

crime. A chair presented as having been made to enlarge a set ought to be accompanied by at least one true antique and should emulate it carefully, almost too carefully. Otherwise it is a reproduction married to an antique, or it is a fake, designed not to enlarge a set but to enrich a faker's purse.

Among the many collectors who fell victim to the cry "I found a mate" was Maxim Karolik, who made possible the splendid M. and M. Karolik Collection at the Museum of Fine Arts, Boston. In 1939, the same year du Pont bought his repro, Karolik bought a chair (fig. 167) that he believed was a mate to an armchair his wife had earlier given the museum. Despite a long provenance purporting to unite the two chairs, measurements show that they are not mates.

The bird carvings on the two Karolik chairs (fig. 168) point up

FIGURE 168:
Detail of armchair shown in figure 167 is on the right. The bird on the left is from the eighteenth-century armchair.

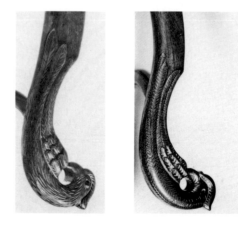

the loose carving of the original (left) and the more rigid work of the copyist (right). (Genuine carvings are usually more than a cut above the fake.)

Not only do the birds on the two upholstered-back armchairs differ, but the chair that arrived in 1939 is not old. It was built around two old legs. All the nails and nail holes attest to wire nails and a few cut nails. Because chairs with upholstered frames have all the nail-holes and most of the body hidden beneath fabric, strip searches are necessary. When these birds raised questions, Jonathan Fairbanks, the curator, had the chair frame stripped of its upholstery. Except where original upholstery is present, *strip upholstered frames*. (More on pages 165–167, in "Some Good Stuff and the Strip Search.")

The secondary surfaces that were visible without stripping — the seat rails and the corner blocks, which can be seen from underneath — were "aged" on the 1939 chair. Unlike the parts of an honestly made reproduction, which are crisply sawn, unstained, and obviously modern, the faked seat rails are of reused oak, and the stained corner blocks emulate old ones.

Apparently the 1930s was a good time for birds, and carvers had a field day. The several fakers with ornithological bents made New York birds (figs. 164 and 166 are New York chairs) and New England birds (the old Karolik chair is from Massachusetts). Bird arms can show up anywhere; a Chippendale-style settee that was sold as Victorian (but was probably made early in this century) has bird arms as arm supports (fig. 169). It's enough to give any furniture detective a fear of flying.

FIGURE 169:
Detail of a settee at an auction preview. (Photograph courtesy Maine Antique Digest.)

THE WITNESS TELLS MORE THAN ONE STORY

Would you believe the chair in figure 170? Parts of it are old. A witness who tells more than one story is unreliable, and this enhanced antique gives mixed messages.

Long regarded as a rare example of Philadelphia transitional (Queen Anne to Chippendale) style, this elaborately carved chair illustrates a plethora of unrelated decorative motifs. Similar motifs adorn elegant eighteenth-century Philadelphia chairs, but the designs are more unified — for example, a Philadelphia chair from New Jersey's Lambert family (fig. 171) has similar foliage, but on the Lambert chair the foliage meanders over both stiles and crest. Good examples feature fewer, more unified motifs. *Watch out for antiques with too much; often it masks too little.*

The structural separation between the crest and the rest of the

FIGURE 170:
Side chair; mahogany.
H. 42; W. 20½; D. 20¾.
(Henry Francis du Pont
Winterthur Museum, Study
Collection.)

chair did not dictate a design separation to the makers of fine furniture of the period. In fact, they sought to erase the structural separateness with integrated design (look at the design at the joint of the crest and splat, figs. 171 and 172).

Focusing on the decoration, the sleuth sees that the "transitional" chair doesn't look unified. In fact, it is not a unit. The defrauder began with a more modest Queen Anne chair, possibly missing its crest and splat, and added a crest and splat similar to those on a turn-of-the-century labeled reproduction made by Ferdinand Keller, a Philadelphia manufacturer of antique-style furniture (fig. 173). The tassel carvings on the crests of both our enhanced antique and Keller's reproduction do not extend to the splat to unify the design (as do those in fig. 172). Makers of reproductions often failed to integrate designs successfully. *Be wary of furniture with such non-integrated design motifs.*

The defrauder recarved the stiles, creating the trailing vegetation that is completely unrelated to the other motifs on the chair. On the seat rails, he added carving to the upper edge and applied a central shell. Then he added the only thing that the various parts of the chair have in common — the thick, dark varnish.

The carved shell he applied is of three pieces of wood; antique

shells were of one piece. Restorations of missing ornament are often composed of several pieces. If a central shell is missing (fig. 172), the inspector knows it by the signs the applied carving left behind — gouges in the front rail for the glue that held the shell. The squad, alert to antiques with replaced or missing enhancements, is even more concerned with furniture, like the witness in figure 170, that has been fraudulently enhanced.

FIGURE 172:
*Side chair; mahogany,
1760–1780, Philadelphia.
H. 40; W. 23½; Seat
D. 17⁷/₁₆; Seat H. 16¹³/₁₆.
(Yale University Art Gallery,
Mabel Brady Garvan
Collection.) The front
seat rail is missing its
shell drop.*

FIGURE 173:
*Side chair; mahogany,
1885–1910, Philadelphia.
Made by Ferdinand Keller.
The glued label on this chair
is printed: "FERDINAND
KELLER, / ANTIQUE FURNI-
TURE, / Silver, China and
Delft. / 216-218-220 S. 9th
St. / PHILADELPHIA, PA."
Keller had about sixty em-
ployees at one time, all
turning out reproductions.*

FIGURE 174:
Upholstered side chair; rosewood, mahogany, ash seat rails, 1850–1860, New York. H. 37¼; W. (at seat) 18¼; Seat D. 17⅛; Seat H. 13¹¹/₁₆. (Yale University Art Gallery, Mabel Brady Garvan Collection.)

Another chair with carved vines (fig. 174), a mid-nineteenth-century upholstered example, provides the rookie with solid information on a very different style of seating. This witness can help collectors pursue Belter and Belterish rococo furniture.

Chairs like this are usually attributed to the New York shop of John Belter, a German who brought to America the wood-bending techniques and rococo carving style that have sometimes garnered for him credit for all such objects. Yet several competitors also produced robustly carved furniture of laminated rosewood. No attribution is made for this unlabeled, grapevine-carved rosewood chair.

Shells (at the knees), C curves and a flower basket (at the crest), florets (at the seat rail and crest), and grapevines abound, most of them carved in a curved laminate of rosewood. On the bent-wood back, the laminate is five plies thick. Detectives look carefully at the edge of the bent wood to see and count the layers.

Two screws fasten an upholstered board to the laminated rosewood back. Some such chairs retain original underupholstery, a few original upholstery. This chair does not.

The losses sustained are typical. The toes of the two front feet are replacements — copied from another museum example — as are the casters. Casters, even original ones, take a heavy toll on old toes. The experienced detective checks such feet carefully, looking for consistency in the carving. Checking for breakage or replacement of the floral carvings takes time and is an eyes-only assignment, which the handsome carvings make well worthwhile.

FIGURE 175:
Sofa; one of a pair, 1808–1809, Boston. H. 36; W. 81⁹/₁₆; Seat D. 26⁹/₁₆. (Private collection.) The sofa retains all of its original underupholstery. A sofa back comprising three separate and removable frames is very unusual; most were upholstered, as were easy-chair backs, as one nonremovable frame.

FIGURE 176:
Loose back frame as seen from the rear. Detail of sofa shown in figure 175. Loose seat frames look like this when seen from underneath. The frame has its original early nineteenth-century upholstery.

SOME GOOD STUFF AND THE STRIP SEARCH

A handsome Federal sofa (fig. 175) exemplifies one of the best buys on the antiques market — many were made, large pieces of furniture sell slowly, and upholstered pieces tend to sell cheaply. The sofa was a newly popular form in the Federal era, so an early neoclassical example such as this one, made in 1808, is about as old a sofa as the collector is likely to find.

This sofa is extremely unusual in that it is one of an extant pair and is in exceedingly fine condition. The refined and delicate proportions of early neoclassical design often proved too fragile for daily use, and many Federal sofas and chairs have become wobbly and broken. Nevertheless, some not only have survived but have even kept their upholstery innards intact for almost two centuries. The savvy collector retains surviving original underupholstery — be it a layer or two or only a small area — because any original upholstery enhances the value of the antique. Sofas and chairs made later in the nineteenth century quite often retain their original underupholstery in sufficiently sound condition that it can be preserved beneath new cover fabric, making the seats usable and beautiful again.

An upholstered chair seat can be inspected without removing the upholstery because the seat rails can be seen from underneath (plate 1). A good detective insists on inspecting the rails and blocks, and requires that any "dust cover" beneath the seat be removed.

On a loose- or slip-seated chair, of course, the inspector removes the seat frame, inspects the chair rails, and checks out the upholstered frame — without its dust cover — to see whether it is old. From underneath, a loose-seat frame with original upholstery looks much like a back frame of this sofa as seen from behind (fig. 176). An

FIGURE 177:
Easy-chair frame; black walnut, maple rear posts and seat rails, birch, and white pine, 1755–1770, Newport or eastern Connecticut. H. 51³/₈; W. 35³/₄; Seat D. 23¹/₂; Seat H. 15¹/₂. (Society for the Preservation of New England Antiquities.)

astute inspector recognizes the original underpinnings for stuffing — the widely spaced, narrow strips of girt web and the coarse linen it supports.

Upholstered chairs and sofas should be examined in a state of undress, either stripped to the frame if no original upholstery survives or stripped to what remains of the original fabric. *Strip away all reupholstery. Examine the entire frame, excepting only the parts covered by original upholstery.*

An easy chair is the easiest kind of chair to inspect (fig. 177). In the strip search, the old frame tells all freely. Old wood looks it,

FIGURE 178:
Knee joint with wedged
dovetail tenon. (Society for
the Preservation of New
England Antiquities.)

new wood too. Added wood — many upholsterers add reinforcements or rails and stiles to help in (re)upholstering — is not a deficit; replaced or missing elements are. Filled nail holes and glued and cloth-wrapped rails are common.

The detective carefully checks the exposed and finished elements — here the legs and stretchers — because replacements to finished wood are more difficult to detect. Check medial and rear stretchers from underneath; the latter are frequent casualties. A rear stretcher that looks like a piece of mop handle probably is.

The rear legs may be of primary wood, joined to rear stiles of secondary wood. Or, as here, the rear legs may be of a piece with the rest of the rear post, all of secondary wood, and merely stained to match the primary wood.

To check a front leg, examine the joint to the seat frame (on this chair, a quarter-round tenon; on another, fig. 178, a wedged single dovetail). Different craftsmen chose different joints for the junction of the front rail, side rail, and front leg. The inspector looks for an undisturbed joint, whatever its type.

CORNERING THE WITNESS

The squad gathers important clues at seat corners, where a leg meets two seat rails. Three pieces of wood must be joined soundly enough to support the weight of the sitter. So, in original construction, many craftsmen reinforced corner joints with wooden blocks or cleats.

Missing or replaced corner supports are minor problems, and corner blocks added where there were originally none are no cause for concern; nevertheless, it is important to check corner blocks. Modern ones are easy to spot and are quick clues to repairs (fig. 179) or reproductions. Many reproductions have stained and varnished corner blocks (fig. 35); antique corner blocks were never finished.

Inappropriate corner blocks can also help corner a fake; eighteenth-century craftsmen in certain cities used certain shapes for their blocks (figs. 180–182), so the style of the block should be consistent with the style of the chair. Triangular blocks of horizontal wood, glued and nailed, are typical of Boston work (and are also seen on some New York chairs). Blocks of vertical softwood, two pieces wide, cut to a quarter round and glued, are characteristic of Philadelphia and Connecticut chairs (and of some chairs from the South and New York). Cleats that cross the corner are typical of Portsmouth, New Hampshire, or English work (though the other types

of blocks can also be found in Britain). The smart cop on the beat knows each block and checks every corner.

Fakers did not always know their blocks, and this can work to the detective's advantage. A supposedly Chippendale chair (birds' heads on the crest and splat immediately set off an alarm) has old-looking "Massachusetts" corner blocks, carvings that resemble Philadelphia work, and through tenons typical of Philadelphia and some Connecticut chairs (fig. 162). This fraud of old parts and new ones has "wear" on the claw-and-ball feet that miraculously spares the usually vulnerable talons, which are neither chipped nor abraded. Though fakers routinely impose "wear" (often on parts not subject to wear in normal use), some workmen can never quite bring themselves to inflict damage on the details they labored most meticulously to create.

FIGURE 181:
Detail of corner block, Pennsylvania and Connecticut type. A vertical softwood block, two pieces wide, cut to a quarter round and glued in place.

FIGURE 182:
Side-chair frame, stripped; mahogany, maple seat frame and cleats, 1760–1790, Portsmouth. H. 38⅛; W. 22¼; Seat D. 18¹/₁₆; Seat H. 18. (Society for the Preservation of New England Antiquities.) Often the tops of front legs protrude above the corners to help the upholsterer in forming a neat edge and corner. Knowing the popular nailing patterns helps the detective decipher the series of nail holes on stripped rails.

Topless Tables and Other Concerns of the Board

9

TABLE furniture, perhaps because it is reasonably simple in form, seems to entice fakers and defrauders, tickle their imaginations, and challenge their egos. There is a lot of ego behind fakery. The perpetrators take pride in their abilities and get their kicks as well as their money from fooling people.

The members of the fakes-and-fraud squad have their own pride and pleasures. Happy to be able to protect themselves from bad purchases, they also relish uncovering fakery. Their satisfaction in spotting a fake or figuring out a fraud is almost equal to the pleasure of ascertaining that a good antique is just that.

Tables may seem barely a challenge. They are relatively small and easily handled; they have few surfaces to be examined, all of them accessible. Much of the wood, however, is finished and so not very informative. Tables are the true test of the determined detective.

TOPLESS TABLES AND BASELESS PLANKS

When "a good base in old red paint"[1] (fig. 183) sold at a 1978 auction to a dealer for $300, it probably had not long to live as a mere base. The painted base — four rails and four stretchers joined with pinned rectangular tenons to four turned legs — was missing only a tabletop and a cleat, which had fit in notches in the two long rails. A glimpse at one lot at another auction (fig. 184) tells the story of what awaits topless tables.

Tops are what tables are all about, the very reason the bases exist. Tops get the wear and the workout. They often break, warp, or split and are removed. Some are wantonly removed. The famous collector George Dudley Seymour (1859–1945) sent a table to a restorer who, without Seymour's permission, replaced the old top, saying it was not original. Seymour thought otherwise. "Those who repair old furniture are always in quest of fine pieces of old wood," he wrote. "If the old top was removed and reserved by the man on the job for use on some other job on account of its age and quality, that would not be the first time in the history of Antiques Furniture Reparation."[2]

Baseless tops and topless bases have a way of getting together. There are new tops on old bases, new bases with old tops, marriages of old tops and old bases, and complex mix-and-matches like the "wonderful country Queen Anne table"[3] (fig. 185), really an old skirt, a new top made from an old plank, and new rounded legs spliced to the posts below the frame.

Look for splice-lines on table legs. One-piece legs are standard; splices to extend table legs are never original. A common enhancement, however, is the "exchanging" of plain legs for more stylish ones, with the splice usually being made at an indent in a turning, where the joint is hard to see. You can wring the truth from a leg. *Try to turn the bottom of the leg while keeping the top still.* Old glue dries out, so old doweled repairs and frauds frequently loosen and "turn" themselves in. This important technique is also useful for checking on ended-out feet of turned chairs, a common problem.

FIGURES 183, 184:
Table base and tabletops at auction. (Photographs courtesy Maine Antique Digest.*) The pale shadow left by a rectangular base is clear on the round top; all but one of the rectangular tops have breadboard ends.*

FIGURE 185:
"Country Queen Anne." (Photograph courtesy Maine Antique Digest.*) "Country" pieces are fakery favorites.*

You can try the thread trick too. Attempt to work a thread (there's one in the needle in your kit) into the unseen crack of the possible joint.

Legs or stiles that are made of two boards spliced together instead of being formed from a single square post are not original. But vertical splicing is original to some Spanish feet (fig. 31) and to a few early Queen Anne cabrioles (fig. 186). In the second quarter of the eighteenth century, some craftsmen making furniture legs added wood to the outer edges at the foot or knee so they could carve toes or knees that were broader than the post being worked. Turning or carving the legs from thicker posts would have been less efficient and less economical.

When an old top, like that on the "wonderful country Queen Anne" (fig. 185), is basically rectangular, check the end-grain edges for nail or wooden-pin holes. Was the top originally a true square or rectangle edged with "breadboard" ends (see the tops in fig. 184)? To be sure about a top, you may have to do what the buyer of the "wonderful country Queen Anne" did when he brought it home: *take off the top and see if the old plank bears the pale, unaged shadow of the old frame.* Once the top was off, the purchaser found foul play, returned the table, and got his money refunded.

QUESTIONING THE BOARD FURTHER

Wooden pins, screws, or glue blocks hold the tabletop to the frame. You can check glue-block evidence with the top in place (fig. 187). Finished or painted blocks are never period work. Often blocks are missing, but have left behind telltale shadows. *Compare the shadows under the top to those on the inside of the frame.* To check pin or screw holes, you have to remove the top. *Demand corresponding fastener holes in the top and the frame.*

The able detective reads the underside of the top — the shadows of the frame on the aged undersurface and the holes made by fasteners or the shadows of fastening blocks — like a book. *If the underside of the top has been completely finished or painted, condemn it.* Complementary shadows or holes are easy to align. A replaced top or a reused plank doesn't read well.

The shadows or holes may tell of a top that shrank and was refastened, or of top boards that warped and were recut at their common edges to help them lie flat. Fastener shadows or holes may tell of top boards that have been reversed and reattached. Such changes to the top are usually acceptable and welcome evidence of a normal history of wear.

Underside of a drop-leaf table; mahogany, birch, and white pine, 1770, Boston. (Society for the Preservation of New England Antiquities.) A series of small blocks is glued to both frame and top, and all of the blocks remain in place. Usually fewer blocks are used, and at least some are lost. These hinges are evidently undisturbed. The feet, which now have glides, have little wear; nevertheless, those on the legs that swing show more wear than those on the stationary legs.

FIGURE 188:
Butterfly tables have enjoyed great popularity with collectors and fakers.

FAVORITE PRANKS OF THE UNPRINCIPLED

In sophisticated furniture, the savvy sleuth expects the top of the table (or the table-high top of a case) to be of the same wood as the base (or case) below. Replacers of tops, though they ideally aimed at using the same wood, frequently settled for substitutes. Original, unrestored walnut furniture does not have mahogany top boards, and vice versa.

A wonderful old top on a card table in a museum collection bears, in old chalk, an inscribed "£26" on its undersurface. The figure is not the original cost of the card table; much of the underside of the top is tooth-planed, but not where the chalk is. The defrauder, in putting a replacement top on the old table, carefully retained the old writing as he planed a reused board to make it fit.

A popular form for fakers is the one-leaf drop-leaf. Usually made from a drop-leaf table that has lost one leaf, the "rare" form gained such favor among collectors that fakes were made from scratch with only one hanging leaf.

Another drop-leaf with great appeal is the butterfly table (fig. 188). Harold Sack, president of Israel Sack, Inc., cautions that this type was the first American antique to be widely faked, "in part because it was easily converted from an abundant supply of tavern tables."[4] A base like the "old red" one (fig. 183) is a fine candidate for receiving top, leaves, and butterfly supports. Among all the butterfly tables that flit around, genuine supports are rare.

Let's turn over a handsome gateleg drop-leaf (figs. 189). Placed on its top (fig. 190), the gateleg tells a completely satisfactory story. It is not necessary to remove the top from the base. In an inverted inspection, the frame is visible; if the top is fastened with glue blocks (fig. 187), the blocks (or the shadows of missing blocks) are visible; the unfinished wood of frame and top is ready to be checked for wear and aging; sometimes the pins that secure the mortise-and-tenon joints of the frame are uncut and very apparent. *Always put a table on its top to get the facts.*

If the table has a drawer, remove it and inspect it before you upend the table. Drawers may be replaced, or they may be the only part that is old. Set the drawer aside, but don't forget it. After examining the table you will reinsert it to check for any changes in color left by the drawer supports (fig. 191) and to check the tabletop for color changes left by the drawer.

Legs — carved or turned — are also best examined when the table is on its top. *Look for wear on the protruding parts of the feet. And look at areas that are protected when the table is in its normal position, and that consequently should not show wear.* This is the way to spot gratuitous "wear," the faker's favorite device.

On gateleg or swing-leg tables, the several feet wear differently. Feet on swing legs rub against the floor and wear much more than those that are stationary. Warping, too, may cause extra wear to one foot. On a leafed table, the legs that do not swing may retain

FIGURE 189:
Gateleg drop-leaf table;
maple and pine, 1715–1740,
coastal Massachusetts or
New Hampshire. H. 28;
W. 41½; D. 50. (Historic
Deerfield.)

all their original height and may even show marks from the craftsman's tools (fig. 56).

Much of the inspection of a drop-leaf table will concern the hinged leaves, which are so tentatively attached to the tabletop that they are even more at risk than the top itself. *Check the hinges or the fastener holes that tell the hinges' history.* The butterfly hinges on this gateleg (fig. 190) are "Colonial" replacements. Beside them are the corresponding shadows and holes of the old rectangular hinges.

The color and texture of the undersides of leaves and top are solid clues to a common history. Check the leaves for wear caused by the supports rubbing them as they swing. Fakers have been known to simulate an eroded arc by staining the underside everywhere else and leaving a line of "wear." *Feel the wear. Actually work the supports.* On an inverted table, this must be done gently while lifting the leg slightly.

And check the shape of the leaves. Shapes vary with the style of the table but conform to general rules. If the otherwise oval top of a William and Mary or Queen Anne table has flat or truncated ends, the leaves are not in their original shape. If the support extends beyond the leaf (fig. 192), the leaf is either replaced or not all there. The square or rectangular tops of Chippendale tables had right-angle

FIGURE 192:
Table legs that extend beyond the leaves are a sign of
a replaced or cut leaf. (Photograph courtesy Maine
Antique Digest.)

corners (fig. 187); if such a table has rounded corners, someone sawed the originals or replaced the leaves.

TAKING THE STAND

Tables on baluster supports (fig. 193) and similarly supported stands (fig. 194) usually have three legs single-dovetailed into the pillar, which, on the other end, tenons into a plate. On a table with its top tipped up (fig. 193), you can see the square top of the tenon where it comes through the plate. The plate may be fastened (usually screwed) directly to the top (as in fig. 194) or hinged to cleats that are screwed to the top (as in fig. 193). Every part commands inves-

FIGURE 193:
Tilt-top table; mahogany,
maple plate, 1760–1790,
Newport. (Society for the
Preservation of New Eng-
land Antiquities.)

FIGURE 194:
Inverted candlestand, 1790–1810, New England. H. 26³/₈; W. 17; D. 17⁵/₈. (Society for the Preservation of New England Antiquities.) The base never had a metal triangle, and the dovetail joints are visible.

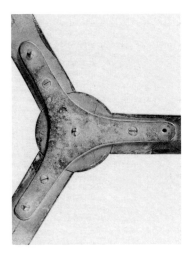

FIGURE 195:
Triangle brace. Detail of the tilt-top table shown in figure 193.

tigation, but the greatest problems are at the bottom and at the top.

The dovetail joints are usually hidden by a reinforcing metal triangle (fig. 195). The fact that triangles were used, often in original construction, points to the frailty of the base of the pillar. Even when the metal looks undisturbed (note the area around the nailheads in this triangle), the pillar may have cracked.

Many pillar stands and tables have a replaced or repaired leg. The alert detective notes the way the wood grain runs on the cabrioles (diagonally, down and out from the top of the knee) and checks along the grain for cracks and replacement splices.

The sturdy plate above the pillar is infrequently replaced even though, on tilt-tops, one end of the plate is sorely tested. (The pintles on which the cleats rotate are an integral part of one end of the plate and bear the weight of the top when it is tilted.) The wood of the plate can be very informative because American tables and stands were almost always made with plates of a secondary wood, often maple. There may be some American tables or stands that are exceptions, but almost every example with a mahogany plate is British.

To ascertain beyond a shadow of a doubt whether the top is original, remove the screws that hold a cleat or the plate. At least a few of the screws should be old, the cleats or plate should have left a shadow on the underside of the top, and the screw holes should match up or show a logical history of readjustments for shrinkage.

FIGURE 196:
Candlestand; ca. 1920.
H. 24³/₁₆; W. (of top) 14¹/₂;
W. (at base) 20¹/₄. (Society
for the Preservation of
New England Antiquities.)

FIGURE 197:
Candlestand. Made by Wal-
lace Nutting. (Photograph
courtesy Maine Antique
Digest.)

Fortunately for the detective, the plate sometimes scratches the cleat and scars the top (fig. 193). Such marks plus the presence of old screws can preclude the need to remove the top.

BALUSTER BUNKO

You don't have to invert all baluster-based stands to get their stories. One example that reveals its past while still standing on its feet (fig. 196) features a baluster that is William and Mary in form and cabrioles that are sort of Chippendale. The mix, which makes no sense today, said "Colonial" in the 1920s.

A Wallace Nutting creation (fig. 197) — note the crisp edges and the thick top — is just that, a creation. It's not a re-creation or a reproduction. Nutting himself noted the problems with this form in *Furniture Treasury*: "The variety of these wooden stands is endless. The author saw in one shop twelve different patterns, all of them new, all purporting to be old. Good patterns were rare, and the demand always finds itself met by a certain sort of supply."[5] *Beware of "primitive" stands.* Very popular early in this century, they were made in large numbers, and still are.

The turned feet on some stands (fig. 198) look like those on a spinning wheel (fig. 2). Defrauders dismembered so many spinning wheels to create stands from the old turnings that they created a fad for such stands. This example of the style was, in fact, newly turned.

The "small, early-looking tripod . . . bounced around from dealer to dealer in Maine," reported Sam Pennington in his *Maine Antique Digest* in January 1980. Starting at about $300, it "went to about $1500, and was returned, then went the whole cycle again, reaching a reported asking price of $2800 in Ohio before it again came back to roost."[6]

All this money changed hands despite the fact that the undersides of the pine top had "random nail holes which have no reason to be there."[7] Pennington suggests that the top, which has parallel saw marks from a pre-1840 mill saw, is actually a reused board from the attic of a pre-1840 house. Now there's a reason for the old nail holes!

Pennington reports that at least nine of these were made. And he located the maker in Woolrich, Maine. The man bills himself as a "Cabinet and Chair Maker," doing restorations, custom work, and quality reproductions, and says he sells his products as what they really are.[8] He just likes to work in old wood.

You may want to collect spinning wheels and yarn winders as fine examples of the turner's art. Some have handsomely turned pillars. An attractive yarn winder or clock reel (fig. 199) illustrates both the appeal of the form for collectors and also the potential of the form for defrauders.

Old candlestands stand some 26 to 29 inches tall, just the right height for someone sitting in an antique chair. But today's seating is lower, and we use lower tables. (Early-twentieth-century coffee tables are lower than old tea tables, and contemporary cocktail tables are lower still.) The base — the legs and baluster — of this clock reel is 20½ inches tall and so is convertible to a 22-inch table, a "perfect" height for current tastes. Twentieth-century dimensions on an "eighteenth-century" or "nineteenth-century" stand may be an instance of a pilfered pillar.

A BASE DECEPTION

FIGURE 199:
Clock reel; maple and white
pine, 1780–1810, southern
New Hampshire. H (to top
of post) 20½; H. (to top of
arm) 40¼; W. 26; D. 15.
(Historic Deerfield.) This
yarn winder has a nice low
pillar.

The tops of eighteenth- and nineteenth-century tables are almost always larger than their bases, and though many tops overhang the skirt only a bit, they are at least no smaller. The top of the one-drawer table in figure 200 doesn't quite look the part of the table's most important surface because it is smaller than the base. And it is set within a molding, which is very different from its having a molding or molded edge (as in fig. 201). This table was photographed with its side slides partly extended and flanking candlesticks placed on them, because otherwise it looks most unusual.

Once you are style-smart, heed your first impressions. To a detective with a sharp eye for style, the cramped top and the surrounding molding on this Federal table look a bit odd. In selling antiques, "odd" becomes "rare," and when a related example was sold in 1984 it was called a "rare Federal inlaid mahogany mixing table" — "mixing" because of the marble top.

The purposes of a mixing table would be better served by a raised molding that made the top more secure for glassware. And a table that is to hold china or glass is ill served by a drawer that must be pulled open and pushed closed. *Think of how the furniture was used, and demand that its several parts make sense.*

The "mixing table" at the 1984 sale had once been owned by an esteemed New England antiques dealer; it had been sold in 1957 for $3500, now carried an estimate of $15,000–20,000, and ultimately reached $55,000 (plus a ten-percent buyer's premium). Although

two years later a Chippendale tea table (fig. 201) became the first piece of American furniture to sell for more than a million dollars, $55,000 was still a hefty price, especially for a table that wasn't a table.

What was it? Let's look again at the unusual molding that uncharacteristically confines the top to a smaller area than the base. The molding recalls those on two-part cases — on a desk-on-frame (plate 5), at the waist of a high chest (plate 3), at the waist of a desk and bookcase (fig. 119). Its shape bridges the difference between the broader lower case and the narrower upper case. In fact, it does belong between two cases; it's a waist molding.

If it is a waist molding, then the mixing table is merely a base. A base for what? An answer comes from a piece in the collection of the Philadelphia antiques dealer Joe Kindig, Jr. — a desk supported by a base just like the one that sold as a table for $55,000. Years ago, apparently, a number of desk-on-frames came on the market, perhaps from a state legislature. Their value as desks was deemed by someone to be less than their value as "rare Federal inlaid mahogany mixing tables," so desk sections were removed, and the bases were fitted with new marble tops. The slides at the sides are full-depth — distinctly deeper and broader than the shallow candle-slides with which many eighteenth-century tables were equipped — because they provided flat spaces for documents beside a tilt-top desk. (They open wider than they are extended in fig. 200.)

For determined detectives, the clearest clues to the true nature of

this old part / new object are the top and its molding, a waist molding no longer at a waist, containing an undersized top, and sporting a shape that says that all below is a base. *Stay alert to base deception.* This trick need not be restricted to Federal furniture. The base of a Queen Anne desk-on-frame (plate 5) could materialize as a table.

COMING TO GRIPS WITH THE GRIFFIN

Try to do the impossible — disregard even splendid provenances. An impressive provenance can grow without a critical inspection ever having been made. A card table (fig. 202) — featured in the 1929 sale of the famous Howard Reifsnyder collection, illustrated in *House and Garden* two years earlier, and known to collectors as number 1030 in Nutting's *Furniture Treasury*, as number 1516 in Edgar Miller's *American Antique Furniture*, and as a star of the 1947 Baltimore furniture exhibition and catalogue — was not skeptically examined until the 1960s.

Then John Kirk, in his book *Early American Furniture*, and Yale's Garvan Collection staff, in the "Eye of the Beholder" exhibition, revealed that the table that had seemed a masterpiece was a fraud with a few old parts. The old, probably eighteenth-century English

FIGURE 202:
The "griffin" card table. H. 29½; W. 36½; D. 35½. (Yale University Art Gallery Study Collection.)

FIGURE 203:
Corner table; mahogany, ash, and undetermined inlay woods, ca. 1920. H. 29³/₁₆; W. 33; D. 20⁵/₁₆. (Society for the Preservation of New England Antiquities.)

FIGURE 204:
Bellflower inlay. Detail of a labeled table by John Townsend, 1797, Newport. (Photograph courtesy Israel Sack, Inc.)

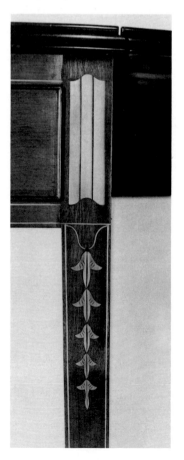

frame was largely of oak with some new veneer and inlay. The top was a reused one whose shadow is inconsistent with the frame. Dowels secure the legs to the frame. The fine inlay of the griffin contrasts with the coarse bellflowers on the legs. The defrauder, possibly from Baltimore, used enough Baltimore motifs to suggest the table's origin in that city in the Federal era.

The table was made in the 1920s, when the Federal style and inlay furniture were much in vogue in both revival pieces (fig. 203) and fakes. The eagles of the 1920s are heavier and healthier-looking than their scrawny Federal forebears; the inlaid flowers of the 1920s are larger and coarser than their delicate predecessors. *Compare the inlay or carving on the Federal-style furniture you examine with that on several period pieces.* When the bellflowers on the griffin table are compared with early-nineteenth-century bellflower inlay (fig. 204), they appear oversized and lack grace.

They also lack grace when compared with the handsome inlaid griffin, a motif found on English furniture and based on Thomas Sheraton's *The Cabinet-Maker and Upholsterer's Drawing-Book*.[9] The griffin created a sensation because it was so rare. (There's that word again.) *Check for consistency by comparing the most advanced aspect of the design to other similarly decorated details.*

THE LYRE IS TRUTHFUL; THE LABEL LIES

This lovely neoclassical worktable (fig. 205) entered the Winterthur collection because of its label, which designated it as the work

of Charles-Honoré Lannuier (1779–1819), émigré of France and cabinetmaker of New York. A handsome table, it was ripe for Lannuier-labeling. Lannuier was a premier cabinetmaker in the "French" style, and his label sizably enhanced the value of the table, which he did not make.

The label also misdated the table. The design, characteristic of the early nineteenth century, was very much in vogue again at the century's end. Without the label, all but the rookies on the squad would have discovered clues pointing to the table's being later-than-period work; with the label, the job is actually made easier. The details do not measure up to the standard suggested by the label. The feet have little of the fully formed, three-dimensional quality of Lannuier's work — for example, no line distinguishes the toenails from the toes.

Deciding that the worktable is not Lannuier's helps the squad determine that the table is not even early-nineteenth-century. It is honestly made revival furniture in the neoclassical style. Those ill-defined feet have the look of later-than-period neoclassical furniture. The drawer sides, back, and bottom are mahogany, not a cheap secondary wood. (The drawers of some New York furniture of the early nineteenth century have mahogany sides, but not mahogany backs and bottoms.) Each foot is doweled to its leg, not tenoned as early-nineteenth-century objects are (see fig. 50). And all of the screws, as befits late-nineteenth-century furniture, are machine-made and have gimlet points.

Screws, rarely used in other furniture, play an important role in the construction of tables, and thus can be of great help to the detective. While some of the screws in a table may be replaced, a few — or at least one old one — should remain. Although a defrauder could theoretically replace machine screws with handmade ones, this is seldom if ever done.

ALL-POINTS BULLETIN: The gimlet points may be cut off gimlet screws. A faker will do this to emulate old ones; a restorer, to make new screws fit in the shallow but broad holes left by old handmade ones.

Luckily for the detective, the dull color and hand-filed threads of old screws do not look, under a magnifying lens, like the shiny, machine-threaded ones from your neighborhood hardware store.

Finishing 'Em Off

10

WHILE investigating style and construction, be alert to how the furniture was finished off. There were several ways of doing the job. If the wood figure was part of the embellishment, the furniture required a clear finish. The walnut high chest (plate 3), whose decoration features carefully matched veneers on the drawer facades and an almost luminous inlay along the meandering skirt, was finished merely with wax. Few pieces were simply waxed, however, and rarely do original waxed surfaces remain. Most stylish furniture was varnished with one of the many formulas created to impart a relatively clear high gloss. Such finishes usually have darkened, become crazed or otherwise damaged, been reworked, or been stripped and refinished. Chances are that a so-called clear finish that looks old and original is new or reworked.

Before receiving the clear glossy coat, the wood was often stained to give it an appearance of better wood or to make it more uniform in color. In refinishing, such furniture loses stain as well as gloss, usually regaining only gloss. For example, the desk-on-frame (plate 5), stripped of its dark reddish stain, appears today in its never-meant-to-show tiger maple under a clear finish.

Painted furniture was much more common than surviving examples suggest. (Little if any of it, however, was covered with the Prussian blue tones — popularly called "Williamsburg" or "Colonial" blue — that were routinely applied to twentieth-century fakes and frauds.) Much original paint has been overpainted, which sometimes proves to be the salvation of the original, much has been stripped, and that which has survived may be very delicate or barely visible.

In recent years, many collectors have become enchanted by old finishes. Some covet an original finish to help prove that the body beneath is original. As a member of the squad, you can evaluate the body on its own merits and cherish an original finish for what it is — another genuine aspect of an honest antique.

The clamor for old paint, like the outcry in the past for ornate objects, has been heard by defrauders. Their answer has been truck-loads of paint-decorated — often grain-painted — furniture, whose "original" finish is in remarkably good shape. Sometimes the furniture beneath the paint is old, sometimes it's new, sometimes it's a little of each. The painted finish, rather than guaranteeing the wood-work beneath, actually doubles the detective work. Painted furniture requires two investigations: *authenticate the furniture, and authenticate its finish*.

For the latter, you may need to become an expert on paint or painted furniture, or you may want to consult one. Which brings up the story of the unicorn.

A PAINTED PAST

An agent, reportedly acting for a famous comedian, bid on a painted "Pennsylvania" chest — dated 1788 in paint, with unicorns on the central of its three front panels (fig. 206) — and won with a bid of $23,000. Surprised when the bidding stopped, the agent decided that he had really lost — that $23,000, in 1985, was too low a price for the genuine article. (A clue overlooked: the auction house had estimated the unicorn chest at $8000 to $12,000.)

Auction-room talk had it that the chest was twentieth-century, perhaps sold by one L. P. Aardrup, a Lancaster dealer in the 1930s, who, by mail, supplied "all-original" painted chests (including some

FIGURE 206:
The unicorn chest and a detail. H. 30; W. 53¼; D. 25½.

with unicorns) for $100. Others thought the chest was too sophisticated to be one of Aardrup's products and suggested that possibly it was the work of Esther Stevens Fraser Brazer, who wrote about decorative painting and encouraged her readers to paint flowers, unicorns, dates, and initials on furniture. In *Early American Decoration*, Brazer introduces the "Pennsylvania Dower Chest" as follows:

> PREPARATION
> *Clean off all old paint from the chest and wipe down
> with turpentine.*[1]

A Brazer preparation put an end to an original finish.

Brazer's fifth stage of decoration (fourteen days after the first stage), called for antiquing, with "age coats" of linseed oil and raw umber being applied every two or three weeks until the chest had "a satisfactory semblance of age."[2]

The most telling episode in the unicorn's story comes from Monroe Fabian, an expert on Pennsylvania painted chests, to whom the high-bidding agent went after the auction. At the preview, Fabian had demurred when asked his opinion by the auction house's cataloguer. As quoted in the *Maine Antique Digest*, he explains why. "A few years ago, a Bucks County dealer asked me to look over a unicorn chest. I . . . spent some time going over it and telling him why it wasn't right. The next week a friend went to see the chest, and the dealer told her that I had been there and liked it very much."[3] Fabian no longer gives oral opinions, which can be misconstrued.

If you want an expert's opinion, get it directly from the expert. After the sale, Fabian gave a written opinion of the unicorn chest to the high-bidding agent for a small ($100) fee. He wrote, in part, "The painting on the front of the chest is late 19th or 20th century."[4]

The auction house, which guarantees paintings but not furniture, is experienced with ultraviolet (a.k.a. UV or black) light; the staff placed the unicorn chest under black light and found nothing suspicious. "Something suspicious" in this instance would have been any change in color not apparent when the painting was viewed in regular light. Newer, added pigments fluoresce differently than older ones; the added work usually shows up as black. Sleuths specializing in painted furniture and those on the lookout for ceramics (glazes, too, fluoresce differently) or paintings will find a UV light necessary equipment. A battery-operated light is lightweight, portable, and especially handy. Most furniture detectives, however, need not arm themselves with one.

The unicorn case illustrates another caution for collectors. *Don't buy an antique just because of an advertisement or a blurb about it.*

The high bidder claimed that he would not have gone after the chest "except that the magazine *Art and Auction* wrote it up as a piece of the month."[5] In December 1985, the magazine's "Previews" featured the chest, describing it as "sweetly decorated with flowers and dancing horses."[6] Whatever the previewer may have known about the chest did not include how to tell a horse from a unicorn.

A BENCH WARRANT FOR A PAINTED MASTERPIECE

While some painted surfaces compound the difficulty of the case for the investigator, paint can and often does help a detective discover old parts that have lent themselves to new objects. Although this painted settle (fig. 207) is not new, some parts are older than the whole. As much of the story as the detective needs to know was recorded in layers of pigment.

The Talcott Settle was so named because it was believed to have been "made in 1769 for the house of Colonel Samuel Talcott, of Hartford, Conn., built in that year . . . made for the kitchen, and the panels in its back correspond to those found in the woodwork of the apartment."[7] Irving W. Lyon, writing in 1891, mentioned alterations but found no reason to doubt the settle, which bore a label proclaiming its history and which had been exhibited in the Centennial Exposition in Philadelphia in 1876.

Although legend said that it was made for a kitchen, and although

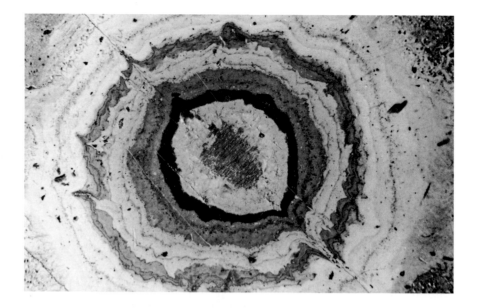

FIGURE 208:
Paint sample of a small
section of woodwork. The
painted surface, initially
scraped with a scalpel, then
abraded with 220-grit sandpaper wetted with linseed
oil and finished up with
600-grit sandpaper, reveals
the sequence of its multiple
layers. (Work and photo-
graph by Morgan Phillips,
architectural conservator,
Society for the Preservation
of New England Antiqui-
ties.) Phillips also removes
paint layers by gently tap-
ping brittle paint with a
hammer or by applying
solvents.

old-time collectors often placed a settle at a fireside to serve both as a seat and as a room divider, this example was photographed in the late nineteenth century standing in an entry hall. About that time, apparently, it acquired leather upholstery on the seat and its last coat of finish, a mahogany stain, both of which it retained in 1962 when it was advertised as "A Masterpiece in Early American Furniture."

The "Masterpiece" was then bought by William Warren, an inquiring antiquary.[8] From underneath, Warren saw, as had Lyon, that the front board and bracket feet were not original. Warren removed the leather upholstery and, finding no mahogany stain underneath, dated the mahogany coat to the time of the upholstering. The seat showed cream paint over a soft green paint. The folding candlestand in the middle had nothing but mahogany stain, so it was at best a replacement.

Detectives begin paint investigations (fig. 208) in small hidden areas. They work slowly to uncover a painted past, scraping with a blade and sometimes following up with sandpaper or using solvents or even gentle hammer taps.

The results in the Talcott investigation were eye-opening. The wings of the settle had several coats; the first (next to the wood) was a dark brown. The edges of the brown boards, however, had never been that color. A brown-painted board had been recut for reuse. *Suspect reused wood whenever a board has a face color that is missing on the edge.*

The panels on the back had a first coat of green paint. The brown wings could not have been original to the green back. Inspector Warren, having revealed the several paint layers in different areas, then removed them, sloughing off the unifying coats of paint.

With the overlayers of paint removed, the green-paneled back showed evidence of dribbling. Whatever dribbled had done so counter to the laws of gravity — upward. The dribbled-upon settle back had begun as a piece of paneled wall, upon which there had been a shelf, from which something had dripped. The wall paneling was inverted when it became a back for a settle.

The wall paneling is post-seventeenth-century and may or may not predate 1769. The question of when the old wall became a settle has not been settled.

BEWARE THE BIEDERMEIER BLONDE!

A new fad for the Biedermeier style (a nineteenth-century European neoclassical fashion) has begun, and the savvy collector is aware of the dangers of this style, especially for chairs like the Corey (fig. 153). The chair was grained to imitate rosewood, a common practice with nineteenth-century chairmakers, and the contours of the chair were outlined and highlighted by a slender gold stripe. This popular decorative finish was applied to maple chairs like the Corey, even handsomely figured tiger maple.

As the finishes wore and as a fashion for light woods — maple and especially tiger maple — grew, many grained finishes and gilt outlines were zealously removed. An early-twentieth-century craze for blond Biedermeier furniture led to a mania for stripping such chairs, which share their neoclassical lines with chairs of the Biedermeier style. The Corey looks today as it was meant to look, as it left the factory, and as it retains its greatest value as an antique. Not all blondes are beautiful.

A KNOCKOUT, AND COMING TO ONE'S SENSES

Its painted finish makes a five-drawer chest from Saybrook, Connecticut, a knockout (plate 6). Its interior is also in excellent condition (fig. 10 is a detail of a drawer). The vigilant investigator, careful not to be bedazzled by the chest's splendors, pursues a complete inquiry and finds a flaw: the chest has replaced feet. Even before turning the chest over, the detective senses — by touch — that at the very least the finish on the feet is not original. The feet simply do not feel like the other painted surfaces. *Use touch to detect replaced parts and refinished surfaces.*

To augment the senses, an investigator needs an understanding of — not necessarily expertise in — finishes. Touching (and seeing,

FIGURES 209, 210:
Armchair and detail of crest; 1742, Milford, Connecticut. Made by David Sanford. H. 44¼; W. 23½; D. 17½. (Museum of Fine Arts, Boston.)

figs. 209 and 210) the alligatored, or crazed, finish on a chair, for example, reveals that some areas are in worse shape than others. Sunlight causes alligatoring. Since less sunlight fell on the lower parts of the chair than on its back, the result is a gradation or variation in the amount of alligatoring. *Do not expect finish deterioration to be evenly distributed.* If caused naturally, it isn't even. No one on the tactile squad has trouble distinguishing between finish deterioration and refinishing. Exposure to sunlight, water, or heat causes logical variations in texture, whereas surfaces finished at different times feel entirely different from one surface to another.

The heart-and-crown chair with the sun-damaged finish is an eighteenth-century product in a nineteenth-century coat. The details picked out in gold are one clue to the date of the finish; the alligatoring is another. Such crazing is especially common on nineteenth-century finishes.

Important information can also come from smell. While eyeing the top of an early-nineteenth-century sideboard and handling its finish, a detective picked up a scent. Touch — the top felt different than the rest of the case — had suggested that the top might not be original. Sight — a few filled holes were spotted at the rear of the top — had suggested a reused board. Smell — an odor of fresh varnish reached the sleuth's nose — revealed that the top had been refinished.

The nosy detective soon solved the case. The top board had been newly refinished to remove shadows left in the old finish by a missing rear splashboard. (Whence the filled nail holes.) With stain and varnish covering the tracks of the splashboard, the sideboard was being auctioned as if it had never had one. A refinished surface frequently has undergone more than mere refinishing.

Not all new painting or finishing is equal, or equally to be abhorred. Overpainting — of which the heart-and-crown chair is an example — and inpainting — touching up damaged areas while leaving original paint in place — have much to recommend them; an inspector need only recognize them.

A Queen Anne chair or Chippendale desk with nineteenth-century grained paint can readily be assessed as what it is. If the chair or desk proves to be period furniture, the nineteenth-century-style paint is evidently overpaint. A fair amount of an original surface may survive beneath new paint (having, in fact, been preserved by it), and the piece can be returned to what remains of its original finish. The finish can be redone, following clues underneath the overpainting, to resemble its original self. Or the furniture can be left as it is, its two centuries of history on view — the stylish shape of the eighteenth century clad in the modish finish of the nineteenth.

WHEN IT'S A CLEAR CASE

In clear finishes the fashion today is for muted surfaces that look somewhat worn, not for a glasslike piano-type finish. Chances are that any muted, somewhat worn surface you see is new, younger than a slick high sheen that was probably applied a couple of generations ago.

Two finish problems that the savvy sleuth addresses are these:

1. Was the finish removed altogether, including the stain under the varnish — the chemical strip-it approach?
2. Was the wood beneath the finish scraped or sanded — mechanically stripped — before the surface was refinished?

The look of a new wood surface helps answer both questions; a hands-on approach helps detect mechanical stripping.

Knowing which woods and finishes were popular when also helps. An antique maple Chippendale chair was originally stained to look like mahogany. If it is still completely covered with mahogany stain, even at vulnerable places — the top edge of the crest, along the top of the front stretcher — then someone surely has restained it. (Some of the original finish may have been retained.) If the maple Chip-

FIGURE 211:
*Rocking chair; 1830–1855,
New England. H. 42⅛;
W. 23⅛; Seat D. 19; Seat
H. 15. (Society for the
Preservation of New England
Antiquities.) The original
painted surface is unre-
touched.*

pendale looks like maple today, you know what happened to it: someone stripped it. Careful inspection in good light and sensitive handling should reveal evidence of scraping and sanding if the offender used harsh mechanical stripping.

The best way to find evidence of the original finish on a case is to open a drawer and look around the front corner of the drawer side or, with the drawer removed, to look just inside the front corner of the drawer opening. Some stain, finish, or paint has usually made it onto such secondary surfaces. The best place to look on an upended table is beneath the top or inside the skirt next to a leg. On a chair, also turned over, original finish will hide beneath the skirt beside a leg or in a spot covered by upholstery. On an attractively decorated rocker (fig. 211), the underside of the wooden seat retains revealing smudges of paint and varnish (fig. 212). The dull dark areas in the photograph are paint; the blacker color is the top coat of clear varnish applied in the original finishing. Nowhere on the chair does any evidence of earlier color show. The well-preserved paint and stenciling on the seat and crest are original.

Furniture that you are sure is old may have a finish that clearly is not and yet may show no evidence of an earlier finish. Such pieces

are veterans of the chemical strip shop. You probably don't insist on an original finish — few of us do — but it is nice to know what has happened to an antique over the years.

DIRTY BUSINESS

The squad looks for dirt on top of and incorporated into most finishes. In hidden corners, in crevices, in up-and-under hideaways, the gummy residues of years of waxing and polishing and just plain dust and dirt accumulate. Dirty build-up, a friend to the detective, is a great challenge to the defrauder. Black paint and dark stain may simulate dirt, but the squad is not fooled. Inspectors soon become adept at searching for genuine dirt and at recognizing it when they see it. They benefit from generations of fussbudgets who roamed the house, dustcloth in hand, constantly polishing and inadvertently assuring dirt in the corners. Detectives who detest dirt under a fingernail delight in the crud in "protected" corners of antiques. Strange joys are everywhere in this business.

The Savvy Collector in Action

11

THE best careers in antique furniture sleuthing combine the shop beat, some print and telephone detail, and the auction beat.

ON THE SHOP BEAT

This patrol is probably the safest and the most rewarding. The conditions in antiques shops often make detective work challenging, but sound investigation is possible. Just a word about some shady characters you may encounter.

The dealer playing the confidence game is easy to spot. He seeks to establish your confidence in him, eagerly pointing out minor flaws but failing to mention the major ones. "The brasses," he says, "are replaced."

So are all four feet, you notice, not distracted by his red herring.

A disclosure of problems by an apparently forthright dealer is no substitute for the scrutiny of the collector's own eyes.

Another clearly recognizable character is the pusher. His hard sell sounds like banter:

"It has been in the same family for generations" (said of a reproduction).

"I tried for years to get this piece and had to pay practically what I am asking for it."

"A prominent collector has his eye on this and is going to be so upset to learn it's been sold."

"I hate to sell it. You can't find any of them anymore."

Amid such talk, savvy collectors slam shut their ears and open wide their eyes.

A pedigree, whether presented in a shop or at an auction, should be evaluated as a bit of history that may well mean nothing. Some of the antiques that are "ex collection" of prominent early collectors are, quite simply, early fakes and frauds.

One story about a pedigree and a dealer should suffice. The dealer sold what were purported to be old, fine, and rare Chippendale chairs to a prominent collector, who quickly discovered that they were copies, not antiques. The collector demanded a full refund for the frauds. The dealer, still claiming that the chairs were genuine, offered instead to buy them back at $1,000 more than the collector had paid. The collector agreed to the strange offer.

Returned to the shop, the chairs resold quickly. With a canceled check to prove their recent purchase, the dealer eagerly divulged the chairs' provenance, which now included the famous name of the prominent collector.

One way to squelch pedigrees and cut down on the banter is to tell the dealer, "I keep a file on everything I buy. When and if I buy this, I want all that information on the bill of sale. Will you write down the history, including your estimate of when the piece was made, while I continue looking it over?"

Always have the dealer write on the receipt all the information he has about the antique. Accept no alibi, neither a broken arm nor a busy shop. If the information isn't on the receipt, you'll never get it. Dealers who promise letters containing all the facts never make it to the post office.

Keep a file on your collection. The receipt now becomes part of the object's history. Every object should have a separate folder, into which you can put any information you subsequently gather about the object: the bill for the reupholstery or repair; the photograph of a similar piece that is advertised or is on exhibit. When the object leaves your collection, its file will enhance its value.

Your dealer's receipt should also state that the sale is not final until a specified date, a day or few in the future. Second only to the fact that it gives you the time for a proper inspection, the great benefit of buying from a shop is that you have a chance to reconsider. Savvy collectors buy from dealers who will hold a check for a day or three to allow the buyer to take the purchase home and see how it looks or fits in the room. Antiques usually look far better at home than in the shop, and the dealer knows it. Purchases that allow for returns are standard with good dealers.

When you get the antique home, or back to the motel if you are on the road, you can unscrew the tabletop that you were reluctant to unscrew in the shop. You can confer with someone else or consult published information. Even when shipping is involved, good dealers allow for returns (shipped back to the shop at the customer's expense, of course). *Always get return privileges from an antiques dealer.*

If you realize, quite a while later, that you are seriously unhappy with something purchased at a shop, you should go back to the dealer. Your patronage is probably more valuable than the one sale. Many reliable dealers will take back a purchased item at the price of the original transaction.

After a dealer gets to know you — you and your 500-watt lights and your tool kit — he's likely to suggest you take the furniture home right off the bat. *Don't take it home yet. Examine it first in the shop.* One, you want to make sure the antique is worth getting into the moving business for; two, you'd be responsible for any injuries to it on the way home; three, you can be a more impartial critic in the shop.

The greatest advantage of the shop beat is the hours. There is time for thorough investigation, and you can make the best use of your time. No need to wait for — or to wait through — an auction. The collector's pace governs the shop beat.

Antiques shows are a variation on, and a useful adjunct to, the shop beat. The great plus is the sheer volume of goods, which necessitates a single-mindedness that an astute auction-goer ought to develop for previews as well. The crowds at shows and auction previews are a drawback. And it is hard to get a conditional sales receipt at a show because the dealer is paying dearly for the volume exposure.

On the other hand, the lighting is good; you can leave your 500-watt bulbs at home and simply augment your tool kit with a strong flashlight. Shows are wonderful opportunities for discovering dealers who trade in the type and quality of antiques that appeal to you.

THE PRINT AND TELEPHONE DETAIL

The print media and the telephone connection are occasionally suited to smart buying. Savvy collectors watch the advertisements when reading the several antiques periodicals that follow the market and publish the latest scholarship. The advertisements make the printed page more informative and more enjoyable. They also imply that the printed page offers a way to shop.

It does, but only if the advertiser will deliver the antique to you for inspection and without any conditions. If the dealer himself will deliver the piece, tell him that you'll need time for your inspection and that he may want to plan to leave the antique with you while he attends to other chores. The dealer who hovers over you in your house, where he really has nothing else to do, is worse than the one who hovers in the shop. Make it clear from the start (from your first telephone call in response to the advertisement) that, for example, a fifteen-minute stop on his way to the Big Show will not give you enough time to look over the desk. For the dealer who does stay with you, prepare a pot of coffee and a pile of old antiques periodicals and set about your work.

The telephone detail allows Californians to remain at home while bidding at New York auction houses. Telephone bidding, based solely on a catalogue picture, can cause one of the many villains to be delivered, unreturnable, at the bidder's doorstep. No catalogue picture or set of pictures can substitute for a full inspection. A cautious bidder who can't attend in person asks an astute and trusted agent to view the object firsthand.

A collector who is able to attend a preview but not the auction itself should do the detective work at the preview and then either leave a high bid with the auction house or bid by telephone. Placing left bids and bidding by telephone — useful alternatives to attending auctions in person — are both easy, almost as exciting as being there, usually safe, and often effective. Left bids seldom win; telephone bids often do.

ON THE AUCTION BEAT

Until you really know your stuff, the auction beat, though it appears attractive, can be treacherous territory. What seems most attractive is the prices; one can expect to pay less at an auction than in a shop, although that is not always the case. Many auction pitfalls are common knowledge: all sales are final; handlers cannily present the best aspects of an object while hiding its flaws; the lights — or lack of them — make even dreadful objects look good. And not all bids at the auction come from people; one auctioneer who claims to have no reserves (predetermined amounts under which the objects will not be sold), seems regularly to accept bids from the large clock in the back of the Elks' hall.

In an entirely different sense, the clock is the greatest danger of auctions. Prospective bidders have little time to examine the items that appeal to them; those in the know go to auction previews early and stay late. If the auction house has previews preceding the day of the sale (the best houses do), there will be sufficient time to adequately examine a few chairs and a table or two, but probably not enough time for more than one large case piece.

Preview the lots as early as possible because the crowd of spectators is largest just before an auction. Someone is always available to help turn over a table, but the crush of people is a menace to critical viewing. A misplaced concern for others or an inappropriate sense of diffidence may conspire to make the collector rush an inspection. *At auction previews, take your time.*

In order to be able to inspect each object thoroughly, inspect fewer of them. The shrewdest auction-goers are very fussy during their first surveys around the gallery and limit the number of objects to be inspected. *Inspect only those lots that truly appeal to you and whose estimated prices (which may be cited in the catalogue or ascertained from the auctioneer) are within your budget and your own estimate of their value.*

The estimated prices — educated guesses that can and very often do wander wide of the mark — are one of only two things the catalogue is good for. Lot numbers are the other. None of those catalogue terms — "antique," "rare," "fine," "style of," "attributed to" — mean anything, although one can probably believe "reproduction."

Catalogue descriptions do not enter into the savvy collector's consideration of any auction lot. Why not? Auction catalogues themselves, in their least perused section, state the reason. The "Conditions of Sale" (printed to protect the house, not the public) state:

> *Neither we nor the consignor make any representation or warranty, expressed or implied, as to the correctness of the description, genuineness, authenticity, or condition of the said property. No statement in the catalogue or at the sale shall be deemed such a warranty or representation or an assumption of liability with respect thereto.*

In other words: *Take no stock in anything said either in the catalogue or by the auctioneer.*

Few auction houses have the same level of in-house expertise as shops that handle antiques of similar quality. Nor need they. They do not have the same investment in what they're selling that the shop dealer has. Yet auction catalogues usually suggest some level of knowledge, claiming that "reasonable care" was taken in the cataloguing. The phrase "reasonable care" means nothing, and doesn't even insure that the auction house is telling all it knows about the lots.

Be especially suspicious of objects or collections that are sold shortly after being included in books or museum exhibitions. The selection of an object for a book or exhibit may not have been based on an unbiased assessment of that object but may have been merely hype for the auction. Publication and exhibition are no guarantees of authenticity, and the short period between your receipt of an auction catalogue and the sale (or between the preview and the sale) leaves you little time to adequately check cited publications, exhibits, and histories.

Sometimes the auction catalogue tells more than there is to tell. In 1985, at Sotheby's sale of the collection of Berry Tracy (who was both a collector and a curator), a pair of New York Federal card tables was said in the catalogue to have a Stephen Van Rensselaer Crosby provenance.

At least one astute auction-watcher remembered the tables from the 1982 Christie's sale where Tracy had acquired them; they were then listed as the property of the Society for the Preservation of New England Antiquities (SPNEA) but had no other history. In three years, a Van Rensselaer provenance had sprouted, though nothing in the SPNEA records could account for such a connection. (Among other lots bearing provenances at the Tracy sale was a "Seton-family" stand [$19,800], which a dealer had sold to Tracy a few years before [$400] without a history.[1]) Bidding was not strong among the cognoscenti. *You can't always be in the know, but you can always be suspicious.*

Auction catalogues may cite a museum as a previous residence of a privately owned lot. Many wonderful, privately owned antiques are in museums because in trying to display the best things museums seek and accept loans from private parties, foundations, and corporations. But the savvy collector is aware that sometimes an antique merely visits a museum on loan because it's on its way to the auction block, even though most museum professionals successfully sidestep the hype-a-privately-owned-antique trap. As a savvy sleuth, you need not pay a premium for the imprint of an institution; you do not need it to assure that the antique is both genuine and worthy.

An antique on the market may have once belonged to a museum. Ex-museum objects (euphemistically called "deaccessions") are appearing ever more frequently on the auction block, and usually — although not always — the catalogue proudly proclaims the museum connection. The savvy collector mentally asks why the lot is no longer in the museum. Some reasons for museum deaccessioning (e.g., the object is one of many of its type in the collection, or it does not fall within the area of the museum's interests) should not discourage interest on the part of the buyer. If the table is not the best gateleg drop-leaf in a museum, it may still be the best one available to the collector. If Hometown Museum is not interested in an out-of-state chair, the collector may well be.

But museums also sell objects their curators have discovered to be fakes, frauds, or reproductions. And museums sell objects that have been so overly restored that they cannot really be considered antique. *While inspecting a museum deaccession, ask yourself why it is being sold.*

Be prepared for an exhilarating discovery — you have become such a savvy sleuth that you can spot the fake, the fraud, the repro, or the reworked antique that once fooled a curator.

Notes

1. THE VILLAINS

1. Worcester, "How to Build a 300-Year-Old-Chair."

3. FALSE IDENTITIES

1. Dyer, "Historical and Documented Antiques from Maine."
2. *The Boston Directory* (Boston: John Norman, 1789), 39, and *The Boston Directory* (Boston: John West, 1796), 90.
3. *The Boston Directory* (Boston: E. Cotton, 1813), 78.
4. *The Boston Directory* (Boston: John West, 1796), 66.
5. Mabel M. Swan, "A Revised Estimate of McIntire," *Antiques* 20, no. 6 (December 1931): 338–343.
6. Margaret Burke Clunie, "Joseph True and the Piecework System in Salem," *Antiques* 111, no. 5 (May 1977): 1006–1013. Clunie reveals the close interrelationship of Salem furniture makers and the superior reputation of Joseph True's carving.
7. Jobe and Kaye, *New England Furniture*, 396.
8. M. Ada Young, "Five Secretaries and the Cogswells," *Antiques* 88, no. 4 (October 1965): 478–485.
9. Comstock, "Frothingham and the Question of Attributions."
10. Kaye, "Marked Portsmouth Furniture."
11. Ibid. All the cited marks and furniture are illustrated.
12. Blackburn, "Branded and Stamped New York Furniture."

4. STYLES AS CLUES

1. Goodbar, "Fakes and Forgeries," 16.
2. Nutting, *Furniture Treasury*, no. 1062, vol. 1.

5. TECHNOLOGY AS EVIDENCE

1. Martin, "Past Masters," *American Heritage* 36, no. 2 (February–March 1985): 36–47.
2. Marsh, *Easy Expert*, 95.
3. Montgomery, *American Furniture*, 27–40.

6. THE CASE OF THE CASE PIECE, PART ONE: JOINERY

1. As quoted by Stillinger in *The Antiquers*, 236.
2. Ibid.
3. Bolles's notes are at the Metropolitan, which does not display the cupboard in its American Wing.
4. Stillinger, *The Antiquers*, 72.
5. Ibid.
6. Fales, *Furniture of Historic Deerfield*, 172, fig. 362.
7. "Exhibition of Arts and Crafts in the Martha Pratt Memorial," in *Pocumtuck Valley Memorial Association, History and Proceedings, IV (1899–1904)* (Deerfield, Mass.: Pocumtuck Valley Memorial Association, 1905), 276.

7. THE CASE OF THE CASE PIECE, PART TWO: CABINETRY

1. Goodbar, "Fakes and Forgeries," 15.
2. "Shop Talk," *Antiques* 43, no. 5 (May 1943): 198.
3. Ibid.
4. Ibid.
5. Michael Varese, "Adapting Furniture to Contemporary Uses," *New York Times*, 25 October 1984, sec. C, 9.
6. Randall, *American Furniture*, 71.
7. *Maine Antique Digest* 13, no. 11 (November 1985), 6-A.
8. Kirk, *Early American Furniture*, 182.
9. Harold Sack, "Authenticating," 1126.
10. *Maine Antique Digest* 6, no. 8 (August 1978), 8-A, and 8, no. 7 (July 1980), 29-B.
11. Nutting, *Pilgrim Century*, 179 and fig. 160.
12. Ibid.
13. An advertisement of about 1915, pictured and quoted in Fennimore, "Fine Points of American Empire," 53.

8. CRIMES DONE TO CHAIRS

1. Fitch to Silas Hooper, London, 23 September 1725; Thomas Fitch Letterbook, Massachusetts Historical Society.
2. Nutting, *Pilgrim Century*, 306 and no. 319.
3. Ibid.
4. Chinnery, *Oak Furniture*, 100, fig. 2:88.
5. Rita Reif, "Buying British," Antiques column, *New York Times*, 23 June 1985, sec. H, 25.
6. Stillinger, *The Antiquers*, 73.
7. Lionetti and Trent, "Chapin Chairs," *Antiques* 129, no. 5 (May 1986): 1082–1095.
8. Trent, "New London County Joined Chairs," 55.
9. Heckscher, *American Furniture*, no. 29.

9. TOPLESS TABLES AND OTHER CONCERNS OF THE BOARD

1. *Maine Antique Digest* 6, no. 8 (August 1978), 21-A.
2. Stillinger, *The Antiquers*, 92.
3. *Maine Antique Digest* 3, no. 9 (September 1975), 10-A.
4. Harold Sack, in a supplement to *The Christian Science Monitor*, 5 November 1984, sec. B.
5. Nutting, *Furniture Treasury*, nos. 1364–1366, vol. 1.
6. Pennington, "Too Good to Be True — A Spurious Tripod Table and Other Notes," *Maine Antique Digest* 8, no. 1 (January 1980), 10-C–11-C.
7. Ibid., 10-C.
8. *Maine Antique Digest* 3, no. 9 (September 1975), 11-A.
9. Sheraton, *Cabinet-Maker*. The griffin appears in "Ornament for a Frieze or Tablet," plate 56 (the second plate so numbered), after page 352.

10. FINISHING 'EM OFF

1. Brazer, *Early American Decoration*, 249.
2. Ibid., 250.
3. *Maine Antique Digest* 14, no. 2 (February 1986), 7-A.
4. Ibid.
5. Ibid.
6. *Art and Auction* 8, no. 6 (December 1985), 84.
7. Lyon, *Colonial Furniture*, 188–189.
8. Warren told the story in "The Talcott Settle," *The Connecticut Antiquarian* 29, no. 1 (June 1977): 23–33.

11. THE SAVVY COLLECTOR IN ACTION

1. *Maine Antique Digest* 13, no. 3 (March 1985), 8-D–9-D.

Bibliography

The entries preceded by an asterisk (*) are for advanced detective work on regional styles; those preceded by a dagger (†) are good general works especially useful for their illustrations.

Arnau, Frank [pseud. of Heinrich Schmitt]. *The Art of the Faker*. Translated from the German by J. Maxwell Brownjohn. Boston and Toronto: Little, Brown and Co., 1961.

*Baltimore Museum of Art. *Baltimore Furniture: The Work of Baltimore and Annapolis Cabinetmakers, 1760–1810*. Baltimore: Baltimore Museum of Art, 1947.

*Benes, Peter. *Two Towns; Concord & Wethersfield: A Comparative Exhibition of Regional Culture, 1635–1850*. Concord, Mass.: Concord Antiquarian Museum, 1982.

Bishop, Robert. *How to Know American Antique Furniture*. New York: E. P. Dutton, 1973.

*Bissell, Charles S. *Antique Furniture in Suffield, Connecticut, 1670–1835*. Hartford: Connecticut Historical Society and Suffield Historical Society, 1956.

Bjerkoe, Ethel H. *The Cabinetmakers of America*. Garden City, N.Y.: Doubleday and Co., 1957.

*Blackburn, Roderic H. "Branded and Stamped New York Furniture." *Antiques* 119, no. 5 (May 1981): 1130–1145.

Boston Furniture of the Eighteenth Century. Edited by Walter Muir Whitehill, Brock Jobe, and Jonathan Fairbanks. Boston: Colonial Society of Massachusetts, 1974.

Brazer, Esther Stevens. *Early American Decoration*. Springfield, Mass.: Pond-Ekberg Co., 1940.

*Burton, E. Milby. *Charleston Furniture, 1700–1825*. Charleston, S.C.: The Charleston Museum, 1955.

*Carpenter, Ralph E., Jr. *The Arts and Crafts of Newport, Rhode Island, 1640–1820*. Newport: Preservation Society of Newport County, 1954.

Cescinsky, Herbert. *The Gentle Art of Faking Furniture*. London, 1931. Reprint. New York: Dover Publications, 1967.

†Chinnery, Victor. *Oak Furniture; The British Tradition*. Woodbridge, Suffolk: Baron Publishing, 1979.

†Comstock, Helen. "Frothingham and the Question of Attributions." *Antiques* 63, no. 6 (June 1953): 502–505.

————. *American Furniture, Seventeenth, Eighteenth, and Nineteenth Century Styles*. New York: The Viking Press, 1962.

*Connecticut Historical Society. *Connecticut Chairs in the Collection of the Connecticut Historical Society*. Hartford: Connecticut Historical Society, 1956.

*Cooke, Edward S., Jr. *Fiddlebacks and Crookedbacks: Elijah Booth and Other Joiners in Newtown and Woodbury, 1750–1820*. Waterbury, Conn.: Mattatuck Historical Society, 1982.

*Cornelius, Charles Over. *Furniture Masterpieces of Duncan Phyfe*. Garden City, N.Y.: Doubleday, Page & Co., 1922.

*Dorman, Charles G. *Delaware Cabinetmakers and Allied Artisans, 1655–1855*. Wilmington, Del.: Historical Society of Delaware, 1960.

Downs, Joseph. *American Furniture, Queen Anne and Chippendale Periods in the Henry Francis du Pont Winterthur Museum*. New York: Macmillan Co., 1952.

Dyer, Walter A. "Historical and Documented Furniture from Maine." *Antiquarian* 14, no. 5 (May 1930): 60–62, 80, 88.

The Eye of the Beholder: Fakes, Replicas and Alteration in American Art. New Haven: Yale University Art Gallery, 1977. (Exhibition catalogue)

†Fairbanks, Jonathan L., and Elizabeth Bidwell Bates. *American Furniture*. New York: Richard Marek Publishers, 1981.

Fales, Dean A., Jr. *The Furniture of Historic Deerfield*. New York: E. P. Dutton, 1976.

————. *American Painted Furniture, 1660–1880*. New York: E. P. Dutton, 1979.

Fennimore, Donald L. "Fine Points of Furniture, American Empire: Late, Later, Latest." In *Victorian Furniture, Essays from a Victorian Society Symposium*, edited by Kenneth L. Ames. Nineteenth Century, vol. 8, nos. 3–4. N.p.: The Victorian Society in America, 1982.

†Fitzgerald, Oscar. *Three Centuries of American Furniture*. Englewood Cliffs, N.J.: Prentice-Hall, 1982.

Flanigan, J. Michael. *American Furniture from the Kaufman Collection*. Washington, D.C.: National Gallery of Art, 1986.

Goodbar, Richard L. "Fakes and Forgeries, Marriages and Deceptions / And the Winterthur Museum Battle." *Hunt Valley Antiques Show Catalogue*, 1984: 14–29.

*Greenlaw, Barry A. *New England Furniture at Williamsburg*. Williamsburg, Va.: Colonial Williamsburg Foundation, 1974.

*Gusler, Wallace B. *Furniture of Williamsburg and Eastern Virginia, 1710–1790*. Richmond, Va.: Virginia Museum, 1979.

——*Hageman, Jane Sikes. *Ohio Furniture Makers, 1790–1845*. Cincinnati: J. S. Hageman, 1984.

Hayward, Charles H. *Antique or Fake? The Making of Furniture*. London and New York: Evans Brothers Limited, 1970. Reprint. New York: Van Nostrand Reinhold, 1981.

†Heckscher, Morrison H. *American Furniture in the Metropolitan Museum of Art, II, Late Colonial Period: The Queen Anne and Chippendale Styles*. New York: The Metropolitan Museum of Art and Random House, 1986.

Hoadley, R. Bruce. *Understanding Wood*. Newtown, Conn.: The Taunton Press, 1980.

*Horner, William MacPherson, Jr. *Blue Book of Philadelphia Furniture*. Philadelphia: Graphic Arts Engraving Co., 1935.

*Jobe, Brock, and Myrna Kaye. *New England Furniture: The Colonial Era*. Boston: Houghton Mifflin Co., 1984.

*Kane, Patricia E. *Furniture of the New Haven Colony: The Seventeenth-Century Style*. New Haven: New Haven Colony Historical Society, 1973.

†———. *300 Years of American Seating Furniture*. Boston: New York Graphic Society, 1976.

*Kaye, Myrna. "Marked Portsmouth Furniture." *Antiques* 113, no. 5 (May 1978): 1098–1104.

†Kirk, John T. *Early American Furniture, How to Recognize, Evaluate, Buy, and Care For the Most Beautiful Pieces: High Styles, Country, Primitive, and Rustic*. New York: Alfred A. Knopf, 1970.

———. *The Impecunious Collector's Guide to American Antiques*. New York: Alfred A. Knopf, 1975.

†———. *American Furniture and the British Tradition to 1830*. New York: Alfred A. Knopf, 1982.

Labaree, Benjamin W., ed. *Samuel McIntire*. Salem, Massachusetts: The Essex Institute, 1957.

*Lionetti, Joseph, and Robert F. Trent. "New Information about Chapin Chairs." *Antiques* 129, no. 5 (May 1986): 1082–1095.

Lockwood, Luke Vincent. *Colonial Furniture in America*. 2 vols. New York: Charles Scribner's Sons, 1901, 1913. Reprint. New York: Castle Books, 1951.

Luther, Clair F. *The Hadley Chest*. Hartford: Case, Lockwood, & Brainard, 1935.

†Lyon, Irving Whitall. *The Colonial Furniture of New England.* Boston: Houghton Mifflin Company, 1891. Reprint. New York: E. P. Dutton, 1977.

*_Made in Ohio: Furniture 1788–1888._ Columbus: Columbus Museum of Art, 1984. (Exhibition catalogue)

Marsh, Moreton. *The Easy Expert in Collecting and Restoring American Antiques.* Philadelphia: Lippincott, 1959.

*McClelland, Nancy. *Duncan Phyfe and the English Regency.* New York: William R. Scott, 1939.

†Miller, Edgar G. *American Antique Furniture, A Book for Amateurs.* 2 vols. Baltimore: Lord Baltimore Press, 1937.

*Miller, V. Isabelle. *Furniture by New York Cabinetmakers, 1650–1860.* New York: n.p., 1956.

*Monkhouse, Christopher, and Thomas S. Michie. *American Furniture in Pendleton House.* Providence: Museum of Art, Rhode Island School of Design, 1986. This collection catalogue is rich in Rhode Island examples.

Montgomery, Charles F. *American Furniture, The Federal Period in the Henry Francis du Pont Winterthur Museum.* New York: The Viking Press, 1966.

*Moses, Michael, and Liza Moses. *Master Craftsmen of Newport.* Teaneck, N.J.: MMI Press, 1984.

*Myers, Minor, Jr., and Edgar deN. Mayhew. *New London County Furniture: 1640–1840.* New London, Conn.: Lyman Allyn Museum, 1974.

*_Neat Pieces: The Plain-Style Furniture of 19th-Century Georgia._ Atlanta: Atlanta Historical Society, 1983.

*Newark Museum, *Early Furniture Made in New Jersey 1690–1870.* Newark: Newark Museum Association, 1958.

*_New England Begins: The Seventeenth Century._ 3 vols. Boston: Museum of Fine Arts, 1982.

†_19th-Century America: Furniture and Other Decorative Arts._ New York: The Metropolitan Museum of Art, 1970.

Nutting, Wallace. *Furniture Treasury.* 3 vols. Framingham, Mass.: Old America Company, 1928.

————. *Furniture of the Pilgrim Century.* 2 vols. 1924. Reprint. New York: Dover Publications, 1965.

Peterson, Harold L. *How Do You Know It's Old?* New York: Charles Scribner's Sons, 1975.

*_Plain & Elegant, Rich & Common: Documented New Hampshire Furniture, 1750–1850._ Concord, N.H.: New Hampshire Historical Society, 1979.

Randall, Richard H., Jr. "Seymour Furniture Problems." *Museum of Fine Arts Bulletin* 1959, no. 310: 102–113.

*———. "Works of Boston Cabinetmakers, 1795–1825: Part I and II." *Antiques* 81, nos. 2 and 4 (February and April 1962): 186–189 (I), 412–415 (II).

*———. *The Decorative Arts of New Hampshire, 1725–1825*. Manchester, N.H.: Currier Gallery of Art, 1964.

†———. *American Furniture, in the Museum of Fine Arts, Boston*. Boston: Museum of Fine Arts, 1965.

†Sack, Albert. *Fine Points of Furniture: Early American*. New York: Crown Publishing, 1950.

Sack, Harold. "Restorations in American Furniture; What Is Acceptable?" *Antiques* 89, no. 1 (January 1966): 116–121.

———. "Authenticating American Eighteenth-Century Furniture." *Antiques* 127, no. 5 (May 1985): 1121–1133.

*St. George, Robert Blair. *The Wrought Covenant: Source Material for the Study of Craftsmen and Community in Southeastern New England, 1620–1700*. Brockton, Mass.: Brockton Art Center, 1979.

Sheraton, Thomas. *The Cabinet-Maker and Upholsterer's Drawing-Book*. London: Gibbings and Company, 1895.

Smith, Nancy A. *Old Furniture*. New York: Bobbs-Merrill, 1975. Reprint. Boston: Little, Brown and Co. 1976.

Stillinger, Elizabeth. *The Antiquers*. New York: Alfred A. Knopf, 1980.

Stoneman, Vernon C. *John and Thomas Seymour: Cabinetmakers in Boston, 1794–1816*. Boston: Special Publications, 1959.

Titmuss, F. H. *Commercial Timbers of the World*. 3d ed. London: The Technical Press Ltd., 1965.

*Trent, Robert F. *Hearts & Crowns: Folk Chairs of the Connecticut Coast, 1720–1840*. New Haven: New Haven Colony Historical Society, 1977.

*———. "New London County Joined Chairs." *The Connecticut Historical Society Bulletin* 50, no. 4 (Fall 1985).

*Weidman, Gregory R. *Furniture in Maryland, 1740–1940*. Baltimore: Maryland Historical Society, 1984.

Worcester, Wayne. "How to Build a 300-Year-Old Chair." *Yankee* (January 1978): 94–99, 152–158.

Yates, Raymond F. *Antique Fakes and Their Detection*. New York: Harper & Brothers, 1950.

Photography Credits

Robert J. Bitondi: figures 33, 84, 135, 136, 137–139, 161, 207

J. David Bohl: figures 18, 35, 37, 38, 54, 60, 62, 65–67, 108, 109, 121, 158, 175, 176, 179, 194, 196, 203, 211, 212

Richard Cheek: plate 3; figures 4, 5, 11, 31, 32, 43, 69, 74, 75, 85, 92, 94–97, 100, 104–107, 113, 114, 117–120, 122, 134, 140–143, 157, 159, 164, 165, 168 (left), 177, 178, 180, 182, 187, 193, 195, 209, 210

Geoffrey Clements: figure 91

Jock Gill: figure 131

Helga: plate 6; figures 70 and 127

George Milkowski, Radiographic Services: figure 51

Joe Ofria: plates 5, 7–10; figures 2, 10, 13, 30, 40, 41, 49, 53, 63, 64, 73, 76–83, 88, 93, 99, 128, 130, 149–151, 190, 191, 199

Robert B. St. George: figures 132 and 133

Taylor and Dull: figure 189

Drawings
Jonathan S. Nerenberg

Index

Page references to illustrations and captions are in boldface type.

Eagle (motif), 182
Early American Decoration (Brazer), 186
Early American Furniture (Kirk), 38, 181
Easy chair(s), 165–167, 166–167; bill of sale for, 34; British, 11
Economy of labor, 17–18, 60–61, 108, 109, 141
England. *See* Britain
English furniture, 3, 11, 19, 51, 143, 143, 148–149, 149
Enhancements, 3, 9, 10, 163, 171
Enlarged set, 8–9, 159–160
Escutcheons, 83, 84, 91, 110
Essex Institute, print from the, 152
Evans, Nancy G., 32

Fabian, Monroe, 186
Facades, case, 41. *See also names of individual types*
Fairbanks, Jonathan, 161
Fan. *See* Shell
Fasteners. *See* Cotter-pin fasteners; Hinges; Nails; Screws; Wooden pins
Federal style, 41; attributions to, 26; brasses, 81, 83; casters and, 85; inlay, 73, 75; sofas in, 164, 165
Feet: full height of, 93, 143–144, 143; pieced, 42; vulnerability of, 96, 107. *See also* Ball feet; Bracket feet; Claw feet; Spanish feet; Turned feet
Fennimore, Donald L., object from the collection of, 133
Finishes. *See* Paint; Stain; Varnish; Wax
Finishing nails. *See* Nails, cut; Nails, wrought
Flayderman, Harry, 158
Fluting, 41
Ford, Henry, Museum, the, 4, 6, 24, 29–30; objects from the collections of, and Greenfield Village, 5, 24
Frothingham, Benjamin, William, and "Walter," 29, **pl. 2**
Furniture of the Pilgrim Century (Nutting), 129, 148
Furniture parts, illustrated glossary of, 36–39
Furniture Treasury (Nutting), 39, 41–42, 178

Garvan, Francis Patrick, 92, 94
Garvan, Mabel Brady, 92
Gilmanton, New Hampshire, 28–29
Glass, 85–86, 86
Glue, 48, 55, 65, 75–76, 107, 142
Glue blocks, 107, 107–108, 118, 128; under a case top, 122; under a drawer, 132, 133; under a tabletop, 172, 173, 174
Grant, Erastus, 132
Grant, Samuel, 34

Greenfield Village, the Henry Ford Museum and. *See* Ford, Henry, Museum
"Griffin" card table, 181–182, 181
Guilford, Connecticut, area, **pl. 6**
Gum, sweet (wood), 158

Handles (pulls), 35, 76, 80–84, 81, 95, 97, 110; design of, 81–84, 81; evidence of, 57, 82; iron, 103, 103; restoring appropriate, 111, 114; wooden, 97
Handle history, 57, 81, 82
Hardware, designs of, 81. *See also* Casters; Escutcheons; Handles; Hinges; Locks; Nails; Screws
Hart, R. (Richard), 30–32
Hartford, Connecticut, 102, 187
Hartshorn, Ebenezer, 45, 114
Heckscher, Morrison, 158–159
Henry Ford Museum. *See* Ford, Henry, Museum
Heritage Center of Lancaster County, the, object from the collections of 14, 15
Hickory (wood), in a Windsor chair, 145
High chair. *See* Windsor(s)
High chest(s), 19, 19–20, 39, 40, **pl. 3** (details, 92, 118); enhanced, 9; losses on, 114; mixed styles in, 44, 45; remade, 9, 113–114; skirt/ stretcher design on, 39, 40. *See also* High-chest base; High-chest top
High-chest base (lower case), 8, 9, 116, 120, 121
High-chest top (upper case), 9, 10, 74, 116–120, 118, 119
Hinge(s), 79–80, 80, 131, 131; cleat-and-pintle, 89, 90, 176, 177; cotter-pin, 47, 88, 95, 96; on desk lids, 80, 127; iron strap, 79–80, 103, 103; on tabletops, 173, 175, 175
Historic Deerfield, 100; objects from the collections of, 91, 95–98, 101, 103, 132, 135, 149, 174, 179–180, **pl. 6**
Homer, Andrew, 24; "label" of, 24, 30
Hosmer, Walter, 45

Ink stains, 92, 124
Inlay, 73, 73–75, 117, 181–182, 181–182; as enhancement, 10; metal, 74
Inpainting, 191
Inscription(s), 10, 25, 27–29, **pl. 2**
Ipswich, Massachusetts, 87, 88, 90
Irish furniture, 11
Iron, 47, 47. *See also names of individual types of hardware*
Iron strap hinges, 79–80, 103, 103

Jefferson, Thomas, 158–159
Jobe, Brock, 34

Joints, 61–64, 61–65; locking, 62–65, 63; simple, 61–63, 61–62; sliding, 62, 63. *See also names of individual joints*

Karolik, Maxim, 160
Keller, Ferdinand, 162, 163
Kelly, Cornelius, 103
Key escutcheon(s). *See* Escutcheons
Kindig, Joe, Jr., 180
Kirk, John, 38, 40, 114, 120, 181
Kneehole bureau table, 12, 111
Knife boxes, 113
Knowlton, Ebenezer, 23–24

Label(s): as documentation, 27; as enhancement, 10, 23–25, 23–25, 183; genuine, 25; Keller's, 173; obliterated, 12–13
Lambert family, 161
LaMontagne, Armand, 4–7, 5
Lancaster County, Pennsylvania, furniture made in, 14, 15, 16, 185
Lannuier, Charles-Honore, 183
Lap joint, 61–62
Leather upholstery, 42, 42
Leather washers, 131, 131
Lock(s), 76, 84, 84, 90, 91, 99, 110; wooden spring, 91–92, 92; missing, 96
Lockwood, Luke Vincent, 99
London: chair made in, 143, 143; shop practices in, 19
Lyme, Connecticut, 155
Lynn, Massachusetts, 152
Lyon, Irving W., 102, 152, 187

Machine-age (or Victorian) style, 41
Machine tools, 24; marks of, 67
McIntire, Samuel, 26
M.A.D. *See Maine Antique Digest*
Made-up set(s), 3, 8–9, 150–151, 155
Mahogany (wood), 49, 52, 53, 54, **pl. 10**; in cases, 9, 28, 80, 111, 118, 127, 132–133; in chairs, 158–160, 162–164; with other woods, 45, 114, 173; in a sofa, 164; in tables, 173, 176, 177, 182–183, 183
Maine Antique Digest, 115–116, 147, 178, 186; photographs from, 8, 12, 57, 63, 108, 115, 121, 123, 146–147, 161, 171, 176, 178, 179
Maker's mark(s). *See* Brand(s); Label(s); Signature(s)
Maple (wood), 51, 52–53, **pl. 7**; feet, 109; figure of, 189; in cases, 20, 91, 102, **pl. 5**; in chairs, 42, 140, 145, 150, 151, 154, 156, 166, 169; in tables, 174, 176, 177
Marblehead, Massachusetts, 158
Married pieces, 3, 10–11, 19, 19, 20, 129–131, 130
Marshfield, Massachusetts, 94
Mechanick Exercises (Moxon), 66